TROUBLED ALLIANCE

AEI-Hoover
policy studies

The studies in this series are issued jointly
by the American Enterprise Institute
for Public Policy Research and the Hoover
Institution on War, Revolution and Peace.
They are designed to focus on
policy problems of current and future interest,
to set forth the factors underlying
these problems and to evaluate
courses of action available to policymakers.
The views expressed in these studies
are those of the authors and do not necessarily
reflect the views of the staff, officers
or members of the governing boards of
AEI or the Hoover Institution.

E 183.8
T 8
H 3

TROUBLED ALLIANCE

Turkish-American problems in
historical perspective, 1945-1971

George S. Harris

American Enterprise Institute For Public Policy Research
Washington, D. C.

Hoover Institution on War, Revolution and Peace
Stanford University, Stanford, California

NOV 2 8 1972

172432

AEI-Hoover Policy Study 2, June 1972
(Hoover Institution Studies 33)

Library of Congress Catalog Card No. L.C. 72-83379

© 1972 by American Enterprise Institute for Public Policy Research,
Washington, D. C. Permission to quote from or to reproduce materials
in this publication is granted when due acknowledgment is made.

Printed in United States of America

To
Barbara, George, and Betsy
who cheerfully surrendered
their claims on my time
during the lengthy gestation of this book

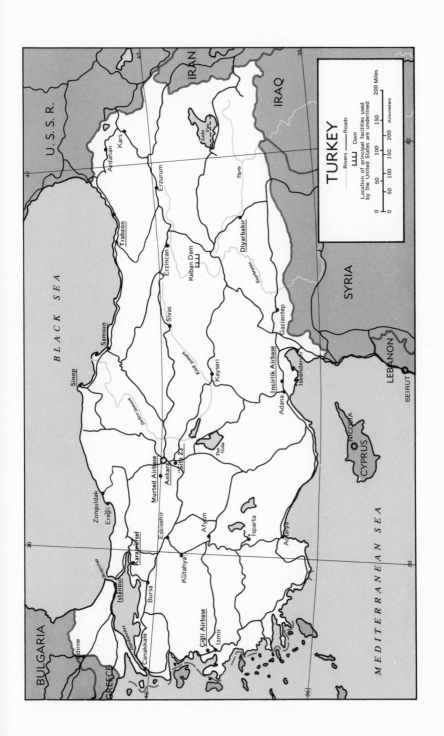

Abbreviations Used

CPSU — Communist Party of the Soviet Union
DCA — Defense Cooperation Agreement
DP — Democrat Party
JP — Justice Party
MLF — Multilateral Force
NTP — New Turkey Party
NYU — New York University
OECD — Organization for Economic Cooperation and Development
RPNP — Republican Peasants Nation Party
RPP — Republican People's Party
SACEUR — Supreme Allied Commander Europe
SOFA — Status of Forces Agreement
TBMM — Türkiye Büyük Millet Meclisi
TGS — Turkish General Staff
TIAS — Treaties and Other International Acts
TL — Turkish Lira

Partial Key to Turkish Pronunciation

c = j as in jail

ç = ch as in church

g = g as in get

ğ = y, or lengthens the preceding vowel

ı = i as in sir

j = zh as in measure

ö = eu as French deux

ş = sh as in shell

ü = as in French rue

A circumflex accent softens preceding consonants.

Contents

PART THREE: LOOSENING THE BONDS

PART FOUR: SUMMING UP

Plates follow page 136

Preface

To Americans, alliance with Turkey came as part of a global endeavor to consolidate support in face of the challenge of the Soviet Union. This collaboration was thus only one among the many close relationships with smaller states which marked the determination of the United States to remain an active world power after the Second World War. Although the Truman Doctrine might have pride of place as the forerunner of the postwar military structure erected by the United States, association with Turkey was not the cornerstone of American defense arrangements. Other concerns of American policy always held the limelight.

This emphasis has been reflected in the relative paucity of work on Turkish-American relations available in the United States. For many years Americans generally appeared not to perceive a need to investigate the bases of alliance with Turkey. In the main, studies on NATO focused on the more highly developed states of Western Europe. Aspects of U.S. economic assistance to Turkey did command somewhat more attention in the United States, although this topic was for the most part treated in technical terms. Scholars versed in Turkish affairs almost to a man preferred to concentrate on the country's domestic concerns. Evidently the prevailing notion that in Turkey "politics stops at the water's edge" discouraged systematic investigation of the intimate bonds established with the United States. Only after problems in the alliance boiled up in a severe dispute over Cyprus did a more general recognition of the complexities of the relationship begin to dawn. Yet even now there has been little effort at comprehensive analysis of the difficulties in maintaining this intimate collaboration between a superpower and a distant, much smaller state.

The following study attempts to span only a part of this gap. As will become clear in succeeding pages, it focuses on the difficulties of the Turkish-American association, and particularly on the perception of these problems by various segments of Turkish society. Admittedly this is to view the "worm" not the "apple," as a colleague once put it, but this approach may offer useful insights.

The present book is a revised version of a report written for the U.S. Department of State in December 1970 and supplemented to deal with developments through December 1971. It was originally conceived as an independent personal survey of available unclassified literature bearing on Turkish-American relations. Undoubtedly informed by the author's nearly six years of residence in Turkey—much of which was on assignment to the American embassy in Ankara— nonetheless this work is by no means an official appraisal; it does not necessarily reflect the policy or views of the U.S. government.

In composing this work I have benefited from the counsel and assistance of persons too numerous to name, both in the United States and in Turkey. Members of the Faculty of Political Sciences of Ankara University were outstandingly generous with their time and ideas. Leading figures of the major Turkish political parties also were helpful in contributing to my understanding of the issues involved. I was fortunate as well in being able to consult a number of Americans who had previously served or resided in Turkey. Among those who were kind enough to comment on the manuscript in draft were three past American ambassadors to Turkey: Raymond A. Hare, Parker T. Hart, and Robert W. Komer. My special thanks go likewise to Edward Lampson, who allowed me to consult his unpublished study of the U.S. economic assistance program in Turkey, and to Philip Stoddard for his unflagging encouragement and help at every stage of this endeavor. For suggestions from all these sources I am most grateful, though I alone am responsible for the views expressed herein.

Last, but not least, I would like to acknowledge the daily ministrations of my wife, who shared both my experiences in Turkey and the process of producing this book. Her patience and understanding support were an essential ingredient in the completion of this work.

G. S. H.

Westmoreland Hills, Maryland
May 1972

Introduction

Conceived in the cold war, born in the context of the U.S. policy of containment, the postwar collaboration of Turkey and the United States once seemed a model of international cooperation. At the outset, this relationship appeared solidly grounded on mutual interests and shared aspirations, not only for defense, but for development as well. Washington had the resources and the willingness to commit them to satisfy, to a reasonable if never complete degree, Ankara's urgent desires for both economic and military assistance. There was an intangible unity of purpose, a devotion to the open society, which marked this association from the beginning. All this combined with warm personal relations to impart the peculiar intimacy that struck observers as the outstanding characteristics of this alliance. In this atmosphere, those disagreements that did crop up were dwarfed by the impressive coincidence of interests of the parties and their commitment to each other.

Today, much of this essence remains. Turkish-American cooperation still stands as an impressive edifice—even if it is no longer all it once was. The solid core of mutual interest has proved resistant to erosion. At the same time, the collaboration has demonstrated a flexibility which so far has allowed it to weather the challenges that have arisen. Over the years the relationship has taken on an institutional life of its own, imparting momentum to every level of the association. In short, the alliance continues to show impressive permanence and strength.

Yet, while the heart of the association has not been vitally affected, there have nonetheless been significant changes in Turkish-American relations. In the first place, the international climate has altered significantly during the past twenty-five years. The threat of foreign attack against Turkey no longer seems immediate. The relaxation of tensions in Turkey's relations with the U.S.S.R. has provided an atmosphere in which diverging interests could make and have made themselves apparent. For Turkey, regional concerns—particularly the fate of Cyprus—have become of central importance. Moreover, since 1960 Turkey has been in the throes of a mounting social ferment that has challenged old assumptions in foreign as well as domestic policy. In this situation, questioning of U.S. motives has become common among the Turkish elite; a radical, though tiny, fraction of the Turkish populace has even resorted to violence in an effort to disrupt Turkish-American collaboration. Although the Ankara government remains committed to close ties with the United States, it too is making a shrewder calculation of its own.interests and is reinspecting the facets of the alliance.

For their part, Americans are voicing more reserve about their general international role. Economic and military assistance programs are losing their former congressional support; President Nixon himself has called for a recasting of U.S. involvement overseas at a level more in keeping with this mood. As regards Turkey, American economic and military assistance have been significantly reduced, though military equipment costs are soaring and the continuing modernization of the Turkish forces strains their already tight budget. At the same time, however, Washington is not interested in disengaging from Turkey in any fundamental way.

To put the relationship into full perspective is beyond the scope of this study. What is *right* with the alliance would require another lengthy treatise to detail. The strengths of the alliance are every bit as real as its problems, and no less important, even though for the most part they will not receive major stress in the following analysis. Likewise this work is not designed to provide a systematic exposition and assessment of the myriad programs or projects undertaken over the past several decades by the United States in Turkey. American activities have been so numerous and multifarious that it would take this study far afield to carry out such a comprehensive task. Only where U.S. programs have provoked significant problems or have had major impact on Turkish development will they find mention in the ensuing pages. Hopefully, enough will be said to impart some flavor of the wide range of American involvement, but the present investigation does not attempt a thorough program analysis.

Instead, this study focuses on the problems of the alliance. Setting the stage with a consideration of how the association came about, the work will seek to trace the course of difficulties that have developed in the relationship over the years and to analyze their causes. For this author believes that if Turkish-American collaboration is to be as productive as possible for both parties, the points of difference and of friction must be well understood. It is to this end that the following analysis is directed.

Sources for this study are vast, particularly in Turkish. Although neither side has yet seen fit to make public the confidential record of relations since 1946, much of the record is open. Increasingly in recent years, press conferences by the prime minister and other cabinet officials in Ankara, as well as congressional testimony by administration spokesmen in the United States, have contributed significantly to public understanding of the Turkish-American association. Beyond official revelations there has also been an avalanche of material—sometimes quite polemical in nature—by scholars and politicians in Turkey directed toward explaining or justifying Turkish foreign policy. Much of this has appeared in the daily or periodical press. But by now the unrestrained atmosphere of the late 1960s has spawned memoirs and occasional papers that seek to reinterpret the earlier period as well. Taken together, this material, despite its inevitable tantalizing gaps, nonetheless serves to delineate the broad shape of the major difficulties facing the allies and especially to reveal the shifting Turkish viewpoint toward collaboration with the United States.

At first sight, heavy reliance on the press may appear dangerous. It is true that there is much idle speculation of the flimsiest sort in these sources. But in the end, the turn of events has usually served to permit a detached observer to separate wild surmise from the realities of the situation. Moreover, in Turkey the press is the mirror and source of a great deal of the unease in urban society. Indeed, ideas launched in the most restricted circles of extremists have had a way of percolating beyond their own limited milieu. It is, to be sure, hard to determine just how far views of this sort may spread. But in Turkey there are few fingers on the levers of power; Turkish society is predominantly urban-oriented and elitist. Based on the 1970 census, a reasonable rough estimate may be that of a total population of some 36 million there are not many more than a million living high school graduates in Turkey today, and perhaps not over a quarter of a million university graduates. This is an interrelated and interconnected elite, bound by family and school ties of an enduring sort. And, as far as one can determine, these urban literati who are the decision makers rely on the press as an important channel of information. Thus, even though the journals may not provide much insight into the thinking of the Turkish masses, their literate audience is nevertheless one of central importance in determining Turkey's fate. The very flights of fancy and obvious exaggerations in the press, therefore, are important in attempting to construct a full and convincing picture of the problems that have troubled Turkish-American cooperation.

Part One:
SEARCH FOR SECURITY

1
Forging the Ties

The origins of the alliance between the United States and Turkey are already subjected to two principal conflicting views. Many, especially foreign observers, tend to regard the Truman Doctrine as a mammoth rescue operation. In their view, the U.S. military assistance program played an essential role in preventing Turkey from being swallowed by the Soviet colossus to the north. This was the rationale underlying much of the testimony of the congressional hearings in 1947. Time has sanctified this picture. Since the mid-1960s, on the other hand, some Turks disillusioned with the United States have bitterly rejected this view. They vociferously maintain that the years of maximum danger were 1945 and 1946, i.e., before America had any special formal connection with Turkey, and hence that it is quite unjustified for the United States to take credit for "saving Turkey." [1]

On a more sophisticated level, this argument raises questions about the concept of deterrence: what was it that in reality persuaded the Soviets not to use force to satisfy their demands on Turkey? Was it the Turkish will to resist, the level of Turkey's military and economic strength, Soviet global considerations, the threat of U.S. and perhaps other Western retaliation? Or did the Soviet Union perhaps never really intend to use force in any event? As Henry Kissinger has suggested, to such questions no final answer is possible.[2] Yet a review of the

---

[1] The respected commentator Ahmet Şükrü Esmer argued in this vein in his "Türkiyeyi Amerika mı Kurtardı?" *Yön,* March 25, 1966, p. 2. This claim was echoed, for example, in the series of articles by professors Mehmet Gönlübol and Halûk Ülman, "Dış Politikamız," *Milliyet,* July 30–August 14, 1966. Doğan Avcıoğlu, *Türkiye'nin Düzeni* (Ankara, 1969), p. 262, also accepts this argument.

[2] Henry A. Kissinger, *The Troubled Partnership: A Re-appraisal of the Atlantic Alliance* (New York, 1965), p. 19.

historical evidence can go a long way toward suggesting to what degree these various factors may have been involved.

The close collaboration of Turkey and the United States in the aftermath of the Second World War was not built on a lengthy tradition of intimate relations. On the official level, diplomatic ties had been interrupted by the First World War, when both sides withdrew their ambassadors, but without formal declaration of war. After 1919, the United States was represented in Turkey by the somewhat anomalous office of American High Commissioner; ambassadors were not again officially exchanged until 1927. The idea of the United States as a mandatory power for Armenia was also broached during the negotiations that followed the First World War. This scheme foundered on the rock of Turkish reality and American unwillingness to underwrite the costs after the Harbord mission, dispatched by President Wilson to inspect the feasibility of this venture, recommended broadening the proposed mandated area to include most of present-day Turkey as well. U.S. economic interests in Turkey had never been significant. American entrepreneurs connected with the Chester Concession project of railroad and mineral development failed to raise the promised capital to carry out their engagement with the Turkish government in 1923. This spelled the end of prospects for major U.S. economic involvement in Turkey.[3] It was principally as a field for educational activity—notably on the part of Robert College and a handful of missionary-run secondary schools—that Turkey seemed of interest to the United States during the interwar years.

In Turkish eyes, the United States emerged from the First World War with a relatively positive image. The particularly close association of America with the Armenian community in Turkey seems to have roused little animosity among the Turks. Nor did the U.S. slowness in formally abandoning its capitulatory privileges in the postwar era engender major response—though Turkish sensitivity ran high over these unequal arrangements which had shackled the Ottoman Empire so painfully in its last days.[4] To judge from the surge of support for the

---

[3] On the Chester Concession see John A. DeNovo, *American Interests and Politics in the Middle East 1900–1939* (Minneapolis, 1963), pp. 58–87, 210–28; Roger R. Trask, *The United States Response to Turkish Nationalism and Reform, 1914–1939* (Minneapolis, 1971), p. 130.

[4] For a detailed discussion of the capitulations, see Nasim Sousa, *The Capitulatory Regime of Turkey* (Baltimore, 1933).

10

proposed American mandate by some of the nationalist leaders, a broad constituency among the elite in Turkey regarded the United States as a power without territorial ambitions or the imperialistic aspirations of European states. Even Mustafa Kemal Atatürk, the heroic leader of Turkey's independence movement, evidently did not wish to close the door completely on the idea of an American mandate if all else failed.[5] But after the nationalists managed to establish secure political independence, expelling the Greek invaders and winning their main points at a peace conference with the European powers in 1923, Turkish interest in an intimate American connection rapidly evaporated. The United States again came to be generally regarded as a friendly but remote power. Over the next two decades significant reaction against America was visible only in those rare instances when U.S. missionary activity ran afoul of the rising tide of Turkish nationalism.[6] Even then, resentment was quickly submerged in the underlying current of favorable feeling toward the United States.

The guiding principle of Turkish foreign policy during these decades was set by Atatürk: "peace at home and peace in the world." But this aphorism was obviously far too general to order any specific line of action. In practice, the precept was translated into a foreign policy of: (1) seeking to preserve friendship with the young Soviet regime which had offered support during the critical days of Turkey's struggle for independence after the First World War; (2) trying to restore normal relations with France and especially Great Britain, whose parliamentary practice formed something of a long-range model for the Turkish political process (this trend culminated in the conclusion of a defensive alliance with the United Kingdom and with France in 1939); (3) concluding regional defensive alliances closer to home with Balkan and Near Eastern states; and (4) resuming friendly relations with Germany.

---

[5] The Sivas Congress in September 1919 sent a request to the U.S. Senate for a mission to inspect the situation of the nationalists. This request was never acted on in Washington. By 1927, in his historic four-day speech, Atatürk passed over this request with the less than frank explanation that he could not "remember exactly whether it was sent off or not." Mustapha Kemal [Atatürk], *A Speech Delivered by Ghazi Mustapha Kemal, President of the Turkish Republic* (Leipzig, 1929), p. 100. See also Lord Kinross, *Atatürk* (New York, 1965), pp. 218–19.

[6] The most acute outburst of nationalist sentiment against the United States during this era was triggered by the incident involving the conversion to Christianity of three Muslim girls in the American school in Bursa in 1928. See Henry E. Allen, *The Turkish Transformation* (Chicago, 1935), pp. 153–60; Kemal H. Karpat, *Turkey's Politics* (Princeton, 1959), p. 61.

11

America, however, was too far away to figure in this picture in any major role. No leading Turkish figures traveled to the United States; Army Chief of Staff General Douglas MacArthur was the sole prominent American to include a visit to Atatürk on his itinerary in this period.[7]

Impact of the Second World War

The Second World War, although it did not immediately change the level of U.S. involvement in Turkey, did set the stage for the intimacy of the postwar era.

In the first place, the war marked a watershed in Turkish-Soviet relations. Conclusion of the Nazi-Soviet Pact of 1939 gave concrete evidence that the Kremlin had not abandoned the traditional Russian ambition to control the Black Sea Straits. This project hung fire after Hitler launched his attack on the U.S.S.R. in 1941,[8] but the Ankara regime fully expected the Soviets to reopen the matter when the time appeared more propitious. Yet this specter did not induce the Turkish government to abandon its rather legalistic application of the Montreux Convention, which was concluded with the major maritime nations of the world in 1936 to regulate passage through the Straits: on the basis of its interpretation of this instrument, Ankara permitted German merchant ships to enter the Black Sea during the war. Ankara also maintained diplomatic and commercial ties with the Nazis until almost the closing days of the conflict—of particular note was a thriving trade in strategic chrome. Moscow was irritated as well by the machinations of the tiny but emerging Pan-Turanist wing in Turkey, which displayed sympathy for Nazi aims to dismember the Soviet Union. By the end of the war Soviet leaders had begun to condemn Turkey's neutral posture as a central failing, although during most of the conflict the Kremlin had taken the view that Turkish participation in the actual fighting would

---

[7] In Turkish eyes MacArthur's trip was one of the most celebrated visits of the Atatürk period. During their conversation in 1932, these two successful generals predicted the outbreak of the Second World War, thus giving occasion to recall this meeting long afterward.

[8] The Kremlin demanded a base in the Straits during secret talks with the Nazis in November 1940. Hitler disclosed these designs after his invasion of the U.S.S.R. in 1941. On this, see U.S., Department of State, *Nazi-Soviet Relations, 1939–1941: Documents from the Archives of the German Foreign Office* (Washington, 1948), pp. 217–59.

not be very significant.[9] Stalin also opposed Turkish operations in the Balkans, an area he had earmarked for the Soviet sphere. In sum, by the end of the war it was obvious that the former Turkish-Soviet friendship had vanished in an air of suspicion and mutual distrust.

As for relations with the Western powers, Turkey had encountered problems in this sector too. President İsmet İnönü, who took the leading role in Turkey after Atatürk's death in 1938, was cautious by inclination and loath to see a repetition of the disastrous experiences of the First World War, when Turkey had sustained such tremendous losses in men and materiel as an active belligerent. He thus played the part of a balance wheel between the pro-German party, of which Foreign Minister Numan Menemencioğlu was perhaps the most prominent exemplar, and the pro-British faction where İnönü's own sympathies appear to have lain. As a result, much to the disappointment of Churchill at Cairo and Adana in 1943, İnönü set a high price for entry into the war: no less than the total reequipment of the Turkish military establishment. It was unquestionably true that Turkey's army was extremely outmoded—as Secretary of War Robert P. Patterson would later say, perhaps of 1910 vintage.[10] This failing was magnified by the rapidly developing technology of the Second World War. But İnönü's firm insistence on a level of assistance obviously impossible for the Allies to fulfill also reflected his distaste for committing Turkey to a course whose ultimate implications were not completely clear. As a result, Turkey approached the end of the war with its ties to its ally, Great Britain, somewhat strained.[11]

If Turkey focused its attention primarily on dealing with the British in these matters rather than addressing itself to Washington with the same urgency, this was because the United Kingdom was a formal ally and in fact served as the main channel for equipment during the war. Of course the Turks did seek to take advantage of American lend-lease as well. Here, too, they met with bureaucratic frustrations and shipping difficulties that limited their acquisitions. By the end of the war, equipment allocated to Turkey under this program amounted to

---

[9] Harry N. Howard, "The United States and Turkey: American Policy in the Straits Question," *Balkan Studies*, vol. 4 (1963), p. 240.

[10] Walter Millis, ed., *The Forrestal Diaries* (New York, 1951), p. 257. See also Sir David Kelly, *The Ruling Few* (London, 1952), p. 328.

[11] A. Suat Bilge et al., *Olaylarla Türk Dış Politikası (1919–1965)* (Ankara, 1969), pp. 193–95.

a total of some $95 million, but only about half this figure had actually been delivered, the remainder having been "diverted to more urgent war needs." [12] The struggle to arrange this aid left a feeling of unfulfilled expectations on the part of Turkish officialdom.

On the other hand, for the Turks the image of the United States was greatly enhanced by the American performance in the war. Capping it off was the explosion of the atomic bomb, which imparted to the United States an aura of invincibility that would not be questioned in Turkey for many years to come. Moreover, the victory of the Allied cause was widely regarded by the Turkish elite as a measure of the superiority of the democratic system. It was, then, the victory of the democracies that the Turks celebrated. At the same time, the United States was generally depicted by the Turkish press as the defender of right, justice, and humanity. This view was tinged by concern lest the United States revert to a policy of isolationism after the conclusion of the fighting. And it was in this frame of mind and with these concerns that the Turkish government finally took the decision to declare war on the Axis on February 23, 1945, to meet the deadline for joining the victorious powers in the new world organization that was to be the United Nations.[13]

In American eyes, Turkey and its future did not loom large during the Second World War. As a general rule, the United States considered Turkey to lie in the British sphere of interest. Washington, however, did not share Churchill's enthusiasm for launching an assault on the "soft underbelly" of the Balkans as an avenue into Eastern Europe. For the Americans, therefore, Turkish neutrality was not a particular irritant. But if there was no great pressure from the United States to propel Turkey into the war, there was equally little sense of urgency in Washington to extend openhanded assistance. After all, neutrals were still neutrals, however much the Turks, especially toward the end of the war, might declare their attachment to the Allied cause. Nor did Turkey enjoy any vocal and influential advocacy in Washington. Essentially what American policy makers desired was to see Turkey

---

[12] William A. Helseth, "The United States and Turkey: A Study of Their Relations from 1784 to 1962," unpublished Ph.D. thesis presented to Fletcher School of Law and Diplomacy, April 1962, pp. 211–12.

[13] For a convenient compilation of Turkish attitudes at the time of the declaration of war, see *Ayın Tarihi,* February 1945, pp. 50–64.

act in such a way as to avoid raising issues that could foul the peace-making atmosphere.[14]

Enter the Soviet Union

By war's end, it had become clear that questions involving Turkey would have to occupy the Allies in their settlement of the conflict. As the fighting drew to a close, the Soviet Union engaged in an effort to probe the attitudes of the Western powers toward Turkey's future status. Neither Churchill, Roosevelt, nor Truman had given the Kremlin a very definite picture of Western intentions in this regard. For example, whereas Churchill explicitly demanded that Greece be understood to form part of the British sphere, he had made no such specific pronouncement regarding Turkey. Moreover, both the British and the Americans repeatedly voiced a willingness to accept changes in the regime of the Black Sea Straits established by the Montreux Convention of 1936. In the verbal fencing on this matter at Yalta, neither Stalin nor the Western leaders attempted to define precisely the nature of any acceptable changes, leaving the field open for the Soviet Union to propose extreme alterations.[15] All this must have heightened Stalin's uncertainty about the firmness of Western support for the integrity of Turkey's territory.

The first Soviet move to test the Turkish issue came on March 19, 1945, when Molotov gave notice of Soviet intention to denounce the 1925 Treaty of Friendship and Nonaggression with Turkey. That the Kremlin was still feeling its way was indicated by the fact that it did not mention the Treaty of 1921, which had established the frontiers between the two states.[16] The results of this probe must have seemed encouraging to the Soviet leaders, for the United States and the United Kingdom found it difficult to react firmly to what ostensibly was a matter of consequence to the contracting parties alone.

---

[14] For a general statement of U.S. policy toward Turkey at the war's end, see *Foreign Relations of the United States: The Conference of Berlin (The Potsdam Conference), 1945* (Washington, 1960), vol. 1, pp. 1015–17 (hereafter cited as *USFR: Potsdam*).

[15] For the proceedings at Yalta, see *Foreign Relations of the United States: The Conferences at Malta and Yalta, 1945* (Washington, 1955), pp. 498–506, 771–82, 897–906, 910–18, 931–33, 940, 982 (hereafter cited as *USFR: Malta and Yalta*).

[16] For a more lengthy exploration of this point, see Feridun Cemal Erkin, *Les relations Turco-Soviétiques et la question des détroits* (Ankara, 1968), pp. 286–92.

To the Turks, however, Moscow's action was an ominous portent of demands to come and an indication that victory in the war would not lead to Soviet magnanimity. As such, it pointed up the necessity of improving ties with the West. When İnönü gave special instructions to his delegation to the San Francisco Conference to announce an early liberalization of Turkey's one-party regime,[17] however, the pledge was not designed merely to improve Turkey's image in the eyes of the world. It also reflected İnönü's own commitment to complete the Atatürk revolution, which had set the attainment of European-style democracy as a long-term goal. İnönü had shown his interest in moving in this direction on the eve of the war, but the exigencies of the conflict had forestalled basic experimentation. Now the time had come to proceed. Moreover, İnönü very likely was already aware that the future leaders of the Democrat Party (DP) were preparing themselves in the wings.[18] Hence his instructions to the Turkish delegation were far more than a maneuver to curry favor with the West; they were solidly grounded on a keen appraisal of the imperatives of Turkey's domestic scene.

The Turkish delegation to San Francisco received a further charge to stop in London on its return to apprise the British more urgently of the Soviet danger.[19] (The delegates passed up a stop in Washington under pressure of boat schedules.) For on June 7, 1945, the Kremlin had advanced another demand, far more alarming than the first, even though it was couched in terms allowing room for maneuver and was not accompanied by "concrete threats," at least not in the view of U.S. officials.[20] Now Moscow was demanding a base on the Straits and border rectifications in the east as the price for renewing the Treaty of Friendship and Nonaggression.

Although concerned over this mounting pressure on Turkey, Washington did not immediately signal to Moscow American interest in Turkey's territorial integrity, lest such a move disturb the atmosphere of the Potsdam Conference scheduled to convene in July 1945. Instead

---

17 *Vatan,* March 24, 1945; George S. Harris, "A Political History of Turkey, 1945–1950," unpublished Ph.D. thesis presented to Harvard University, 1956, p. 184.

18 *Dünya,* March 26, 1956; Harris, p. 184.

19 Erkin, p. 296.

20 When Acting Secretary of State Joseph C. Grew told Turkish Ambassador Hüseyin Ragıp Baydur that the United States was pleased that the U.S.S.R. had not made any "concrete threats," Baydur replied that he would like to know how America would react to demands for "Boston and San Francisco." See *USFR: Potsdam,* vol. 1, pp. 1044–46.

the United States sought to calm the Turks and did not join the British in a démarche indicating concern to the Kremlin. The Department of State also rebuffed Turkish desires to brand the Soviet demands as contrary to the U.N. Charter, a move that Ankara felt would have had a great effect on Moscow. Acting Secretary of State Joseph Grew even went so far as to voice the hope that talks between Turkey and the U.S.S.R. would be conducted in a friendly fashion and with due respect for the views of both parties. But this suggestion led the Foreign Office in Ankara to express incredulity that the United States would encourage Turkey to discuss the cession of territory and bases.[21]

At the Potsdam meeting, Churchill raised the question of Soviet pressure against Turkey, eliciting a mollifying response from Stalin. Truman, for his part, was concerned with the issue of free passage through the Straits. But despite the agreement of the Big Three on the need to bring the Montreux Convention up to date, the meeting broke up without resolving the matter. The conference merely authorized each party to attempt to work out its desires with the Turks in bilateral negotiations.[22]

The Ankara government had not been sanguine about seeing the Big Three debate its intimate concerns in its absence. The results of the Potsdam Conference, which were privately passed to Turkish officials by the British, did nothing to allay this concern. In Ankara the Foreign Office interpreted the U.S. position on the Straits as according the Black Sea powers increased authority over passage through this waterway, hence raising questions about the inviolability of Turkish sovereignty. Moreover, in the view of the Turkish government, the American stand tended to parallel Soviet desires to turn the Black Sea into a *mare clausum* with Turkey sharing responsibility as doorkeeper.[23]

Turkish efforts to involve the United States

In this situation, the Ankara regime set itself two urgent objectives: first, to bring the U.S. position on the Straits into harmony with the minimum Turkish view and, second, to involve America in defending Turkey against the Soviet Union.[24] To this end, the İnönü government

---

[21] Ibid., p. 1034.
[22] Ibid., vol. 2, passim.
[23] Erkin, pp. 312–17. See also Metin Toker, "Türkiye Üzerinde 1945 Kâbusu," *Milliyet,* January 24–February 23, 1971, especially February 15, 1971.
[24] Ibid., pp. 324–25.

stepped up its consultations with the United States, attempting to drama-tize the Soviet threat, arguing that the Kremlin would be deterred not by concessions but by firmness. In August 1945, the Foreign Office in Ankara solicited the U.S. view of Soviet-Turkish relations. Later that month the Turkish ambassador chided the State Department over an apparent slackening of American interest in Turkey, a charge which U.S. officials denied. In September, the Turks seized occasions to point out that evident Soviet interest in the Mediterranean (manifested especially by Moscow's desire for Tripolitania) proved that Turkey was a top-priority target for the Kremlin. In the final analysis Ankara's argument rested on the proposition that Turkey's geographical position made it the key to the Middle East, a refrain echoed frequently thereafter by both the Turks and their Western allies.[25]

The Turkish campaign quickly bore fruit. In October 1945, reports from Ankara of a major Soviet troop buildup in the Balkans and in the Caucasus led W. Averell Harriman, then U.S. ambassador to the Soviet Union, to raise this matter with Soviet leaders.[26] Harriman's démarche elicited a firm denial by the Kremlin of threatening intentions; within a short time even Ankara officials conceded that the apparent concentration had been a troop rotation and not a net increase in Soviet forces. When in November 1945 the United States presented its views on the regime of the Straits as authorized at Potsdam, the American position represented in Ankara's eyes an improvement over the Truman formula for internationalization. Even though Washington's proposals were not entirely in accord with the views of the Turkish Foreign Office—as the Turks frankly conceded to the British—nonetheless the Turkish government, publicly and to the United States, registered its approval in principle while reserving its position on details. In this way, Ankara hoped to encourage the U.S. Department of State to move the remaining distance to the Turkish view. Significantly, Turkish officials warned Washington not to put any stock in lukewarm or hostile press reactions in Turkey, though in fact the reaction turned out to be generally quite favorable, some Istanbul commentators even construing the U.S. note as a complete espousal of the Turkish cause.[27]

---

[25] *Foreign Relations of the United States, 1945* (Washington, 1969), vol. 8, p. 1239 (hereafter cited as *USFR, 1945*).

[26] Ibid., pp. 1260–64, 1268, 1270–71.

[27] Erkin, pp. 316–17; Helseth, pp. 302–3; *Ayın Tarihi,* November 1945, pp. 78–89.

A further opportunity to involve the United States was afforded by the grandiose territorial claims put forward by two Georgian professors on the eve of the foreign ministers' meeting in Moscow in December 1945. Soviet press and radio gave wide publicity to the issue, lending the impression that the Kremlin intended energically to press territorial demands. In this context, the Turkish Foreign Office urged the United States and the United Kingdom to take a clear stand on the matter. At the end of December 1945, Acting Secretary of State Dean Acheson gave private assurances to the Turks that the Soviet territorial demands extended into "spheres of world peace and security" in which the United States took the "deepest interest." However modest the scope of Acheson's words may now appear, Turkish officials described this statement as "the first concrete proof of effective U.S. interest in Turkey." [28]

The Ankara government was also successful in securing British pledges of support. British Secretary of State for Foreign Affairs Ernest Bevin matched the private U.S. assurance by a statement in the House of Commons on February 21, 1946. He declared that the 1939 Treaty of Alliance was still in force and that he did "not want Turkey converted into a satellite state." To emphasize this point, Hector MacNeil, Bevin's undersecretary, reaffirmed on March 25, 1946, that the 1939 treaty obliged the United Kingdom to extend aid in the event of aggression against Turkey. With these declarations, the Ankara Foreign Office concluded that Turkey's postwar isolation had finally been overcome. [29]

In Washington, hopes of meaningful cooperation with the U.S.S.R. had collapsed in the wake of the unsuccessful conference of foreign ministers in December 1945, especially as a result of Soviet intransigence over Iran. Truman himself early in January 1946 gave notice of his disillusionment with the Kremlin in a famous memorandum to Secretary of State James F. Byrnes. The president bluntly warned that there was "no doubt that the Soviets intend to attack Turkey." Unless they were "faced with an iron fist and strong language, another war [was] in the making." [30] Truman gave public evidence of this new mood in his

---

[28] Erkin, p. 326; *USFR, 1945,* vol. 8, p. 1288.

[29] Great Britain, *Parliamentary Debates* (Commons), vol. 419, no. 87, February 21, 1946, cols. 1357–59; vol. 421, no. 109, March 25, 1946, cols. 6–7. For the Ankara Foreign Office view, see Erkin, pp. 335–38.

[30] Harry S. Truman, *Memoirs,* vol. 1: *Years of Decisions* (Garden City, N. Y., 1955), p. 522. By 1969, when some circles in Turkey had come to espouse a revisionary view of history, Professor Türkkaya Ataöv construed the tougher

Army Day speech on April 6, 1946, in which he warned "that the sovereignty and integrity of the countries of the Near and Middle East must not be threatened by coercion or penetration." [31] And in token of the new American stance, the battleship *Missouri* was dispatched to Istanbul bearing the remains of Turkish Ambassador Münir Ertegün, who had died in Washington during the war.

Turkish reaction to the arrival of the *Missouri* on April 5, 1946, was ecstatic. To the man in the street here at last was tangible proof that Turkey did not stand alone, despite the refusal of the American visitors to confirm openly that their mission was more than a mere courtesy call. The Turkish press hailed the United States as the defender of "peace, right, justice, progress, and prosperity." For its part, the Ankara government used the occasion to emphasize Turkey's solidarity with the United States, stressing Turkish devotion to "the ideals cherished by America." [32] Significantly, President İnönü took the opportunity to reveal that Turkey had requested a $500 million credit from the Export-Import Bank. At the same time, he disclaimed any urgent desire for American military equipment, saying that he "hoped it would not be needed." [33]

İnönü's statement did not mean that Turkey was uninterested in obtaining arms. In fact, Ankara was actively seeking to acquire all the assistance, both military and economic, that it could. But the Turkish government still looked to the United Kingdom as its main source of military equipment, though difficulties in this regard were soon to convince the Turks that they would have to turn increasingly to the United States. As for economic assistance, it was obvious to the Turks that large-scale aid could come only from America. In the spring of 1945 the Ankara regime had already begun to sound out Washington's attitudes toward providing economic aid. [34] By October these conversations led to a Turkish request for a credit of $500 million from the Export-

---

U.S. stance as imperialist aggression. Passing over Soviet demands from Turkey for territory and a base in the Straits with only the barest mention, he asserted that America "consciously and willingly" launched the cold war as a means of gaining dominance over those states that became its allies. See his *Amerika, NATO ve Türkiye* (Ankara, 1969), passim, especially pp. vii–viii.

[31] U.S., Department of State, *Bulletin*, April 14, 1946, p. 622 (hereafter cited as *Bulletin*).

[32] *New York Times*, April 7, 1946. Text of Prime Minister Saracoğlu's speech is in *Ayın Tarihi*, April 1946, pp. 61–62.

[33] *New York Times*, April 7, 1946.

[34] *USFR, 1945*, vol. 8, pp. 1309–10.

Import Bank for industrial development and infrastructure projects. At that time the Turks were informed that the stated amount far exceeded the total resources available to that lending agency and that much more detailed justification would be required in any event. In March 1946, Washington sent word that Turkey was likely to receive no more than $25 million.[35] Nonetheless, the Ankara government, though deeply disappointed, did not lose hope of securing much more in the end. İnönü's statement to the delegation that had arrived on the *Missouri* represented a further effort in the campaign for an American commitment to assist Turkey.

If the United States was still not prepared to extend large-scale economic or military aid to Turkey, it had become willing to take a firm diplomatic stand against the threat of Soviet encroachment, a posture that had paid great dividends in Iran. U.S. policymakers were beginning to fear that without strong American backing Turkey might be transformed into a "springboard for political and military expansion by the U.S.S.R. into the Near and Middle East."[36] Thus, by the time the Soviets launched a diplomatic offensive in preparation for the tenth anniversary of the Montreux Convention, the United States had determined to stand solidly behind the Ankara regime.

On August 7, 1946, the Kremlin sent a strong note to Turkey, reiterating complaints over the administration of the Straits during the war and repeating demands for shared control of the waterway. Moscow's request was punctuated by a flurry of military activity in the Black Sea and in the Caucasus. But because the Soviets did not follow the procedures specified for amending the convention, the Turkish Foreign Office concluded that the Kremlin recognized it could not prevail at a conclave of the signatories.[37]

To reinforce its position in the face of these threatening gestures, the Ankara regime sought urgently to coordinate its response with those of the U.S. and British governments. Turkish officials were particularly

---

[35] *USFR, 1946*, vol. 7, pp. 902–3.

[36] Ibid., p. 894.

[37] Erkin, pp. 344–50; *USFR, 1946*, vol. 7, pp. 830, 832. Ibid., p. 827, reported a message from the U.S. embassy in Moscow to the War Department saying: "We do not believe that an attack on Turkey will be made at present." See also p. 836, for Stalin's assurances to Jan Masaryk, Czechoslovakian minister of foreign affairs, that the U.S.S.R. had no intention of attacking Turkey. Text of the Soviet note is in U.S., Department of State, *The Problem of the Turkish Straits* (Washington, 1947), pp. 47–49 (hereafter cited as *Straits*).

anxious to bring the American position fully in line with their own.[38] In this effort Ankara was successful. When the U.S. reply to the Soviet note came on August 19, 1946, it firmly backed the Turkish stand. Washington stressed the need for Turkey to maintain sole control over the Straits and rejected the idea of a regime controlled by the Black Sea powers alone. Moreover, in line with the American president's willingness to go "to the end" in opposing any Soviet actions against Turkish integrity, the U.S. note pointed out that attacks or threats of attack against the Straits would clearly be matters for action by the United Nations Security Council.[39] At the same time, the United States ordered an increase in the level of naval activity in the Mediterranean. In September 1946, British and American warships took part in ostentatious maneuvers in the Aegean.

The firmness with which Washington and London joined the Ankara regime in treating the first Soviet note was well received in Turkey; it apparently also gave pause in Moscow. The Kremlin contented itself with sending a somewhat perfunctory reply on September 24, 1946, repeating much of its earlier argumentation with added emphasis on the Black Sea as a *mare clausum*. Again the Turks coordinated their response with the United States and the United Kingdom. This time Ankara enlisted Washington's assistance in convincing the British not to stray from the Turkish position. Once more, all three rejected the main Soviet demands, though reiterating their willingness to convene a conference to update the Montreux Convention.[40] This time the Kremlin did not reply directly. Toward the end of October 1946, Moscow passed the word to London that it deemed it premature to call a conference on the Straits.

This result, coming as it did on the heels of the withdrawal of Soviet troops from northern Iran, contributed to the growing feeling of confidence in Turkey that the U.S.S.R. would not attack. Yet the Turks were far from satisfied with U.S. reluctance to provide liberal military and economic aid. Ankara's efforts to break down American

---

[38] Erkin, p. 324. For the Turkish reply of August 22, 1946, see *Straits*, pp. 50–55.
[39] *USFR, 1946,* vol. 7, pp. 840–42. For the text of the U.S. note, see *Straits*, pp. 49–50.
[40] Erkin, pp. 354–62. The United States of course was not a signatory to the Montreux Convention, but nonetheless expected to participate in any revision of that instrument. For the texts of the Soviet note of September 24, 1946, the U.S. and U.K. notes of October 9, 1946, and the Turkish note of October 18, 1946, see *Straits*, pp. 55–68.

reserve did not result in any immediate success. The Export-Import Bank signed an agreement in November to provide supplier credits of $25 to $50 million, the higher limit being offered as a result of unused Polish allocations. The Turkish government also asked for naval assistance on a large scale, but this request led the United States in October 1945 to reach an agreement with the United Kingdom, to the effect that Britain would have the chief responsibility to supply weapons, whereas the United States would try to provide economic help.[41]

Easing of pressure

By the end of 1946 the pressure on Turkey seemed considerably less urgent than it had been during the previous two years. The United States, though still preferring to have the British furnish direct military aid, had moved significantly closer to Turkey. The British had on a number of occasions reaffirmed the 1939 alliance. Soviet pressure seemed to have stabilized on a high but tolerable level; to the Turkish Foreign Office, there seemed no indication that the U.S.S.R. was seriously considering recourse to force.

Internally, the Turkish regime appeared to be in no immediate danger. Political liberalization was continuing apace. The opposition Democrat Party (DP) was picking up steam, emerging as a potent rival for İnönü's Republican Peoples Party (RPP). The government had advanced the date of elections by a year to July 1946, thus precluding the possibility that the nascent opposition could win a majority in parliament. Although the postelection government appeared excessively authoritarian to the DP, the political contest did not seriously threaten the political system. Nor did these growing pains extend to Turkey's basic foreign orientation. In fact, the Soviet threat led to a closing of ranks against the external danger.

This closing of ranks affected especially the left wing of the political spectrum. There had been a strong upsurge of socialist activity in the period immediately following the war. Some of the most active and vocal opponents of the one-party system had been of this persuasion. But the prospects that these elements might dominate the opposition movement had been decisively set back by the violent student demonstrations against the left in December 1945, actions that were tolerated,

---

[41] *USFR, 1946*, vol. 7, pp. 893–97; James F. Byrnes, *Speaking Frankly* (New York, 1947), p. 301.

if not instigated, by the government.[42] Although this pressure did not prevent several small socialist parties from organizing toward mid-1946, these groups merely divided the already small constituency for their point of view. But the inclination of socialists to promote a soft line toward the Soviet Union and Moscow's persistence in echoing approvingly their criticisms of the government imbued the leftist opposition with an aura of disloyalty. In December 1946 these small bodies were dissolved by the martial law command that had been maintained in Thrace and the Istanbul region since the war.[43] This swift and decisive action reflected essentially the legacy of the one-party regime. In the best of circumstances, opposition, even by the DP, tended to be regarded by government partisans as tantamount to disloyalty. Toleration for unpopular causes had no tradition in Turkey, and no voices in the larger parties were raised in defense of freedom of political expression for the left. In these circumstances, the blow to the socialist movement was telling. It would be almost fifteen years before such views could again find a sympathetic hearing in Turkey.[44]

Turkey's economy, despite chronic structural imbalances, did not seem faced with immediate crisis.[45] During the war, Turkey had amassed a reserve of some $270 million in gold and foreign exchange, though at the price of running down its already inadequate industry. This amount was sufficient to defray the cost of imports for more than a year; in the meantime most foreign observers expected Turkish exports to Europe to rise rapidly. Moreover, the new Turkish government had in September 1946 undertaken a substantial devaluation to bring the value of its currency into line with the views of the International Monetary Fund. Economic liberalization became the order of the day; a strong current began to flow against the etatist hostility to private enterprise that had characterized the previous decade. Essentially this movement represented a reaction against the failure of the earlier etatist

---

[42] On the government's role in the demonstrations, see Karpat, pp. 150–51.

[43] Ibid., pp. 357–58.

[44] In recent years some Turkish critics of the United States have charged that American-inspired anti-Communist fanaticism motivated the closing of these socialist organs. See Avcıoğlu, p. 274. There is no evidence of U.S. encouragement of this move against the left; the martial law command, however, may have expected its actions to demonstrate to the United States Turkey's will to resist the·U.S.S.R. Cf. Harris, pp. 386–87.

[45] *USFR, 1946,* vol. 7, p. 922, reports the American embassy's assessment of the economic situation.

experiment to provide a self-sufficient economic base and the restiveness of Turkey's growing entrepreneurs with the wartime restrictions. The sudden relaxation of controls afforded momentary relief to business interests, and provided the possibility of windfall profits as well, giving to the Turkish authorities and Western observers an initial if short-lived surge of confidence. Although these measures soon proved to be the wrong prescription for healthy development, at the end of 1946 Turkey's economic prognosis appeared satisfactory. Short of a Soviet attack, the country seemed to stand in no danger of imminent disaster.

Genesis of the Truman Doctrine

The Truman Doctrine signified the formal emergence of the United States as Turkey's chief support in the West. Despite the strength of Turkey's position, when early in 1947 the British decided to abandon their role as Turkey's principal backer, there was little reluctance within the U.S. government to assume this function.[46] Advocates of a firmer line toward the Soviet Union had been steadily gaining ground in presidential councils, especially with the departure of Secretary of State Byrnes at the end of 1946. By spring of 1947, of the major foreign policy advisers to the President, only George Kennan is recorded as persisting in strenuous objections to taking up the British responsibilities.[47] For the others, fear that the end of British support might permit the U.S.S.R. to seize control of Greece and Turkey finally swamped concern that large-scale American military aid to these countries might appear provocative to the Soviets.

---

[46] Turkey had paid cash for much of the military equipment it had received from Britain since the end of the war. Large-scale rearming of the Turkish force, however, was beyond the resources of either Ankara or the United Kingdom. Recognition of the need to refurbish extensively the Turkish military establishment led London to ask Washington to take over this burden in February 1947. See Helseth, p. 397. For general background on the Truman Doctrine, see Stephen G. Xydis, *Greece and the Great Powers, 1944–1947: Prelude to the Truman Doctrine* (Thessaloniki, 1963), passim.

[47] Joseph M. Jones, *The Fifteen Weeks* (New York, 1964), pp. 154–55. George F. Kennan, *Memoirs 1925–1950* (Boston, 1967), pp. 316–17, explained his reasons for objecting to a "special aid program" for Turkey. He felt that the emphasis should be placed on "firmness of diplomatic stance, not on military preparations." He suspected that "what had really happened was that the Pentagon had exploited a favorable set of circumstances in order to infiltrate a military aid program for Turkey in what was supposed to be primarily a political and economic program for Greece."

The urgency of the Greek situation was responsible for the speed of the transformation of American policy. The specter of the Greek government disintegrating in "skyrocketing inflation, strikes, riots, and public panic" appeared to Washington to leave "the field clear for the increasingly bold and successful Communist guerrillas to take over." [48] The American mission sent to Athens to recommend a course of U.S. action reported in March 1947 that large-scale intervention would be required to forestall chaos. This dramatic message laid the foundation for the momentous shift to a policy of global response to the Soviet Union.

Recognizing that the Turkish case paled by comparison with the crisis facing Greece, Truman made only the barest mention of Turkey in his historic message to Congress on March 12, 1947. Nor did testimony before congressional committees reflect greater emphasis. While admitting that Turkey was not in immediate danger, the administration nonetheless focused on the results of a possible Soviet takeover of Turkey. In addition, the State Department argued that the Turks could not carry out economic development as long as they had to bear the costs of a huge military establishment. This presentation led one witness to note rather wryly before the House Committee on Foreign Affairs that "it almost appears that . . . Turkey was slipped into the oven with Greece because that seemed to be the surest way to cook a tough bird." [49] The Turks themselves understood the delicacy of their position. At the prompting of Ambassador Wilson in Ankara on the eve of Truman's proclamation, the Turkish foreign minister promised not to seek "unnecessary" military aid, but only what would be needed to bring the Turkish armed forces "up to strength." [50] The conclusion is inescapable, therefore, that congressional approval of aid to Turkey was assured primarily because of association with concern over Greece.

Congressional debate on the Truman Doctrine raised several important points for the future of Turkish-American cooperation. In the first place, to quiet fears that Truman's message had circumvented the United Nations, Senator Arthur H. Vandenberg proposed that this aid could be suspended if the Security Council so requested.[51] In this connection, the U.S. representative assured the council that American

---

[48] Jones, p. 76.
[49] Ibid., p. 163.
[50] Helseth, p. 397.
[51] *New York Times,* April 1, 8, 1947.

assistance was emergency relief and would be temporary.[52] Congress also insisted that American journalists and radio reporters be guaranteed free access to cover all aspects of the assistance program. Similarly, U.S. officials were to have authority to supervise the use of aid extended under this act; the President was empowered to suspend the program if he deemed it necessary. And finally, in what was to play a most important role nearly twenty years later, Congress imposed restrictions on the use of American assistance, directing the President to terminate the program if recipient governments failed to carry out their assurances as to the use of U.S. aid.[53]

These provisions complicated the negotiations of the aid agreement between the United States and Turkey. To be sure, the Turks' predominant reaction to Truman's message reflected pleasure, if some surprise, at the sudden urgency accorded assistance to their country. The prime minister and other influential Turks staunchly defended American motives in extending aid.[54] But in some circles the question of granting unrestricted freedom to gather news and to supervise the use of U.S. aid tended to raise the specter of the capitulations that had granted Europeans extensive immunities during the later stages of the Ottoman Empire. If there was one sensitive nerve in the Turkish body politic, it was according privileges to foreigners. Supervision implied control; this in turn implied abandoning sovereignty. The provision for free access to news suggested an independence of action not then enjoyed by Turkish reporters themselves. Criticisms along these lines came not only from left-wing radicals like Mehmet Ali Aybar, editor of the tiny weekly *Zincirli Hürriyet* in Izmir (which was closed in the wake of demonstrations toward the end of April 1947),[55] but from prominent figures in both the government party and the principal opposition. DP leader Fuat Köprülü spoke against these terms as did Hikmet Bayur, the Istanbul deputy elected as an independent on the DP slate.[56] Even Hüseyin Cahid Yalçın, a staunch government supporter

---

[52] Ibid., March 29, 1947.
[53] See Public Law 75, 80th Cong., 1st Sess., Chapter 81. (This was an act to provide for assistance to Greece and Turkey.)
[54] Necmeddin Sadak, "Dünya Siyasetinde Yüzyılın en Ehemmiyetli Dönüm Noktası," *Akşam*, March 14, 1947.
[55] Mehmet Ali Aybar, "Amerikan Yardımını Bizde Kimler İstiyor?" *Zincirli Hürriyet*, April 12, 1947, p. 1; "Yardımın aleyhinde Bulunmak, Her Türk için Mukaddes Bir Vazifedir," *Zincirli Hürriyet*, April 19, 1947, pp. 1, 3. See also, "Yeni Bir Sevre Doğru," *Zincirli Hürriyet*, April 5, 1947, p. 4.
[56] See Helseth, pp. 413–14.

and protagonist of Turkey's Western orientation, gently warned the United States against seeking excessive privileges, although the RPP and the DP made clear their warm endorsement of the Truman Doctrine.[57]

Against the background of these pressures, the Turkish Foreign Office worked to soften the terms of the statutory requirements imposed by the U.S. Congress. In the aid agreement signed in Ankara on July 12, 1947, after considerable bargaining, the Turkish negotiators inserted language making the freedom of reporters to gather news subject to "security" considerations.[58] To remove the suggestion of foreign control, the term "aid administrator" was dropped in favor of the title "chief of mission." Washington also agreed to act discreetly in carrying out its supervisory functions. As a further gesture to Turkish sensibilities, Ambassador Wilson was named chief of mission in an effort to submerge this function in his normal reporting responsibilities.

The Truman Doctrine marked the end of the first phase of Turkey's search for security. Nonetheless, it left a number of unresolved questions. For example, the duration of American aid was not clearly spelled out. The American government worked within the frame of annual appropriations, and suggestions for a multiyear military commitment were not adopted during the period before Turkey's entry into NATO. Indeed, the American assurance to the Security Council that this aid was temporary would contribute to Turkish apprehensions that the U.S. assistance might cease in following years. In addition, the nature of the U.S. commitment also appeared vague to many. Several Turkish commentators sought to clarify this point by calling for a Turkish-American military alliance specifically obliging the United States to assist Turkey against outside attack.[59] Washington rejected this suggestion.

To the U.S. government, the rationale for providing aid was couched in security terms: American interests in the eastern Mediterranean would suffer if Turkey should fall. Under the Truman Doctrine, therefore, Turkey was to receive aid primarily to strengthen its military establishment, and this assistance was to be extended as a grant in order

---

[57] See Yalçın, "Türkiyeye Yardım ve Kontrol," *Tanin*, March 23, 1947.

[58] See Appendix 1 for Art. III, Aid to Turkey, *Treaties and Other International Acts Series* (hereafter cited as TIAS), 1629, July 12, 1947. For comment on the negotiations, see Helseth, pp. 413–20.

[59] See, for example, Abidin Dav'er, "Amerika Türkiye ile Tedafüî Bir İttifak Yapmalı," *Cumhuriyet*, June 23, 1947.

to avoid onerous repayment obligations which it was recognized might delay Turkey's development. On the other hand, the Turkish economy was viewed in Washington as basically healthy; it was thought that the Turks could borrow from the Export-Import Bank and other international agencies for economic development purposes. Also militating against U.S. economic assistance were doubts in America about the nature of the Ankara regime. Turkey's democracy appeared too young to inspire confidence among Western observers; indeed, the Turkish regime was strongly criticized on these grounds during the congressional hearings on the Truman Doctrine. Even the liberalization of foreign capital repatriation restrictions that Ankara announced in May 1947 did not serve to induce the United States to extend large-scale economic assistance.[60]

For the Turkish government, Truman's pronouncement offered a somewhat unexpected but nonetheless welcome opportunity to reequip the antiquated Turkish military establishment in order to improve its mobility and firepower. Conclusion of the treaty with America also provided a means for approaching Washington on a continuing basis for the modernization and maintenance of the Turkish armed forces. Moreover, while the Foreign Office in Ankara appears to have already concluded that the Soviet Union was unlikely to attack, still the formal association with the United States did impart new confidence in Turkey's security. In this frame of mind, for example, Ambassador Selim Sarper made a spirited counterattack against Andrei Vyshinskii at the United Nations in October 1947, for the first time replying to Soviet vituperation in the same coin.[61]

Deterrence

If even before the Truman Doctrine Stalin had felt deterred from seeking to impose Soviet demands by force, it was clearly not because of a fear of the effectiveness of Turkey's military machine. Since the end of the war the Turkish armed forces had remained woefully antiquated, some of their munitions dating from the First World War. They lacked mobility; even the advantage of interior lines of communi-

---

[60] On the change in foreign capital repatriation regulations, see Avcıoğlu, p. 277.
[61] U.N., General Assembly, First Committee, *Summary Records of Meetings* (A/C.1/SR 82, 83, 86), October 18–26, 1947. For the full text of Sarper's speech, see *Ayın Tarihi*, October 1947, pp. 76–78.

cation was largely offset by the poor state of the transportation network. Nor could Moscow have been dissuaded from attack by the state of Turkey's formal alliances with the United Kingdom and France. For until February 1946, Stalin must have been unsure of whether the British or the French still regarded the treaty of 1939 as binding in the changed postwar situation.

At first Stalin may have believed that elements sympathetic to the U.S.S.R. stood a reasonable chance to dominate the emerging Turkish opposition in 1945—a possibility that must have seemed all the more promising as leftists were among the earliest and most vocal opponents of Turkey's one-party regime. By the time those of this persuasion had been isolated from the bulk of the opposition movement at the end of 1945, however, Turkish national determination to reject Soviet demands had crystallized and it was clear that force would be necessary to secure Moscow's desires. Yet until the U.S.S.R. had achieved something of a nuclear capability, Stalin was everywhere unwilling to chance provoking U.S. retaliation by engaging in force of arms against a determined opponent. Especially when the United States by the fall of 1945 had begun to show its unmistakable interest in the fate of Turkey, concern lest American forces come to Turkey's defense must have argued strongly against recourse to arms by Moscow to secure its demands.

Perhaps, as Mehmet Ali Aybar was almost alone in stating at the time, the Soviets were war-weary and could not actually take up arms against Turkey in any event.[62] Certainly the Kremlin was on a fishing expedition to see what profit it could derive. Yet whatever the Soviet intentions, it seems evident that in the calculus of confrontation the ever-present shadow of the United States provided the ultimate margin of security for Turkey. This, more than the might of Ankara's military force, the strength of the Turkish will to resist, or the difficulties of terrain, tipped the balance.

---

[62] Aybar, "Amerikan Yardımını," p. 1.

2
From Marshall Plan to NATO:
Turkish Efforts to Join the Alliance

The same spirit that had led U.S. policy makers to step into the gap left by the British in their withdrawal from Greece and Turkey also predisposed the American government to undertake a massive rehabilitation program for Europe. Proclamation of the Marshall Plan in June 1947 faced the Ankara authorities with the urgent problem of discovering how they might fit into this project.

The Marshall Plan was not designed to deal with Turkey's particular situation. With the Truman Doctrine, American planners believed that Turkey's urgent assistance requirements had been met. The mission under General Lunsford Oliver, which had been dispatched immediately to survey Turkey's needs, had reported that the Turkish economy was basically sound. The team had proposed that Turkey receive military aid for five years, after which time the Oliver group expected the Turks to be largely self-sufficient. In fact these American advisers concluded that, in view of Turkey's low level of economic development, a high rate of investment would exceed absorptive capacity and lead to inflation. For this reason, they believed that international lending agencies could satisfy the limited aid requirements they projected for Turkey.[1]

Under these circumstances, the American policy makers proposed only a small role for the Marshall Plan in Turkey. Truman's advisers felt that Turkey, whose economy had escaped physical damage during the war, would even be able to contribute to European recovery by supplying urgently needed agricultural goods and minerals; thus what they believed necessary for Turkey was an allocation of machinery to

---

[1] William A. Helseth, "The United States and Turkey," pp. 423–24.

stimulate production in those fields. However, in view of Turkey's sizable foreign exchange holdings, Washington judged that this equipment should be provided the Turks on a cash-and-carry basis. In short, concessionary aid was omitted from the initial U.S. conception of how the Marshall Plan should operate in Turkey.[2]

This design raised a number of problems for the Turks. In the first place, the U.S. failure to offer either long-term credits or grant aid to assist economic development was a painful blow, especially given the massive U.S. assistance to be provided Western Europe. Besides, internal pressures for rapid economic advance were mounting. In the context of the bitter political contest unleashed by the move from a one-party state to a functioning multiparty system, economic development was fast emerging as the coin to purchase political success. Pressures on the Turkish government to move ahead very quickly in the economic realm became irresistible. For this, liberal American assistance seemed essential.

Determined to assert Turkey's case for benefiting from the Marshall Plan, the Turkish government sent a delegation to Paris in July 1947 for the meeting of European states to respond to the American proposals. Here, as the first step to rebut the argument that Turkey did not require outside assistance, the Turks unveiled a Five-Year Plan calling for $615 million in foreign aid for economic development.[3] The size of the request did little to bolster the Turkish case, but the Turkish argumentation had some effect. On the one hand, Turkish officials called into question the U.S. estimate of the soundness of Turkey's foreign exchange position; on the other, they shifted the argument for aid from economic to political criteria. Borrowing from the rationale underlying the Truman Doctrine— that Turkey deserved American aid because it served as an outpost of the West against the U.S.S.R.—Ankara pointed to its heavy defense burden. Under the pressure of this reasoning, Washington gave ground. By mid-March 1948, the United States had agreed to extend Turkey $10 million in credits, as the first installment in a program of economic assistance which by 1971 would total nearly $3 billion.[4]

Another point of friction inherent in the Marshall plan was its effort to assure favorable treatment for private enterprise, especially for foreign

---

[2] A. Suat Bilge et al., *Olaylarla Türk Dış Politikası (1919–1965)*, p. 236.

[3] Bilge, pp. 236, 474–83. For details of this plan, see Max Weston Thornburg, Graham Spry, and George Soule, *Turkey: An Economic Appraisal* (New York, 1949), pp. 288–315.

[4] Bilge, pp. 474–88.

investment. The American attachment to private initiative was most clearly expounded in the report of Max Thornburg, who had begun to survey the Turkish economy for the Twentieth Century Fund at the start of 1947. Thornburg even went so far as to call for the dismantling of important state enterprises, such as the Karabük steel mill.[5] But the spirit was reflected as well in the agreement of July 1948 which established the terms of Turkey's participation in the Marshall Plan. Here the Turkish government engaged itself to prevent practices that might "restrain competition, limit access to markets, or foster monopolistic control," and it undertook to reduce barriers to both domestic and foreign trade.[6] These and other analogous commitments led the right-wing oriented *Yeni Sabah* to complain in mid-August 1948 that the United States was pursuing in Turkey a "full-fledged open door policy."[7] From the left end of the political spectrum, Mehmet Ali Aybar—who was to emerge as leader of the Turkish Labor Party in the 1960s—chimed in to condemn the agreement with the United States as reviving the capitulations. Aybar taxed America with seeking control of Turkey's resources in order to be able to exploit the country as a colony.[8]

Once Turkey's eligibility to receive concessionary aid had been established, however, most Turks greeted the Marshall Plan with warm appreciation. Dissenters were few in number and not persuasive with the overwhelming majority of the elite or with the masses. Even the fact that economic assistance was for the first year extended in the form of loans rather than as outright grants did not evoke significant public criticism. Sensitivity on this score was undoubtedly dulled by the fact that repayment was long term (thirty-five years) and the interest rate low (2.5 percent).[9]

True to the original intent of its designers, the program for Marshall Plan assistance in Turkey concentrated on developing agriculture. Of the some $300 million aid provided between 1948 and 1952, almost

---

[5] Thornburg, Spry, and Soule, passim.

[6] See Art. II, *Economic Cooperation with Turkey,* TIAS 1794, signed July 4, 1948.

[7] *Yeni Sabah,* August 10, 1948. The following day *Yeni Sabah* quoted Nation Party founder Hikmet Bayur as agreeing without reservation to these views.

[8] See his articles in *Geveze,* August 15, 24; September 15; October 6, 1948.

[9] Richard D. Robinson, "Impact of American Military and Economic Assistance Programs in Turkey," report to the American Universities Field Staff, 1956, p. 25 (hereafter cited as "Impact of American Programs").

60 percent appears to have been invested in the agricultural sector.[10] Food production rose dramatically; and by 1953 Turkey had become, if only briefly, one of the world's major wheat exporters. Thanks in large part to this achievement, Turkish national income grew nearly 45 percent during the five years following the start of the program, in an atmosphere of only moderate inflationary pressure. This success, however, rested on shaky foundations: much of the extraordinary increase in productivity was due to beneficent weather; crops on the marginal land brought under cultivation proved particularly vulnerable to the unfavorable weather cycle that began in 1954. The operation of the Marshall Plan could also be faulted for such practices as encouraging diversity in the variety of agricultural equipment imported, thus excessively complicating the problem of spare parts. The mechanization of the farmer and of the Turkish military establishment also brought new demands for petroleum imports.[11] Yet overall, the impact of the American aid was clearly beneficial. It served to impart needed dynamism to the agricultural sector, which faced the monumental challenge of a rapidly increasing population.

U.S. assistance also had effects in areas unintended by its designers. Provision of aid on such a scale tended to insulate the Turkish authorities from economic reality. The striking early successes of the Marshall Plan experience gave Turkish policy makers exaggerated expectations of being able to carry out rapid development without compromising a steady growth in the standard of living. As a result, Turkish politicians became increasingly resistant to American insistence that projects be based on economic criteria, thereby preparing the ground for the severe disputes over aid that marred official Turkish relations with the United States during the mid-1950s.

At the same time, the Marshall Plan emphasis on agriculture encouraged the government's orientation toward the peasant masses. Under the Menderes government, which came to power in 1950, this concentration on the rural sector became associated with a growing DP disdain for the traditional elite power centers. In turn, it was the alienation of these important elements by the DP—something that Washington neither

---

[10] Doğan Avcıoğlu, *Türkiye'nin Düzeni,* p. 277, attempts a precise calculation, although the nature of the statistics lends some doubt about the accuracy of his figures. Avcıoğlu finds 20.6% invested directly and 59.7% indirectly in agriculture. See also S. İlkin and E. İnanç, eds., *Planning in Turkey* (METU, 1967), p. 23.

[11] See Robinson, "Impact of American Programs," p. 8.

desired nor for the most part even recognized at the time—which would set the stage for the military revolt that was to bring down the civilian regime in 1960. This alienation also contributed to the eventual casting of the United States in the image of a force opposed to the urban elite, the principal victim of the policy of concentration on rural development. Moreover, in the long run, Turkish critics of the United States would assail the Marshall Plan stress on agriculture in Turkey as a direct challenge to the philosophy of etatism inaugurated by Atatürk.[12] The idea that political independence required a self-sufficient industrial base had become widely accepted by the Turkish elite in the 1930s. But the American recipe for development as expressed in the Marshall Plan seemed to spurn industrial development. Much as there was sound economic justification for concentrating the limited available resources on agricultural and infrastructure projects, recommendations along these lines from American sources would long after the fact be singled out by Turkish radicals as evidence that the West wished to see Turkey remain a producer of raw materials for the industrialized countries of Europe.

The challenge of NATO

By mid-1948 the United States had become interested in establishing a formal collective security arrangement for Europe. This was a momentous shift in American policy. Previously, Washington had on a number of occasions rejected the idea of engaging in an explicit defensive alliance when broached by the Turks. But with the demise of the non-Communist regime in Czechoslovakia and the imposition of the Berlin blockade in 1948, the U.S. stance toward defensive pacts shifted. In March 1948, when England, France, Belgium, Holland, and Luxembourg signed the Brussels Pact for collective defense, the United States announced its support of this arrangement, and by June of that year Washington was actively engaged in laying the bases for the North Atlantic Treaty Organization. NATO, an alliance originally envisaged as restricted exclusively to Western European states, officially came into being in April 1949 with no provision for Turkish membership.

The Ankara government was immediately interested in joining the organization. Perhaps at bottom the Turkish authorities were animated by concern lest Turkey's exclusion lead to a diminution of U.S. interest and consequently to a reduction in American aid. Unquestionably, the

---

[12] See, for example, Avcıoğlu, pp. 270 ff., 284 ff.

size of U.S. assistance had by this time become a central preoccupation in Ankara. Some Turkish leaders also voiced anxiety that the formation of NATO, by barring further Soviet encroachment in Western Europe, might induce the Kremlin to increase pressure on such less firmly protected points as Turkey. Beyond these fears lay the desire to avoid as well the appearance of a diplomatic defeat that could be exploited by the DP opposition inside Turkey.[13]

The RPP government, however, soon found that there were formidable obstacles to acceptance by NATO. In July 1948 the American secretary of state shot down the trial balloon launched by Foreign Minister Necmeddin Sadak who, in a statèment published in the *New York Times* on June 30, 1948, had called for a formal U.S.-Turkish alliance.[14] When the Turks persisted, informally urging that Ankara be among the founding signatories of NATO, the Truman administration again demurred on the grounds that this pact was an Atlantic regional alignment not open to purely Mediterranean states. Basically, the United States was not prepared to "undertake further responsibilities until NATO structure had been firmly established," and feared that a commitment to Turkey might suggest indifference to the fate of Greece and Iran.[15]

For the Turks this rebuff became even more painful when preparations for the signing of the North Atlantic Pact were in their final stages. Although the RPP government openly acknowledged the narrow geographical argument for Turkey's exclusion, the news that Italy and French Algeria were slated to be included under the NATO umbrella caused much unhappiness in Turkey early in 1949. The Ankara regime hastened to renew pressure on the Department of State, demanding that Turkey receive equal treatment. But Washington, while expressing sympathy, continued to insist that the time was not ripe for Turkey to join; the United States undertook merely to "accord friendly and careful consideration to the security problem of the Turkish Republic." Disappointment over America's reluctance to fortify relations with Turkey even led one right-wing commentator in the RPP newspaper *Ulus* to call

---

[13] Abidin Dav'er, "Atlantik Paktının Tekâmülüne Doğru," *Cumhuriyet*, March 11, 1949. See also Metin Tamkoç, "Turkey's Quest for Security through Defensive Alliances," in Ankara University, *The Turkish Yearbook of International Relations*, vol. 2 (Ankara, 1963), p. 19.

[14] *New York Times,* June 30, July 3, 1948; Helseth, pp. 440–49.

[15] Tamkoç, p. 20; U.S. Senate, *Congressional Record,* 82nd Cong., 1st sess., March 21, 1951, pt. 2, p. 2759 (remarks of Senator Harry P. Cain).

on the Turks to pull away from the West and adopt a neutralist stance.[16] Most other journalists did not go that far in voicing their dissatisfaction; *Ulus* itself made it a point to explain that this article represented a personal, not a party, position.

To try to disguise the magnitude of this diplomatic reverse, the RPP government now floated a proposal for a Mediterranean pact centering on Turkey as a "continuation" of NATO. Foreign Minister Sadak himself advanced the notion, arguing that European security was indivisible and could not be assured without providing for Turkey's defense.[17] Obviously the idea of a Mediterranean pact did not mean that Turkey was reconciled to its exclusion from the Atlantic community. Rather, the Turkish strategy was to get the United States involved in a Mediterranean regional defensive arrangement until such time as Turkey could attain full acceptance by NATO. But while Washington made clear for the record that it did not disapprove of the idea of a regional pact, Sadak had no success in enlisting active U.S. support for his scheme during his trip to the opening of the U.N. General Assembly in April 1949. President Truman was not prepared to go beyond reaffirming publicly that, despite Turkey's exclusion from NATO, there was no decrease in American interest in the Turks. Thus Sadak returned home bearing only a letter reiterating Washington's friendship and noting that the formation of NATO also served Turkey's security.[18]

It was the United States that bore the brunt of the disappointment felt in Turkey over rejection by NATO. There were some senators and other influential figures in Washington who strongly favored the Turkish cause, however, and the Turkish government soon came to appreciate the fact that it was opposition from the European members of the alliance, especially the British and Scandinavians, that formed the greatest barrier to Turkish admission.[19] These powers apparently were fearful

---

[16] Ibid., p. 2760; Peyami Safa, "Atlantik Paktı ve Biz," *Ulus*, March 26, 1949.

[17] See Sadak's interview with Agence France Presse on February 17, 1949, in *Ayın Tarihi*, February 1949, pp. 139–40; "Atlantik Paktı bir Akdeniz Paktı ile Tamamlanmalı," *Ulus*, February 18, 1949; Ankara University, *Turkey and the United Nations* (New York, 1961), p. 158.

[18] For the text of the Truman letter, see *Bulletin*, April 17, 1949, p. 482. On this visit, see also Helseth, p. 443; Ali Halil, *Atatürkçü Dış Politika ve NATO ve Türkiye* (Istanbul, 1968), p. 119.

[19] Tamkoç, pp. 19–21; Hamilton F. Armstrong, "Eisenhower's Right Flank," *Foreign Affairs*, July 1951, p. 660. Senator Cain professed to have it on good authority, for example, that "a high official of the State Department confidentially" informed the Turks that their exclusion came at "the insistence of some European members of the pact." See *Congressional Record* (footnote 15), p. 2760.

lest the extension of the pact to nonindustrialized and Muslim Turkey would weaken the unity of the European community. Some also seemed concerned that the effort to bring Turkey's military equipment up to the standards set for Europe would entail a reduction in the arms they were to receive. Moreover, the British hoped that Turkey, rather than being submerged in NATO, would become a point around which a new order in the Middle East could crystallize.

These European attitudes presaged the difficulties that Turkey was soon to experience in its efforts to participate in the Council of Europe. Despite Ankara's strong interest in taking part in that modest experiment at forging an international parliamentary forum, Turkey was not invited to be a founding member of the council at its organizational meeting on May 5, 1949. The Turkish press complained bitterly of this slight; an editorialist writing in the authoritative *Ulus* even went to the point of wondering why the United States had not prevented this humiliation.[20] And when, after much behind-the-scenes activity, Greece and Turkey did receive a call in August 1949 to join the council after all, some voices in Turkey grumbled that this act was meager consolation for being left outside of the Atlantic alliance. Given the atmosphere in Turkey, it was hard to consider the Council of Europe, which disposed neither economic nor military resources, in any way an acceptable substitute for NATO.

The Democrat Party and the Korean gambit

The final phase of Turkey's Western odyssey took place only after the RPP regime had fallen. İnönü's party bore far too heavy a legacy of past faults to retain the allegiance of the majority of the country once a legitimate alternative was available in free elections. The atmosphere of change was irresistible. Under the leadership of Celâl Bayar and Adnan Menderes, the DP skillfully claimed credit for forcing all the major moves toward political liberalization made by the RPP government in the years before 1950. Rapidly expanding its organization across the length and breadth of Turkey, the DP emerged as the most powerful vote-getting organization the country had ever seen.

The urge to change administration also drew on an unspoken desire to show the world that Turkish democracy had come of age. In this,

---

[20] Hüseyin Cahid Yalçın, "Avrupa Birliği Müessisleri ve Türkiye," *Ulus,* May 8, 1949. See also Bilge, pp. 242–43.

38

some observers have seen the fine hand of the United States: Geoffrey Lewis claims that USIS made a "gentle attempt to influence the Turkish electorate" by publishing shortly before the elections a pamphlet titled *A Government Founded by the People,* in which the right of the people to change their government was asserted.[21] This pamphlet, which could not have had more than a minuscule audience at best, passed virtually unnoticed at the time; and the DP's landslide victory on May 14, 1950, came in elections that were hailed throughout Turkey for their honesty. The new DP government soon proved that it merited the confidence expressed in it by the Department of State which, in commenting on the results of the elections, had hastened to affirm U.S. intentions of continuing "very friendly and close relations" with Turkey.[22]

Hardly a month after the Menderes cabinet took office, the Korean War broke out. When the U.N. Security Council called for support of South Korea, the DP leaders welcomed the appeal. Following a cabinet meeting hastily convened far from the capital at the summer resort of Yalova on July 25, 1950, the Menderes government announced its decision to send a 4,500-man unit to join the U.S. troops in Korea. This move was taken without consulting the opposition parties or gaining parliamentary approval—omissions that would draw persistent fire from İnönü and his associates.[23] Some in the RPP, as well as the leaders of the tiny Nation Party, criticized the dispatch of troops as inappropriate and even dangerous to Turkey's security. A handful of self-styled "peace

---

[21] G. L. Lewis, *Turkey* (New York, 1955), p. 129. Karpat distorts Lewis's explanation of this incident, claiming that a balancing statement was included in this pamphlet to the effect that governments should not be changed for frivolous causes. In fact, quite to the contrary, Lewis specifically notes that the sentence containing this idea was omitted from the passage quoted from the Declaration of Independence in the USIS brochure. See Kemal Karpat, *Turkey's Politics,* p. 241.

[22] For the text of the Department of State press release of May 16, 1950, and of Acting Secretary James E. Webb's statement of May 19, 1950, see *Bulletin,* May 29, 1950, pp. 869-70. In a more general context, Secretary of State Acheson reaffirmed U.S. "determination to continue our policy of supporting" Turkey. See his statement of May 20, 1950, in *Bulletin,* June 5, 1950, p. 883.

[23] Kasım Gülek, secretary general of the RPP, stated the party's official position in a release carried by the press on July 26, 1950. For İnönü's statement, see Sabahat Erdemir, ed., *Muhalefetde İsmet İnönü* (Istanbul, 1956), pp. 18, 32–33. See also Nihat Erim, "Hükümetin Son Kararı," *Ulus,* July 27, 1950. Among those in the RPP most critical of the Korean expedition was former Foreign Minister Necmeddin Sadak, "Kore Savaşı ve Türkiye," *Akşam,* July 16, 1950. For the Nation Party's views, see "Hatalı Kararın Akisleri," *Yeni Sabah,* July 28, 1950. For defense of the DP position, see Ali Fuad Başgil, *La Révolution militaire de 1960 en Turquie (ses origines)* (Geneva, 1963), pp. 83–85.

partisans" addressed a public appeal to the parliament to rescind the decision. They insinuated that Turkey's action had been dictated by a U. S. senator, Harry Cain, who was then passing through Istanbul.[24] But these objections were soon swamped by an upsurge of pride in the conduct of the Turkish contingent in Korea and gratitude for the prestige that this venture had won for Turkey in the Western world. Once Turkish troops were actually engaged in combat, DP deputies sought belatedly to regularize the cabinet's decision by passing a "sense of parliament" resolution in December 1950.[25] In this atmosphere appeals to national unity prevailed, and objections to the commitment of Turkish troops petered out.

From the first, the Menderes government recognized that the Korean gambit offered the opportunity it was seeking to force the gates of NATO. However objectionable the DP tactics might have appeared to the domestic opposition, Ankara's decisiveness greatly enhanced its standing with its Western associates. To take full advantage of this opportunity, the Turkish Foreign Office approached the U.S., British, and French ambassadors on August 1, 1950, with a request that Turkey be accorded NATO membership.[26] Foreign Minister Fuat Köprülü accompanied this démarche with a declaration published the following day in the *New York Times* warning that Turkish public opinion regarded entry into the North Atlantic pact as "an acid test of United States interest in Turkey." He argued further that "extension of the Atlantic Pact to include Turkey is essential to close a breach in the defense system laid down in the pact."

These Turkish moves signified the DP government's recognition that the Mediterranean pact notion urged by its RPP predecessors was totally impracticable in view of the deep differences dividing the states of the eastern Mediterranean, particularly the Arabs and Israel. It also connoted realization by the Menderes cabinet that the past pattern of quiet

---

[24] For the text of the declaration distributed by Behice Boran, leader of these "peace partisans," see *Ayın Tarihi,* July 1950, pp. 8–9. See also Fethi Tevetoğlu, *Türkiye'de Sosyalist ve Komünist Faâliyetler* (Ankara, 1967), pp. 624–26.

[25] Türkiye Büyük Millet Meclisi (hereafter cited as TBMM), *Tutanak Dergisi,* dönem IX, vol. 3, pp. 136–205, session of December 11, 1950. The resolution was voted 311 to 39 with one abstention. RPP, Nation Party, and independent deputies cast negatives votes. The resolution was published in *Resmi Gazete,* no. 7694, December 28, 1950. See also Mümtaz Soysal, *Dış Politika ve Parlamento* (Ankara, 1964), pp. 196–204.

[26] Bilge et al., p. 245.

diplomacy, urging behind the scenes that Turkey be brought under a formal security umbrella, would not achieve success. The problems of NATO were too many and too varied to lend themselves to a consensus on anything as controversial as membership for Turkey and Greece. Besides, some in the alliance feared that the extension of NATO to the eastern Mediterranean—indeed, to the very borders of the Soviet Union —might appear unduly provocative to the Kremlin at this critical juncture with war in Korea.[27] Only a frontal assault by the Turkish government could hope to overcome these objections from the various NATO powers.

Halfway in

As it turned out, Turkish tactics carried the day. While the NATO foreign ministers at their meeting in September 1950 could not bring themselves to accept the Turkish demand for membership, they felt that some concession was required. As a compromise Turkey (and Greece as well) was invited to take part in NATO military planning for the Mediterranean area. And at the start of October 1950 the Ankara government announced that it would participate in this activity.[28]

The DP leaders were highly disappointed at getting only half a loaf. But the undeniable gain they had scored encouraged them to press further with the same tactics. Their resolve to regularize their relationship with the West was reinforced as well by the doubts engendered in Turkey by an article by General Omar Bradley published in the *Reader's Digest* in October 1950. The American chief of staff, in discussing U.S. military policy, warned that Turkey and other Asian states were likely to become involved in "local wars" in the years ahead. Bradley, however, cautioned against committing U.S. troops to such conflicts outside the main Western defense perimeter, lest the diversion of forces dissipate the strategic reserve necessary to defeat the Soviet Union. Shocked by this line of argumentation, the Turkish press vigorously challenged the notion that an attack against Turkey by the U.S.S.R. or its allies could be considered simply a "local war." The respected newspaper *Cumhuriyet* even exchanged telegrams with U.S. Secretary of State Dean Acheson in an

---

[27] *New York Times,* May 26, June 2, 1951.

[28] For the text of the *notes verbales* exchanged between Secretary of State Acheson and Turkish Ambassador Erkin on September 19, and October 2, 1950, see *Bulletin,* October 16, 1950, pp. 632–33.

attempt to clarify the American position.[29] And this furor offered Ankara renewed opportunities to insist that Washington make clear its commitment to Turkey's defense.

During a round of visits of high-ranking U.S. military and diplomatic officials in January and February 1951, Turkey proposed that the United States join the British-Turkish and Franco-Turkish alliances of 1939. This initiative, made public at the beginning of March 1951, obviously did little of practical significance to add to Turkish security, and was probably not intended as a serious suggestion,[30] for the 1939 security pacts excluded action against the U.S.S.R. on the part of Turkey. Yet this démarche served well to raise the issue of Turkey's position in respect to NATO and to force a U.S. response.

The last push

On May 15, 1951, Washington proposed to its NATO partners that Greece and Turkey be accepted as full members. The rationale for this decision as leaked to the press was that the Turkish armed forces would fill an otherwise exposed flank, and that without such ties Turkey "possibly could be drawn toward a sort of 'neutralism' " in view of its common border with the U.S.S.R.[31] In fact, however, the Turkish tactics had left the United States with little choice. Once NATO had accepted Turkey in something akin to "associate" status, it was hard to argue against full membership, particularly when Turkey was already linked by formal alliances with the United Kingdom and France. Beyond the absence of any convincing reason for turning Turkey down, the military benefits of Turkish association had made themselves apparent during the efforts of the Turkish planners and their NATO associates to design a common Mediterranean defense. Not only would Turkey's adherence to the Atlantic Pact impel the Soviet Union to divert additional forces from Eastern Europe, but Turkish air fields would be available for NATO allies.

---

[29] *Cumhuriyet,* November 11, 1950, carried the texts of these telegrams. A spokesman for Bradley also explained that the general's meaning had been distorted in condensation and that the United States could not remain a bystander if Turkey were invaded by a "communist" power. See Mümtaz Faik Fenik, "General Bradley'in Son İzahı," *Zafer,* November 16, 1950; General Omar Bradley, "U.S. Military Policy: 1950," *Reader's Digest,* October 1950, pp. 143–54.

[30] James Reston, "Turkey Invites U.S. to Join Treaty of Mutual Aid with Britain, France," *New York Times,* March 2, 1951.

[31] Walter H. Waggoner, "Turkish-Greek Bid for Full Ties Gains," *New York Times,* March 18, 1951.

At that time, when the Strategic Air Command was in the process of constructing a base system ringing the U.S.S.R., this consideration obviously held important weight.[32]

Under this U.S. pressure, the British weakened in their opposition to extending NATO to the eastern Mediterranean. The United Kingdom was particularly concerned with defense of the Middle East, especially with protection of the Suez Canal. These considerations loomed even larger after the start of the Anglo-Iranian oil crisis in 1951. England was interested in forming a Middle East defense organization embracing not only the Arab states but Israel as well. In this connection, the British projected a key role for Turkey, which was seen in London as the bellwether of the Middle East. Thus the U.K. leaders insisted that any plan to include Turkey in NATO be conditioned on Ankara's willingness to cooperate in a Middle Eastern regional arrangement at the same time. The Menderes government was willing to play such a role, as Foreign Minister Köprülü publicly affirmed in July 1951, on receipt of assurances that London would support Turkey's application.[33]

Although agreement in principle to accept Turkey and Greece into NATO was subsequently given without dissenting voice by the foreign ministers meeting at Ottawa in September 1951, there remained several matters of detail to be settled. Most thorny was the question of the command to which Turkish and Greek forces should be assigned. Again, the British interest in constructing a Middle East defense system underlay the difficulty. London wanted Turkish and Greek forces assigned to a British general under a separate command whose authority could be extended to the armies of other states they hoped would join the Middle East Command. Turkey, on the other hand, desired its forces to report to a U.S. general and to be part of the regular NATO European army.[34] This impasse was partially overcome when in October 1951 the Egyptian government unceremoniously rebuffed the joint appeal by the United States, Great Britain, France, and Turkey to participate in a Middle East Command. Arab opinion generally registered its unmistakable hostility to joining with Turkey and the Western powers, thus scotching any possibility that the projected command could be formed. Yet the British did

---

[32] C. L. Sulzberger, "Atlantic Parley Will Strive to Bolster Europe's Flank," *New York Times,* September 2, 1951. Cf. George F. Kennan, *Memoirs, 1925–1950,* p. 411.

[33] "F. Köprülünün Atlantik Paktına dair Demeci," *Cumhuriyet,* July 21, 1951.

[34] Bilge et al., pp. 247–48.

not immediately give way; they still insisted on a separate command for the Turkish and Greek forces under a British general. Only after a compromise was devised to create a separate South European Command under an American general was it possible to reach agreement. As a result, Turkey was able to enter NATO officially on February 18, 1952, as a full-fledged member.

Implications of NATO membership

The Turks greeted their adherence to NATO with general rejoicing. Even the tiny left wing was either so intimidated or in such disarray that it could not make its voice heard as it had in times past. Two aspects of the Turkish reaction appeared particularly significant for the future. On the one hand, Turks characteristically regarded NATO as an extension of the United States. Hence, for example, the chief editorialist of *Zafer,* the semiofficial organ of the government party, emphasized that "with the Atlantic Pact, should Turkey now be attacked, America's aid is automatically guaranteed." On the other hand, much was made of the recognition of Turkey's equality with West European nations inherent in the agreement to include her in NATO. For the Turks, acceptance by the Atlantic alliance was an act confirming their cherished belief that they were, and should be recognized as, an integral part of Europe.[35]

Turkey's search for a formal Western commitment was now thus successfully concluded. But it was not only the gain in physical security from the Soviet Union that was important. From Ankara's point of view, an important advance over previous connections with the West lay in providing assurance that Turkey would continue to receive aid in quantities that could spell the success of the government's ambitious development plans.

The new alliance system was viewed by the Turks as of the broadest scope. Both the DP leaders and their Republican predecessors had worked to involve the United States as intimately as possible in Turkish affairs. Obviously the Turkish leadership believed that Turkey stood to benefit more from a comprehensive association than from a bare formal security guarantee. To bring the somewhat refractory United States to this conclusion, the Turks were willing to take on a wide range of obligations. Especially the Turkish agreement to pursue an active role

---

[35] Mümtaz Faik Fenik, "Dış Politikada Büyük Zafer," *Zafer,* September 22, 1951. See also, Altemur Kılıç, *Turkey and the World* (Washington, 1959), p. 211.

in the Middle East—a sharp break with past patterns of policy—demonstrated that, initially at least, Ankara regarded the Western alliance as having connotations far beyond matters directly touching on the Soviet Union.

The establishment of intimacy with a large foreign power was a new departure for Republican Turkey. While there was always great sensitivity about sacrificing Turkey's rights, especially where privileges in any way reminiscent of the Ottoman capitulations were involved, the Turks had been the suitor in this instance, and after their hard wooing were not inclined to insist on more restrictive arrangements than West European countries had imposed in regulating the alliance. In fact, Turkish opinion makers felt the greatest confidence in their new allies. The image of the United States as the protector of small nations appears to have been widely accepted in Turkey. Moreover, there was no doubt that Foreign Minister Köprülü expressed the general view when he told the parliament in December 1951: "Our national interests are identical from every standpoint with the joint interests of the North Atlantic Treaty Organization and with its geographic and military requirements." [36] In this frame of mind, many Turks, especially those in the DP, readily assumed that Turks and Americans were intrinsically alike and that Turkey could and should become a "little America." Of course, if the American way was to be exalted as the model, it is not surprising that little need was felt to insert stringent qualifications on the scope of U.S. activity in Turkey.

For the United States as well, the assumption that Turkish-American interests were entirely congruent now became accepted as the basic tenet of the relationship.[37] In consequence, American planners thereafter tended to overestimate U.S. freedom of action in Turkey; they did not easily foresee the difficulties that would arise from using the alliance for purposes that did not appear to be directly connected with "containing" the Soviet Union. Hence, one of the central and enduring problems of the Turkish-American cooperation has been to define the scope of this association, a scope that has demonstrably changed in the years since the alliance first came into being.

Nor was it clear from the NATO commitment what economic goals

[36] Turkey, Turkish Information Office, *Turkey's Foreign Relations in 1952* (New York, 1952), p. 6.

[37] George C. McGhee, "Turkey Joins the West," *Foreign Affairs,* July 1954, pp. 617–30, notes the "remarkable similarity in national aims and policies."

the Western allies, and especially the United States, were expected to meet. The Atlantic alliance implied that Turkey was a Western nation on a par with Europe. This was not true in terms of living standard, education, and the cultural level of the masses. Therefore, the question remained open. What sort of program would the NATO allies undertake in order to build up Turkey (and Greece, too, for that matter) to bring these underdeveloped states to the level of their European counterparts? The failure to define aims for Turkey's economic development contributed directly to the contretemps over economic assistance that formed one of the outstanding features of Turkish-American relations in the 1950s.

Part Two:
COLD WAR PARTNERS

3

The Menderes Decade 1950-1960

Military Alliance

Once Turkey entered NATO, this connection served as the general foundation for the whole range of political, economic, and military relations between Turkey and the United States. Previous programs, such as economic assistance extended under the Marshall Plan and the military aid provided through the Truman Doctrine, were expanded. But in the eyes of both parties these activities were now considered to be subsumed under NATO. In practice, this meant that both sides recognized these programs to be continuing multiyear engagements with no projected terminal date. Moreover, the NATO connection led to a proliferation of U.S. activities in Turkey, from an array of special bilateral accords ordering more intimate military cooperation to a fanning out of technical-assistance projects to a great variety of areas of Turkish life. It was to be this ungainly sprawl of American involvement that would eventually form one of the festering sores in the relations between the United States and Turkey.

Through NATO membership, Turkey for the first time assumed the obligation to coordinate defense plans with those of a European army under an international command. No longer was the protection of the country a matter for exclusive planning by Ankara; nor was it a function of Turkish forces and their deployment alone. Although Turkish units in peacetime were to remain under their national commanders, their armaments, doctrine, and organization had to be brought into harmony with those of their allies. The association with the U.S. military under the Truman Doctrine had prepared the base for this. Now, however, Turkish officials with their counterparts from other NATO states met regularly to debate issues relative to these matters in a much more intimate way. These multinational conclaves set so-called "force goals" representing the judgment of military planners as to the shape of the military establishment necessary to defend the member countries.

NATO's force goals were targets whose fulfillment, as it turned out, proved always beyond the resources at the command of the alliance. Periodically adjusted downward, they stood as a monument to the changing perception of the threat to the member states. The gap between the force goals and the resources the NATO partners committed to them represented also the measure of the difference between the politically expedient and the militarily desirable. And this gap offered a field for bargaining in which recipient countries could appeal to the accepted force goals in their quest to secure military assistance from their allies. In the Turkish case, this bargaining process proved a source of potential misunderstanding.[1]

When Turkey joined NATO, the experience of the Korean War still dominated the thinking of the allies. Fearing imminent Soviet attack on Europe, the alliance partners had set themselves the goal of fielding a conventional defense force of ninety-six divisions, of which some forty were to be operational at all times; and yet, the Western European states had less than twenty divisions at their disposal. Hence, the prospect of adding some eighteen Turkish divisions—even if not on the crucial central front—was a powerful argument for admitting Turkey in the first place. NATO strategy assumed that the presence of these forces along the frontier of the Soviet Union would cause the Kremlin to divert significant effectives to defend its Caucasus border, thereby reducing the number of Soviet units that could be committed to attack central Europe. Moreover, Turkish troops were the least costly to maintain of any in the alliance—a consideration then also commonly cited in justifying U.S. military aid allocations. Though the Menderes administration argued in a similar vein in its campaign to gain entry into NATO, vaunting its military establishment as an "asset" to the West, Turkish critics a decade or so later seized on American recognition of the cost advantages of

---

[1] For a cogent discussion of force goals, see Francis A. Beer, *Integration and Disintegration in NATO* (Columbus, Ohio, 1969), passim.

Turkish soldiers as evidence that Washington regarded the Turks as expendable cannon fodder.[2]

Even with the accretion of Turkish and Greek effectives, the alliance remained far from its ambitious goals. In recognition of the deficiencies in NATO's conventional forces, the Eisenhower administration soon after taking office proclaimed the doctrine of "massive retaliation." This strategy envisaged that conflict against the Soviet Union and its allies would rapidly and inevitably lead to "total" war. To offset the heavy numerical advantage that the U.S.S.R. enjoyed in men under arms over the European army, it seemed to the American planners necessary to have immediate recourse to nuclear weapons. As tactical nuclear arms that could be used on the battlefield had not yet come into the inventory of the allies, NATO's battle plans provided for strategic strikes against the enemy's heartland from the first, with no design to limit the area of conflict. Soviet aggression on any scale against a member of the alliance thus posed the possibility of a concerted response by all the allies— in effect threatening the onset of a third world war.[3]

This prospect did not dismay the Turkish leaders. On the contrary, they felt reassured that for their enemies the cost of war had become impossibly high. Moreover, in this era most of the Turkish elite conceived of the world as essentially bipolar; viewing their fate as inextricably bound up with that of all their allies, they simply could not imagine it possible to remain outside of any conflict that might develop between the U.S.S.R. and the West. Obviously the idea of a limited Soviet attack against a NATO target that would not concern Turkey was beyond any of Ankara's calculations at that time. In part this outlook represented the assumption that Turkey itself was a prime target of Soviet cupidity. For among the Turks the then predominant strategic view held that their country occupied a particularly important position astride two continents and at the gateway to a third, hence that Turkey was destined to be a prize in any major world conflict.[4] Recalling Stalin's demands for

---

[2] Doğan Avcıoğlu, *Türkiye'nin Düzeni,* p. 267, quotes a cost benefit analysis showing Turkish troops to be eight times cheaper to maintain than equivalent U.S. forces. For Turkish propaganda of the time, see *News from Turkey,* August 10, 1950, p. 1; supplement, March 15, 1951, p. 3; H. F. Sarhan, letter to the editor, *New York Times,* March 15, 1951.

[3] Roger Hilsman, "NATO: The Developing Strategic Context," in Klaus Knorr, ed., *NATO and American Security* (Princeton, 1959), pp. 27–28.

[4] See, for example, M. Faik Fenik, "Amerika'nın Emniyeti ve Türkiye," *Zafer,* January 17, 1952.

Turkish territory, this strategic appraisal seemed solidly grounded on reality.

NATO's "new look" plans called for the use of conventionally equipped ground forces (the "shield") to defend allied territory, while the air forces (the "sword") delivered the strategic nuclear counterpunch to knock out the enemy. In this concept Turkey's large land army— most of which was "assigned" to NATO, i.e., would come under allied command in wartime—was to hold as close to the borders as possible at reasonable defensive points. Of course, until the Turkish military establishment had been trained and equipped, and until roads and other infrastructure facilities needed to support a defending army had been constructed, NATO plans had evidently envisaged large-scale withdrawal, if faced with superior Soviet forces. No allied ground forces were to be stationed on Turkish soil, but periodic maneuvers were scheduled to show that American and other NATO units could quickly come to Turkey's aid. According to this formula, the air force was to receive heavy stress. Construction of air fields and other infrastructure projects necessary for strike aircraft had already been under way since the Truman Doctrine. And by the time Turkey joined NATO, a network of fields radiating from İncirlik airbase near Adana was nearing completion. With Turkey's entry into the alliance, the procurement of modern equipment was accorded urgent priority. Following the selection of Izmir as the headquarters of NATO's new Southeastern Command in 1952, the headquarters unit of the Sixth Allied Tactical Air Force was established there. It was not long before the U.S. Strategic Air Command was using the newly constructed İncirlik facility for training and periodic exercises.[5]

Under the NATO arrangement the Americans were the primary element involved in the Turkish military establishment. The other Atlantic Pact allies had little day-to-day contact with Turkish armed forces and furnished relatively little to bolster Turkish military capabilities in this period. The European powers were still in the postwar recovery phase and had no significant military surplus to offer Turkey even at a price. The Canadians were able to supply modern aircraft, but during

---

[5] *New York Times*, March 9, 1951; March 19, 1955. The status of the İncirlik airbase and of American rights to use it became later a perennial subject of concern among prominent elements of the Turkish elite. See, for example, Abdi İpekçi, "Üsler Sorunu," *Milliyet*, May 21, 1970; "İncirlik Üssü, Türkiye için Büyük Tehlikedir!" *Devrim*, September 15, 1970, pp. 1, 5; Ahmet Şükrü Esmer, "Dış Politika: İncirlik Üssünün Esrarı," *Ulus*, November 21, 1965.

the first decade of the alliance, other suppliers who later became important, such as the West Germans, did not become purveyors of arms on any scale to Turkey. In fact, the Turks preferred it that way. Like their NATO associates in general, they saw the United States as the essential force to lend credence to the alignment; they also trusted in Washington's disinterest perhaps more than in that of the Europeans. Thus they ever urged strong U.S. leadership and a prominent rolé for America in the alliance.

The United States was eager to help improve the efficiency of the Turkish military establishment. To this end, American military assistance had from the first been directed toward bolstering fire power and increasing mobility, so that the size of the Turkish ground forces could be cut back significantly without any loss in military capability. Indeed, rapid progress was made in this endeavor; within a few years the number of men under arms was reduced from about 700,000 to some 400,000.

The Americans advising the Turkish armed forces naturally drew on their own experience and sought to bring the Turkish military establishment as close as possible to the American model. Besides attempting to inculcate new attitudes toward equipment and techniques, they urged liberalization of archaic personnel policies to provide more rapid advancement for able officers and noncommissioned officers. This was a delicate process and one fraught with pitfalls. It was difficult to prevent friction between officers trained in modern methods and their superiors who often remained steeped in the old ways. The use of American noncommissioned officers to instruct Turkish officers also required uncommon tact. But irritation from these sources was far overshadowed by the essentially good working relationships that from the first prevailed between the Turkish and American military establishments.[6]

Many years later Turkish critics would attack the American effort as a slavish imitation of U.S. practices. One extreme example cited in support of this contention was the translation of organizational manuals calling for the institution of regimental *imams,* as the equivalent of chaplains in the American army—a notion that violated the laic tradition laid down by Atatürk.[7] After the U.S. image had become tarnished in the mid-1960s, occasional complaints would be heard that American advisers, ignorant of Turkey's past military glories, had unnecessarily

---

[6] Richard D. Robinson, "Impact of American Programs," p. 6.
[7] Avcıoğlu, p. 268.

undermined Turkish military tradition: proposals to abbreviate the staff officer training course were cited for particular reprobation in this connection. And finally the more radical protagonists of this point of view alleged that the military changes initiated at the behest of the United States compromised the ability of the Turkish armed forces to maintain their independence.[8] But charges of this nature were largely confined to a handful of civilians and retired officers; they were not overtly voiced by those on active duty.

Bilateral agreements

A more important problem for the future, however, lay in another aspect of the military relationship. The NATO agreement was soon complemented by bilateral understandings dealing with specific facets of Turkish-American military cooperation.[9] Some of these understandings were full-fledged agreements, openly published and ratified by the Turkish parliament: for example, the Status of Forces Agreement of June 1954, which provided privileges and immunities for nondiplomatic personnel in the service of the U.S. government. Other understandings took the form of public exchanges of notes indicating agreement on certain procedural questions. But in addition, there were secret exchanges of notes and executive agreements concerning such matters as the deployment of weapons systems in Turkey and the right of U.S. personnel to carry on activities of a military or intelligence nature. These secret accords were negotiated either with the Foreign Ministry, with the particular ministry involved, or with the Turkish General Staff; none was ratified by the parliament. Most basic of these was the Military Facilities Agreement of June 1954, an understanding concluded in accordance with a Turkish cabinet decision.[10] Where these formal agreements left gaps or provided merely a general framework, Turkish and American officials often worked

---

[8] See, for example, Orhan Erkanlı, "Türk Ordusu Yeniden Düzenlenmelidir," *Milliyet*, February 19, 1968. For a listing of other articles on this subject, see Muammer Aksoy, "Atatürk'un Işığında 'Tam Bağımsızlık İlkesi'," in Siyasal Bilgiler, Fakültesi, *Abadan'a Armağan* (Ankara, 1969), pp. 689–799.

[9] Prime Minister Demirel gave a useful review of the bilateral relationship at his press conference on February 7, 1970. Text in T. C. Dışişleri Bakanlığı, *Dışişleri Bakanlığı Belleteni, Ocak-Şubat 1970*, pp. 98–140. For the abridged version in English which appeared in *The Pulse*, February 9, 1970, see Appendix 5.

[10] Turkish cabinet decree 9/1363 of August 27, 1953. See Dr. Hamza Eroğlu, "Türkiye ile A.B.D. arasında İmzalanan İkili Temel Anlaşma," *Ulus*, February 4, 1970; Sezai Orkunt, "İkili Anlaşmalar: İttifak Tarihinde Müspet Bir Adım mı?" *Cumhuriyet*, July 14, 1969.

54

out their own mutually agreeable procedures. As a result, a web of verbal understandings and precedents based on modes of action permitted by various levels of authority took shape. While these informal arrangements frequently related to specific matters of operational detail, on occasion they governed broader activities, such as permission to operate the American armed forces postal system and authority to open schools for the dependents of American personnel.[11]

Under these circumstances, neither state exercised close and comprehensive control over American activity in Turkey. There were no full records of the verbal undertakings to which either was committed; knowledge of some of the more sensitive activities was extremely closely held on both sides. The Turkish General Staff was not organized to provide centralized coordination of U.S. activities in Turkey. Nor, indeed, was any responsible senior American commander named to oversee all the various U.S. military elements active in Turkey. Until the 1960 coup led to wholesale changes in the Turkish military establishment, pointing up the lack of comprehensive knowledge and control of American activities, the dimensions of this problem appear to have passed largely unrecognized by the Turkish authorities.[12]

The secrecy surrounding many of these understandings between the United States and Turkey had pernicious political implications as well. Generally, Menderes and his colleagues felt little need to keep the opposition fully informed of foreign policy developments.[13] In some instances, security considerations must have argued strongly against any public disclosure; in others, reluctance to offer the political opposition a chance to raise objections may have discouraged recourse to parliament. Whatever the reason, the secrecy of these accords would eventually arouse suspicion in Turkey about their content. And already before the end of the 1950s, the opposition would begin to attack on constitutional grounds those understandings not ratified by the parliament.[14] While at first these attacks were directed far more at the DP

---

[11] For a highly critical and somewhat sensational account treating these aspects of U.S. military relationships with Turkey, see Doğan Avcıoğlu, "Türkiye'deki Amerikan Üsleri," *Yön*, November 26, 1965, p. 8.

[12] See Foreign Minister Çağlayangil's senate speech, Senato, *Tutanak Dergisi*, 1969, vol. 51-1, p. 40.

[13] Mümtaz Soysal, *Dış Politika ve Parlamento*, p. 196.

[14] Coşkun Kırca was one of the first to challenge the constitutionality of such military accords. See *Vatan*, October 18, 1959, where Kırca argued the need to bring before parliament any agreement authorizing the stationing of intermediate range missiles in Turkey.

administration than at the United States, in the 1960s it would be only a short step to centering fire on America as well.

The American presence

Particularly after the conclusion of the Status of Forces Agreement in 1954, the number of American personnel in Turkey began to rise significantly. At its height the total would reach some 24,000 U.S. officials and dependents.[15] At first these Americans were involved in completing projects begun in the days of the Truman Doctrine—for example, construction of the net of air fields, the expansion of the naval base at Gölcük, and modernization of port facilities at İskenderun. But this activity and the organization of field training teams sent to advise operational units of the Turkish armed forces were not responsible for the main influx of U.S. personnel. It was rather when American combat and reconnaissance aircraft began to be stationed in Turkey, when a chain of electronic installations was set up especially along the Black Sea coast, and when the deployment of intermediate range ballistic missiles (IRBMs) was in prospect that the major increase in the numbers of Americans would take place.[16] With this influx, support personnel too began to burgeon, and headquarters of other U.S. regional activities were attracted by the welcoming climate in Turkey.

This increase in personnel evidenced a shift in American interest in Turkey. Initially, Washington had seen defense of Turkey and the blocking of Soviet expansion in the area as its main concerns. Now American officials would increasingly recognize the benefits from using Turkey as a base of operations to augment the deterrent threat against the Soviet Union and to gain information about it. The concept of Turkey as an "unsinkable aircraft carrier" was coming into its own, a view that would lead American planners to regard Turkey as a possible staging area for operations in the Near East as well. Moreover, when the idea of a "missile gap" was raised by the successful launch of a Soviet satellite in 1957, there was no denying the attractiveness of the benefits to be derived from stationing IRBMs in Turkey.[17]

---

[15] U.S. Senate, Subcommittee on United States Security Agreements and Commitments Abroad of the Committee on Foreign Relations, *United States Security Agreements and Commitments Abroad,* Part 7: *Greece and Turkey* (Washington, 1970), p. 1860 (hereafter cited as *U.S. Security Agreements: Greece and Turkey*).

[16] John White, *Pledged to Development* (London, 1967), pp. 101–102.

[17] George F. Kennan, *Memoirs, 1925–1950,* p. 411.

At this period, Turkish public opinion generally paid little attention to this aspect of American activity in their country. National security concerns tended to induce both the opposition and the government press to de-emphasize coverage of military or related subjects. Soviet allegations in February 1956 that meteorological balloons launched by Americans from Turkey were used for espionage purposes failed to trigger any significant Turkish reaction.[18] The Turks provided effective cooperation in maintaining secrecy of the U-2 program of high-altitude overflights of the Soviet Union from İncirlik air base near Adana. Only when after four years of more or less uneventful operation, Gary Powers was shot down inside the U.S.S.R. on May 1, 1960, did this activity become a subject of public discussion. Then editorialists and politicians expressed some guarded criticisms of the United States, not for having carried on the overflights but for timing the Powers flight on the eve of a summit conference. In the main, however, the Turkish press blamed Khrushchev for deliberately sabotaging the celebrated Paris Summit meeting by overreacting to an activity he had known about for years. Many commentators even strongly defended the need for aerial reconnaissance of the Soviet Union, recalling Eisenhower's "open skies" proposal as essential in an age of missiles.[19]

The Status of Forces Agreement

The expanding U.S. presence in Turkey brought a host of problems, many of which stemmed directly from the application of the rights granted by the Status of Forces Agreement.[20] These were for the most part minor irritants when taken singly, but together they formed a plague of significant proportions.

The agreement provided that in the case of "offenses arising out of any act or omission done in the performance of official duty" a NATO country would surrender jurisdiction to the allied country whose personnel were charged with the crime. For the West European powers,

---

[18] A. Suat Bilge et al., *Olaylarla Türk Dış Politikası* (1919–1965), pp. 337–38. Richard D. Robinson, *Developments Respecting Turkey,* vol. 3 (New York, 1956), p. 94.

[19] See, for example, articles of Şükrü Baban in *Yeni Sabah,* May 15, 21, 1960; Coşkun Kırca in *Vatan,* May 12, 14, 1960; M. Piri, "Amerika-Rusya Hadisesi Nasıl Başladı . . . ?" *Cumhuriyet,* May 18, 1960. For an account by Powers himself, see Francis G. Powers (with Curt Gentry), *Operation Overflight* (New York, 1970), passim.

[20] For the text of the Status of Forces Agreement, see Appendix 2.

the sacrifice of primary jurisdiction involved little in the way of emotional overtones; these countries in practice often waived their rights to try offenders even if not enjoined to do so by reason of duty status. Not so the Turks. With their memories of the Ottoman capitulations still fresh, they often regarded any such sacrifice as a major derogation of sovereignty. They rarely relinquished jurisdiction when not so obliged by treaty.[21] Nor indeed were negotiations with them on matters relating to judicial exemptions ever perfunctory. But Washington insisted on its position that Turkey could not receive terms different from those concluded with other NATO states. In these circumstances, it was more than two years after Turkey joined NATO before Ankara adhered to the Status of Forces convention adopted by its allies in 1951.

From the first, therefore, there was a potential conflict in interpretation of the rights accorded by the Status of Forces Agreement. This problem came to the surface most frequently over the matter of traffic accidents. Here the sacrifice of sovereignty was posed acutely in the definition of duty status and of the right to determine it. Neither of these questions had been clearly settled in the NATO agreement. By 1956, experience in carrying out this accord impelled the Menderes government to secure parliamentary authority to insert language clarifying the phrase "in the performance of official duty," to emphasize that these words meant *while in a general duty status*.[22] This amplification brought the application of the convention into line with the U.S. understanding of the NATO agreement. The Ministry of Justice forthwith sent instructions to judicial authorities throughout Turkey that American officials would be permitted to take jurisdiction upon certification by the senior American commander that the offender was on duty when the offense took place.[23]

Though these instructions removed ambiguity and facilitated the smooth operation of this mechanism, they did not salve the feelings of Turkish opinion makers. For many of Turkey's elite gradually came to suspect that the procedure served to protect Americans from paying a reasonable penalty for misdeeds committed on Turkish soil. The rapidity

---

[21] See Ambassador Hart's farewell press interview, *Milliyet,* October 3, 1968.

[22] Law no. 6816 of July 16, 1956. See *Resmî Gazete,* July 24, 1956, p. 15168. Cf. "Anlaşmanın Tadili için Çalışmalara Başlandı," *Cumhuriyet,* August 29, 1964.

[23] For the text of this instruction, see Muzaffer Kıran and Gültekin Güneri, *NATO, Kanun ve Andlaşmaların Türkiyedeki Mukayeseli Tatbikatı* (Ankara, 1962), p. 59; also Haydar Tunçkanat, *İkili Anlaşmaların İçyüzü* (Ankara, 1970), pp. 264–65.

with which the wheels of U.S. military justice turned as compared to the slow pace of Turkish proceedings perhaps lent the impression to some that the American system operated rather perfunctorily. In a few celebrated cases, indeed, the sentences of American tribunals seemed inordinately light to the Turkish audience. Moreover, as the U.S. military commanders authorized to certify duty status often took a broad view of their prerogatives, few American soldiers stood trial in Turkish courts during the 1950s. To be sure, automobile accident rates for U.S. personnel in Turkey were low as compared with those of Americans stationed in Europe. But incidents inevitably rose with the increase in the American presence, and as publicity about exemptions from Turkish judicial procedure mounted, so too did resentment among the more vocal Turks at what they considered privileged treatment of U.S. citizens.[24]

This sentiment would reach a crescendo with the famous incident of November 1959, when Lieutenant Colonel Allen I. Morrison ran down a contingent of the Presidential Guard, killing one and injuring several others. Morrison was released to American authorities who certified that he had been on duty at the time of the accident.[25] He was subsequently tried in a U.S. military court, found guilty of negligence, fined $1,200, and restricted from troop command for two years. Nonetheless, his immunity from normal Turkish judicial procedure as well as the difference in punishment from what he might have received from Turkish authorities (up to three years in jail) evoked an emotional outburst of protest in the Turkish press.[26] Ever since then, the Morrison

---

[24] For a striking example of this resentment, see *Dünya,* November 12, 1959, where Bedii Faik wrote: "When you meet one of the Americans residing in our country, do you ask, even before learning his name, whether he is 'on duty' or not? No? Then let us warn you at once that you are exposing yourself to great danger. . . . You really don't know what 'on duty' means. . . . In the dictionary the meaning of this word is just 'on duty,' but in the NATO language it assumes many different meanings. It is a kind of insurance policy. It is also unlimited. . . . Just as [these American friends] bring all their foodstuffs, even their salt, from their own country, they never use the local justice! It looks as though one harms their stomachs and the other their heads."

[25] The accident occurred after normal working hours, when Morrison had just left the American officers club.

[26] In addition to a spate of articles in all the major Turkish papers condemning the surrender of Morrison to American justice, one editorial in the provincial press titled "Savulun, Amerikalı Geliyor" ("Take Cover, the American Is Coming") created something of a sensation. The author was tried for "damaging the foreign prestige of the government," but was eventually acquitted after the 1960 military coup. See A. Kemal Yılmaz, *Savulun Amerikalı Geliyor* (Çelikcild Matbaası, 1960), passim; *New York Times,* March 17, 1960.

case has stood for the Turks as a symbol of inequity in the Status of Forces Agreement.[27]

Other military issues

Another problem associated with the increasing American presence was black-marketeering among U.S. personnel. Americans employed in an official capacity enjoyed customs privileges which, if abused, could turn a flood of goods into illegal channels or could permit the illicit export of antiquities. Currency trafficking also offered the lure of great profit, given the enormous disparity between the official rate of exchange and that often obtainable on the black market. It is hard to determine the parameters of such illegality, though these offenses were evidently not uncommon, at least on a small scale, among Americans in Turkey. In 1959 the predominantly military American population around Izmir was rocked with open scandal over disclosures of large-scale black-marketeering.[28] Many vocal Turks resented the windfall profits they supposed most Americans were receiving in this fashion; this feeling increased their distaste for the existence of the post exchanges and the army postal system which were widely accounted the main vehicles for this trade.[29] Indeed, after evidence of abuse mounted toward the end of the 1950s American authorities began to keep systematic records of major items purchased in the post exchanges to check at the time the purchaser departed from Turkey. Eventually in the 1960s such control was extended to embrace a large proportion of the goods sold. The Turkish government, however, never acted to exercise customs supervision over the military postal system.

On another level, conspicuous consumption by Americans in Turkey was also an irritant in the relationship. As a result of the disparity of salaries and standards of living, it was possible for U.S. noncommissioned officers to maintain a style of life equivalent—if not supe-

---

[27] The Morrison-Knudsen Company, which had defense contracts in Turkey, suffered because of its similarity of name. This association also rubbed off on subsequent Prime Minister Süleyman Demirel, who was often called "Süleyman Morrison" by the extremist opposition because of his onetime employment as a representative of Morrison-Knudsen.

[28] For an account sympathetic to the American sergeants arrested in connection with this incident, see the series of articles on this case in *Time,* August 24–October 12, 1959.

[29] Avcıoğlu, "Türkiye'deki Amerikan Üsleri," *Yön,* November 26, 1965, pp. 8–9.

rior—to that of a Turkish general. Especially after a sharp economic crisis in Turkey led to the disappearance of almost all imported consumer goods from the market in the mid-1950s, the opulence of American life styles contrasted painfully with the straitened circumstances of the Turks. Moreover, the competition for scarce goods and services, especially domestic help, grated on the sensibilities of those Turks involved. The apparent insensitivity of the United States in this regard— as shown, for example, by long maintaining the Ankara Post Exchange conspicuously near the center of town [30]—would contribute to eroding the favorable Turkish image of the American abroad. It lent verisimilitude to an emerging picture of materialism as the characteristic value of the American, and in this way helped to lay the basis for later feelings among many educated Turks that the United States had no concern for social justice.

Under pressure of these and other factors, the welcome for the American military in Turkey gradually declined through the decade of the 1950s. Sailors on fleet visits no longer received the enthusiastic reception they had been accorded in the late 1940s. The newspapers increasingly publicized minor infractions by American personnel, particularly incidents involving the Turkish flag or the statutes of Atatürk, both symbols of high emotional charge. But throughout the 1950s the tone of these remonstrations was still generally one more of sadness than of anger.[31] There was little suggestion of assault on the bases of the alliance, nor was there any pronounced indication that Turkish public opinion was as yet concerned over the increase in the size of the American personnel complement in Turkey.

Diplomatic Cooperation

The NATO connection stimulated Prime Minister Menderes to become pact-minded. The DP leaders indeed needed little encouragement in concluding that Turkey's strategic position made it the natural leader of

---

[30] Location of the U.S. movie theater in Ankara on a narrow residential street where it regularly disrupted traffic also attracted unfavorable notice by Turkish critics of the United States. See *U.S. Security Agreements: Greece and Turkey,* pp. 1862–63.

[31] For example, see the plaintive recital of American incidents in *Tercuman,* January 23, 1959, ending with the plea that "foreigners coming on duty in Turkey should be especially educated" to know and respect Turkish mores.

the eastern Mediterranean. Ignoring the renunciation of Soviet claims on Turkey by Stalin's successors in May 1953, the Menderes government embarked on a series of efforts to construct regional alliances to complement the NATO tie.

First of these, after the initial setback in molding the Middle East Command, was the conclusion of the Balkan Pact in 1954. Turkey had been interested in a Balkan grouping since Atatürk had engineered a similar alliance in 1934. Now, with Yugoslavia's defection from the Soviet block and with the reassurance of Turkey's and Greece's NATO ties, it was possible to take up this idea again. The defensive arrangement linking Yugoslavia to Turkey and Greece echoed the provisions in the NATO agreement that an attack on one partner was to be considered an attack on all. In effect, it provided Yugoslavia a tenuous link with the European security system. Besides the commitment for joint defense, however, there was little that the Balkan Pact could offer its members: none had the resources to provide military or economic assistance to the others. After the Kremlin in 1956 began to make friendly overtures to Yugoslavia, therefore, this pact would for all practical purposes fall into abeyance.[32]

The Baghdad Pact

A venture with far more important implications for Turkish-American relations was the formation of the so-called Baghdad Pact. The idea of a defense arrangement for the Near East had not expired with the stillborn Middle East Command. Encouraged by John Foster Dulles, who traveled through this area in 1953 to test the possibility of forming a new grouping, Prime Minister Menderes sought to assemble an alliance based on the "northern tier" states of Iran and Pakistan (with the inclusion of Iraq) to block Soviet advance into the Arab world. To this end, in 1954 the Turks undertook to negotiate the series of agreements with their regional partners that was to culminate in February 1955 in the formation of the Baghdad Pact. Britain joined this alliance from the start, but the United States, largely for domestic reasons, hung back; despite urging from Ankara, it did not accept full membership. Washington did, however, agree to participate broadly in ac-

---

[32] John O. Iatrides, *Balkan Triangle: Birth and Decline of an Alliance Across Ideological Borders* (The Hague, 1968), passim.

tivities of the pact, contributing regular financial support and taking part in the deliberations of many of its various organs.[33]

At home the DP government enjoyed wide support in its endeavors to construct this alliance. With the deterioration of relations with many of the Arab states at this time, and with the sharp decline in amity with Greece as the Cyprus issue began to simmer, efforts to solidify relations with neighboring states appeared welcome to Turkish public opinion. Criticism from the domestic opposition, when it came, was focused largely on matters of detail and on ways in which the government carried out its policy, not on the underlying strategy. For example, one influential RPP journalist cautioned Turkey against appearing to take a "provocative" stance in sponsoring opposition to the U.S.S.R. in the Middle East.[34] İnönü himself, speaking in the name of his party, also warned the DP leadership to pay close attention to reconciling the obligations of Turkey's various security groupings—NATO, the Baghdad Pact, and the Balkan Alliance. But at the outset the DP's domestic critics did not yet seem prepared, as they would become by the end of the ensuing year, to tax the government with alienating the Arab states by seeking Arab members for the Baghdad Pact.

Formation of the Baghdad Pact added fuel to the Turkish confrontation with the Soviet Union, which was determined to gain access to the Middle East. Menderes had evidently misjudged the prospects for Syrian and Egyptian adherence to the pact. Both of these states were propelled toward the U.S.S.R. by Western tactics, thus providing Khrushchev invaluable assistance in leaping over the "northern tier." And with the Egyptian deal to acquire Czech arms in September 1955—a move made partly in reaction to the Baghdad Pact—both the United States and the Turks felt a new dimension of danger in the Middle East. From that time on, the Turkish representatives took the lead in NATO councils in branding the new Soviet policy in the area as both dangerous and provocative.

The Menderes government did not abandon hope that the United States would one day become a full member of the Baghdad Pact. As a first step along this path, Ankara sought to induce its American ally to take a public stand against what the Turkish authorities construed

---

[33] On the Baghdad Pact, see U.S. Department of State, *American Foreign Policy: 1950–1955: Basic Documents* (Washington, 1957), vol. 1, pp. 1253–59.

[34] Falih Rıfkı Atay in *Dünya*, January 29, 1955.

as a growing threat to Turkey from Syria. Particularly after the Suez crisis in the fall of 1956, the DP government became alarmed at the momentum of Soviet advance in Syria, which in Ankara's eyes appeared to be fast becoming a Soviet surrogate. Led by the semi-official *Zafer,* the Turkish press launched a campaign to publicize Soviet "infiltration of Syria"; in December 1956, the Turkish foreign minister publicly warned that Syria had received more arms from the U.S.S.R. "than she could use given her present capabilities." [35]

Turkish fears were echoed in Washington. On November 29, 1956, the Department of State publicly reaffirmed American determination to assist Turkey in meeting aggression, noting that the United States would regard threats to the territory of the Baghdad Pact members "with utmost gravity." [36] This declaration was followed on January 5, 1957, by enunciation of the Eisenhower Doctrine, engaging the United States to defend Middle Eastern countries threatened by "indirect" aggression from "international communism." American commitment was further underscored when on March 22, 1957, during talks with British Prime Minister Harold Macmillan the President announced that the United States would take part in the work of the Baghdad Pact's Military Committee. After the Damascus government expelled three American officials on charges of plotting with Turkey and Iraq to overthrow the Syrian regime, Deputy Under Secretary of State Loy Henderson made a quick trip to the Middle East at the end of August 1957, amid demands in the Turkish press for international action against Syria.[37] Henderson returned to Washington apparently convinced that Ankara's fears about the Damascus government were well founded. And in October 1957 the United States reiterated its pledge to come to Turkey's help without delay in the event of attack resulting from "Soviet infiltration of Syria." [38]

By this time the sparring contest between Turkey and the Soviet Union over Soviet involvement in Syria was almost over. Both Moscow and Ankara had extracted some benefit from the confrontation. Although the Turks had not been able to overcome Washington's reluctance

---

[35] Altemur Kılıç, *Turkey and the World,* p. 196.

[36] *Bulletin,* December 10, 1956, p. 918.

[37] *New York Times,* August 14, 24–28, 1957; U.S. Department of State, *American Foreign Policy, Current Documents, 1957* (Washington, 1961), pp. 771–74; 1037–45.

[38] *Bulletin,* November 11, 1957, p. 741.

to become a full-fledged member of the Baghdad Pact, the United States had increased its level of participation significantly and had gone on record specifically and positively in support of Turkey.[39] In the end, too, the Kremlin had secured Turkey's tacit recognition of its right to supply arms to the Arab world. There was nothing more to be gained by active dispute. Thus both the Turks and the Soviets backed off. After Syria joined Egypt to form the United Arab Republic in February 1958, the crisis rapidly petered out.

The Baghdad Pact clearly was not living up to its advance billings as a bar to the U.S.S.R. in the Middle East. Starting with the Suez crisis in the fall of 1956, opposition within Turkey to this pact began to be voiced, gently at first. But it was the Lebanese and Iraqi events of 1958 that unleashed public attack and called into question the bipartisan nature of foreign policy in Turkey. These crises posed issues that crystallized RPP opposition to the DP foreign policy in the Middle East and by implication—and at times explicitly—to U.S. policy in that region as well.

The Iraqi revolution in July 1958 was a blow to Menderes' Middle East policy. At the same time, the violent overthrow of an allied regime threw a scare into the Ankara leaders. Their own military establishment had been rocked by accusations of plotting, leading to the arrest of nine middle-grade officers in December 1957. Exhaustive investigation through most of 1958 failed to turn up any conclusive evidence, and the accused were released—though some had in fact been engaged in organizing for an eventual coup.[40] But this incident sharpened Menderes' fears that revolution might be a contagious disease and spread to his country. In this frame of mind, he, like the United States, may have felt tempted to consider ways and means to restore the old regime in Iraq; indeed, there were rumors in Turkey on the heels of the Iraqi coup that the DP leaders had ordered their forces to invade Iraq for that purpose. It was not, however, U.S. intervention (as some have alleged on rather inconclusive evidence)

---

[39] Aziz Nesin, in *Akşam,* June 14, 1960, condemned the Menderes regime for having engineered the bombing of the American embassy warehouse in January 1958 during John Foster Dulles' visit to a Baghdad Pact meeting in order to claim that the Communist danger necessitated more U.S. support.

[40] George S. Harris, "The Role of the Military in Turkish Politics," *Middle East Journal,* Spring 1965, p. 173.

that dissuaded Menderes from pursuing such a design.[41] However much he may have wanted to make the move, his forces were not prepared for attack from this angle and could not have been deployed rapidly in numbers sufficient to accomplish this objective, given the difficulties of terrain and lack of roads in the vicinity of the Iraqi-Turkish border. Where the DP chiefs saw international communism and the Soviet hand in Iraq, the RPP began to discern the forces of Arab nationalism. İnönü and his colleagues, therefore, from the first urged a sympathetic stance toward Iraqi Premier Abd al-Karim Qasim and questioned the validity of seeking to apply the Eisenhower Doctrine in cases of Arab revolution. Moreover, they saw the withdrawal of Iraq from the Baghdad Pact as likely to strengthen, not weaken, that alliance by removing a focus of discord with the rest of the Arab world.[42]

Crisis in Lebanon, 1958

It was the Lebanese insurrection that put the United States squarely in the center of this controversy. The shock waves radiating from Baghdad reverberated almost instantly to Beirut, where the regime had for some time been beleaguered by a complex of forces, including rebels based in Syria. In this situation, the Lebanese government lost no time in asking for American troops to preserve it from the fate of the old Iraqi regime. Washington accepted the request and in mid-July 1958 sent some forces from the Sixth Fleet in the Mediterranean as well as some units from Europe. The latter were dispatched in haste to İncirlik air base near Adana to prepare to join the Lebanese action.

Several aspects of that operation require comment, for the repercussions from the use of the İncirlik facility have dogged the American image in Turkey ever since. First was the matter of permission for this

---

41 Richard D. Robinson, *The First Turkish Republic,* p. 187, claims that Menderes had decided to invade Iraq, but was forestalled by Washington. Evidence he cites in this connection (*Cumhuriyet,* May 25, 1961) itself shows that this accusation was based on mere hearsay and was categorically denied by both Menderes and the then foreign minister. The Yassıada court, which heard this allegation, did not pursue the charge, evidently regarding it as unsubstantiated.

42 İnönü explained his views in *Ulus,* August 2, 1958; see also [İsmet İnönü], *1958de İnönü* (Ankara, 1959), p. 8. Another who expressed these views even more strongly was Bülent Ecevit. See his "İflâs Eden Politika," *Ulus,* July 16, 1958; his "Çıkartma ve Sonrası," *Ulus,* July 17, 1958; and his "Dış Siyasetteki Ayrılığın Kayankları," *Kim,* August 8, 1958, pp. 12–13. A. İhsan Barlas, "Nâsir ve Komünizm," *Dünya,* November 23, 1958, explains the link to Arab nationalism. See also *New York Times,* July 29, 1958.

maneuver. Mounted in haste, the troop movement was carried out on notification, rather than consultation, of the Turkish authorities. Although the Menderes government never gave an indication then or subsequently that it considered the U.S. action to have been at all improper on this score, the opposition pressed this issue from two points of view. On the one hand, İnönü and his associates attacked the U.S. operation as an abuse of Turkish sovereignty, on the grounds that the troops had come on the initiative of Washington, not Ankara.[43] On the other hand, the RPP criticisms to the effect that the United States was defending its own interests to the detriment of Turkey's implicitly raised the question of the limits of the NATO collaboration. Was the alliance to be a coincidence of interests of the broad scope that Ankara had sought up to that time—and which the United States had agreed it should be—or was the cooperation limited primarily to matters directly involving the U.S.S.R.? The answer would not be immediately forthcoming, but it was evident that a process of reevaluation had started that would eventually restrict the compass of the Turkish-American alliance.[44]

The other aspect of the use of the İncirlik air base which galvanized attention at the time was a flagrant failure in community relations. The U.S. forces brought European and American correspondents to cover the troop landings for the Western press; these journalists flew in with the American forces and had relatively free access to what was otherwise an exceedingly tightly controlled installation (as the home base of the U-2 detachment in Turkey). Representatives of the Turkish press, on the other hand, coming as they did over land, were stopped by Turkish perimeter guards and refused entrance to the base. Nor were they able to get this procedure overruled. The inequality of their treatment, albeit at the hands of Turkish troops, nonetheless rankled bitterly, forming another in the chain of grievances felt by the Turkish newspaper world against the United States. The Turks had to get all their news of the action at Adana from foreign correspondents.[45] Even a belated tour of the installation after all the activity had subsided did not help matters much. Nor did it head off biting questions by the

---

[43] "Adanadaki Amerikalılar Meselesi," *Akis,* August 23, 1958, p. 13; Bilge et al., p. 326.

[44] By 1966 Bülent Ecevit had come to label the İncirlik landing a maneuver "outside the purposes of NATO." See his "Mektuplar," *Akis,* January 22, 1966, p. 9.

[45] Cf. "İncirlik Askerî Üssünde Neler Gördüm," *Kim,* August 8, 1958, pp. 20–21.

opposition, who demanded two extraordinary sessions of the parliament in July and August 1958 to debate Turkish foreign policy in the wake of these happenings.[46]

Officially, the Menderes regime backed the United States to the hilt in those crucial days in 1958. After a meeting in July with its Baghdad Pact partners, Iran and Pakistan, the Turkish government declared its approval of the American troop landing in Lebanon.[47] Indeed, these three allies seized this opportunity to summon the United States to join the pact as a full member. Washington again refused the invitation, but it promised in a joint declaration at the end of July 1958 that it would negotiate bilateral agreements with each of the pact members to confirm American support.[48] This assurance came at Iranian insistence, as the Shah regarded himself vulnerable without a more explicit alliance. In the interests of equality, similar accords were to be concluded with Turkey and Pakistan as well. Thus on March 5, 1959, with little fanfare, the United States and Turkey signed an agreement titled simply "Cooperation." [49]

The Cooperation Agreement

A signal feature of the Cooperation agreement was the mention in its preamble of the determination of the parties "to resist aggression, direct or indirect." In the Turkish context this term gained special meaning during the course of the ensuing year. As early as 1957 relations between the opposition and the government had begun seriously to deteriorate. The DP had used its large parliamentary majority to pass legislation that imposed ever greater restrictions on the press and on political activities. By May 1959 acrimony had reached such intensity that İnönü was stoned during a political tour and set upon by a hostile crowd apparently instigated by DP partisans. Thereafter, tension re-

---

[46] *Ulus,* July 28, August 22, 1958.

[47] Jay Walz, "Turkey Approves Marines' Landing," *New York Times,* July 16, 1958.

[48] According to the text of this declaration, "the United States . . . agrees to co-operate with the nations making this Declaration for their security and defence, and will promptly enter into agreements designed to give effect to this co-operation." *Bulletin,* August 18, 1958, pp. 272–73.

[49] TIAS 4191. For details concerning the Baghdad Pact organization and the Cooperation agreement, see CENTO, *The Story of the Central Treaty Organization* (Ankara, 1959), passim. The text of the Cooperation agreement is in Appendix 3.

mained near the boiling point as spokesmen for the ruling party began to cast doubt that elections would be held under equitable conditions, or indeed that they would even take place at the end of the normal term. Soon the RPP leaders became concerned that Menderes would dissolve their organization on the pretext of sedition.[50]

In these circumstances, when after long delay the Cooperation agreement was finally brought to the Foreign Affairs Committee of the Turkish parliament in February 1960, it provoked audible reaction. The RPP spokesmen sought assurance that Menderes did not intend to demand American assistance in stifling the opposition. They attacked the agreement as incompatible with Turkish sovereignty and demanded that the term "indirect" (aggression) be clarified.[51] Unaccountably, the government fueled these fears by refusing to define the offending term on the grounds that its meaning had been worked out in secret negotiations with the United States. Foreign Minister Fatin Rüştü Zorlu later added that an imprecise definition was necessary to cover new forms of aggression—a not wholly reassuring explanation to the opposition. It was left to RPP deputy Coşkun Kırca to point out that the body of the agreement—as distinct from its preamble—did not mention "indirect" aggression, hence that this accord could not be used against indigenous dissidents.[52] Significantly, during this controversy RPP commentators took occasion to reiterate their approval of Turkey's ties with the United States, adding only the plea that Washington should make clear to all that the Cooperation agreement could not be invoked against the political opposition in Turkey.[53] In the end, the agreement was ratified by the Turkish parliament on May 9, 1960, in a vote boycotted by the opposition deputies, who were offended that it had gone into force at signature more than a year before.[54]

---

[50] Cf. George S. Harris, "The Causes of the 1960 Revolution in Turkey," *Middle East Journal,* Autumn 1970, pp. 438–54.

[51] *Cumhuriyet,* February 6, 1960. Bülent Ecevit led in demanding this clarification.

[52] *Vatan,* February 11, 1960; Coşkun Kırca, "Birleşik Amerika ve İç İşlerimiz," *Ulus,* February 13, 1960.

[53] *Ulus,* February 26, 1960.

[54] See TBMM, *Zabıt Ceridesi,* devre XI, vol. 13, session of May 9, 1960, pp. 456–59. The date given in A. H. Ülman and R. H. Dekmejian, "Changing Patterns in Turkish Foreign Policy, 1959–1967," *Orbis,* Fall 1967, p. 773, is in error. Also it would seem from the evidence that these authors hang entirely too much on the Cooperation agreement, reflecting the greater emphasis placed on this accord in the latter half of the 1960s.

Clearly at this stage the reaction aroused by the Cooperation agreement was directed primarily against the DP and was by no means sharply aimed against the United States. Few Turks were yet essentially mistrustful of American motives. What the opposition doubted was Washington's ability to fathom Menderes' designs. Within a few years, however, looking back at this agreement with less assurance concerning the benevolence of the ultimate intentions of the United States, some Turks and foreign observers as well began to regard this bilateral understanding as evidence of American perfidy. And by the mid-1960s the Turkish left had come in retrospect to exaggerate the importance of the Cooperation agreement, an accord that never had more than perfunctory significance to the government of either state involved.

The decline of CENTO

After the 1950s the Baghdad Pact Organization—which was renamed the Central Treaty Organization (CENTO) in 1959 following Iraq's withdrawal—faded out of prominence as a facet of the Turkish-American relationship. To be sure, it continued to provide a forum for regular high-level contact and to serve as an umbrella for a small amount of economic assistance. In the sphere of military cooperation, however, ostensibly its chief *raison d'être,* CENTO never fulfilled its promise. Unlike NATO, it lacked regularly constituted forces, and its annual naval maneuvers in the Arabian Sea and semiannual air exercises were relatively small-scale operations. Against this reality, Moscow was able to score little success when in 1961 it tried to portray CENTO as a threatening military alliance by publicizing purported plans of the allies to rain nuclear weapons on the U.S.S.R. The Soviet allegations were categorically denied by Turkish authorities and the Turkish press was unwilling to credit CENTO with aggressive designs.[55] In 1964, Turkey, Iran, and Pakistan formed their parallel but separate alliance for Regional Cooperation for Development, and thereafter

[55] *Cumhuriyet,* September 8, 1961; *Milliyet,* September 9, 1961. The Soviet consulate general in Istanbul attempted to exhibit alleged CENTO nuclear target plans. After an initial press showing, the exhibition was closed at the behest of the Turkish Foreign Office. Both leftist and rightist Turkish student organizations in Istanbul issued statements condemning the exhibition. *Akşam,* September 9, 1961. The Turkish representative at the United Nations formally termed the Soviet allegations "a fantastic story." U.N., General Assembly, *Official Records* (A/PV. 1002), August 24, 1961, p. 86. For the purported CENTO documents, see *Krasnaia Zvezda,* August 19, 1961.

70

CENTO's importance visibly receded. Indeed, given the developing neutralist sentiment in Pakistan during those years, there was a growing question whether CENTO would even long survive.

Yet despite its increasingly innocuous appearance, the CENTO alliance came under periodic attack by the Turkish left after the mid-1960s when it began to be fashionable among the more extreme circles to question ties to the West. In addition to singling out the Cooperation agreement, those fearful of Western machinations saw cause for alarm in CENTO's Counter-Subversion Committee because of its very title if not its activities. But in view of CENTO's unobtrusive course, the main attacks on it usually were reserved for those infrequent occasions when its council meetings brought high-ranking American officials to Turkey; then complaints came not so much against CENTO activities per se as against U.S. policy, particularly in respect to Turkey.

Economic Ties

Economic cooperation formed one of the more abrasive aspects of the Turkish-American relationship in the 1950s. This was a period when the Turkish economy was undergoing serious strain. Pressure inside Turkey for rapid economic growth was mounting, and the DP leaders firmly believed that the rate of development had to be speeded whatever the cost. Regarding free enterprise as essential to this process, Menderes was inclined to view liberalization as an important ingredient in the recipe for development; he made clear that in his opinion any comprehensive state plan—such as the RPP had sought to devise after 1946—unnecessarily fettered essential governmental flexibility.

The DP had from the start been shaped by economic interests. As a party, it favored policies benefiting agricultural producers. In fact, the issue that had crystallized the DP founders was opposition to the land law of 1945. [56] This bias remained once the party came to power five years later. During their decade in office, the party leadership resisted unflinchingly any urging to end the exemption of agricultural income from taxation. Moreover, to woo the more than 70 percent of the population that lived on the land, the DP leaders followed a policy of pumping money into the rural sector through high agricultural subsidies. Their industrial programs had similar domestic political motives.

---

[56] Harris, "A Political History of Turkey," pp. 189–90, 199–200.

Menderes sought high-impact, showy projects; he was particularly noted for scattering state economic enterprises, such as sugar factories, over the countryside to reward the politically faithful, but in locations and numbers that made efficient operation unlikely.[57] This was an exceedingly inflationary course, one which whetted appetites for consumer goods far beyond the capacity of Turkey's own manufacturers. As a result, imports spurted far faster than exports, leading to rapidly mounting foreign trade deficits.

This growing external insolvency posed a critical threat to the Turkish economy, as the Americans continually warned the Menderes government. In part, the unfavorable trade balance had been aggravated by a relaxation of Turkish restrictions on many imports from the Marshall Plan countries. Thanks to this move, originally taken with the encouragement of the United States and of Turkey's European allies, Ankara was unable to control the deficit in its foreign account until the DP government in the fall of 1953 reimposed controls; but before this Turkey had exhausted its reserves and amassed sizable arrears covered by short-term credit. Import restraint did not last long. Menderes' determination to press ahead with large-scale investment without curtailing consumption of consumer goods led him to sanction an importing binge on short-term supplier credits. This brought the Turkish economy face to face with bankruptcy by the end of 1954.[58]

The DP leadership may have embarked on its reckless course with an exaggerated faith in the efficacy of foreign private investment to speed Turkish economic development. Even before the DP came to power, the RPP administration in its quest for ties with the West had eased some of the restrictions on the transfer of foreign capital and enacted guarantees for the repatriation of profits. On August 1, 1951, the Democrat Party regime broadened the scope of these provisions. Nonetheless, foreign investors remained wary; only a few major firms undertook projects in Turkey. But as economic pressures mounted, the Democrats, at the advice of the prominent industrialist Clarence Randall, on January 18, 1954, passed a comprehensive new bill to

---

[57] Kemal H. Karpat, *Turkish Politics,* pp. 306–307; William Nicholls, "Investment in Agriculture in Underdeveloped Countries," *American Economic Review: Proceedings and Papers,* May 1955, pp. 58–73. The left in Turkey was by the mid-1960s harshly criticizing this as "showcase" economic development which benefited the few. See Avcıoğlu, *Türkiye'nin Düzeni,* p. 285.

[58] Robinson, "Impact of American Programs," pp. 15–16.

encourage foreign investment. This act not only removed remaining restrictions on the transfer of capital and profits, but also engaged the government to extend to foreign private enterprise the same facilities that local concerns enjoyed. Moreover, to stimulate the oil industry, which was unable to meet Turkey's rapidly growing demands, the Menderes regime in March 1954 radically altered the petroleum law to end the government monopoly in the development of underground resources. The new bill, drawn up to the specifications of American petroleum expert Max Ball, provided foreign companies attractive concession arrangements. In fact, so favorable were these terms that the RPP accused Menderes of granting new "capitulations"— a theme that figured prominently in the 1954 election campaign.[59] But the DP leaders, who had sufficient votes to enable them to ignore these complaints, obviously hoped that this legislation would open the floodgates of foreign capital.

Further, Menderes and his colleagues apparently expected that the U.S. government would bail them out of their economic difficulties. The DP leadership believed that Turkey's political importance to the West would induce its allies to provide extensive economic assistance even if the Turks refused to follow the course recommended by their partners. Such a calculation was by no means farfetched. While the U.S. aid mission continually pressed the Turkish government to retrench and follow a more rational economic policy, in the end the United States always came forward to provide essential assistance to keep the Turkish economy afloat. Indeed, American aid nearly doubled over its previous rate during these crucial years—averaging about $96 million annually for the period 1953–1959.[60] Nonetheless, Turkey remained on the verge of insolvency, living from hand to mouth, experiencing periodic

---

[59] For the RPP criticisms, see *Muhalefetde İsmet İnönü*, pp. 255–57, 259–61, 266 (speeches of April 13, 15, and 16, 1954). On Clarence Randall and the Law for the Encouragement of Foreign Capital, see his "Can We Invest in Turkey?" *The Atlantic*, November 1953, pp. 48–50; Avcıoğlu, pp. 323–24; Mehmet Gönlübol and A. Halûk Ülman, "Türk Dış Politikasının Yirmi Yılı, 1945–1965," *Siyasal Bilgiler Fakültesi Dergisi*, March 1966, p. 157.

[60] The average assistance provided during the Mutual Security Act period was calculated from U.S., AID, Office of Statistics and Reports, Bureau for Program and Policy Coordination, *U.S. Overseas Loans and Grants and Assistance from International Organizations* (Special Report prepared for the House Foreign Affairs Committee), May 14, 1971, and earlier editions. See also White, pp. 102–103; Leo Tansky, *U.S. and U.S.S.R. Aid to Developing Countries* (New York, 1967), p. 64.

shortages of petroleum and other basic commodities imported from the West.

The stabilization fund controversy

To escape from this straitjacket, Menderes resolved to press his Western allies for a $300 million fund to stabilize the Turkish economy. He first broached this idea during his visit to Washington in the spring of 1954, but American planners firmly rejected the request on the grounds that the Turks must first put their economic house in order.[61] U.S. officials argued that Turkey's parlous economic state was the result of the DP's inflationary policies and took the position that the availability of resources should dictate the rate of development. On that basis, the formula favored by the Eisenhower administration called for the Turkish government to carry out retrenchment in investment, reduction in agricultural subsidies and credit, basic tax reform to raise revenue from the rural sector, and strict import controls. As a capstone to the stabilization program, Washington believed it necessary for Ankara to devalue the Turkish lira to bring it into reasonable relationship with the rate on the world market. But this prescription clashed fundamentally with the philosophy on which Menderes operated; it would mean slower economic growth, and in the short run it would work hardship on the rural population whose support seemed necessary to win elections. He thus remained unwilling to adopt these measures until he had exhausted every other alternative.

For almost four years the Turkish and American governments fought a standoff battle behind the scenes over this issue. On the Turkish side, Fatin Rüştü Zorlu, who was then deputy prime minister, led the attack; at one point he traveled to Washington to press the case personally, amid an apparently carefully staged campaign in the Turkish newspapers excoriating American aid policies.[62] In hopes of increasing pressure on Washington, the Ankara authorities even retained former presidential candidate Thomas Dewey at a cost of $100,000 to represent Turkish interests in securing the additional assistance. Each failure of the United States to agree to extend the $300 million loan was

---

[61] Welles Hangen, "Ankara Seeking Clear U.S. Stand," *New York Times,* March 13, 1955.
[62] *Hürriyet,* April 30, 1955; *Halkçı,* May 4, 1955; "Turkey: A Friend in Trouble," *Time,* October 24, 1955, pp. 24–25.

greeted with hostile outcry in the Turkish press. But Washington stood firm on the main issue, although in order not to jeopardize the Turkish military program it intervened on several occasions to rescue Ankara from defaulting on payments to Western oil companies that were on the point of refusing deliveries of vital petroleum. Yet with each such reprieve Menderes would back away from the idea of basic reform and attempt to muddle through without essential change.[63]

This pattern of continuing confrontation guaranteed a maximum of friction between the American aid mission and the Turkish government. In fact, relations grew so strained that the Turkish authorities virtually ceased meaningful contact with U.S. aid administrators; there was even talk at one time that the chief of the aid mission might be declared persona non grata for failing to espouse the Turkish cause.

Under these circumstances, to avoid ruffling Turkish feelings further, after 1955 the United States preferred to let international agencies like the International Monetary Fund and the European Payments Union take the lead in pressing Ankara to change its economic policy. By 1958 the Turkish economy had slowed almost to a standstill; the Turkish government faced the imminent prospect of being declared insolvent by its creditors around the world. This pressure left no alternative. Menderes in August of that year finally agreed to economic retrenchment and an imposition of controls accompanied by devaluation. He even privately invited European experts to draw up a preliminary economic plan—something the opposition party had been demanding for years.[64] To assist him in carrying out these measures, his allies provided a package of $359 million in credit and worked out a consolidation of existing debt to extend the repayment period significantly.

This was a landmark event. Not only did it ease the economic crisis in Turkey, permitting a renewed flow of consumer goods and a renewed sense of economic well-being; it also set the stage for the creation of the international aid consortium that was to operate in the 1960s. As a legacy to this international venture, the Turks were left with the reputation of being ever recalcitrant in the economic field and hence willing to conform to the wisdom of the world's economists only *in extremis*. This impression received additional impetus when Menderes soon gave evidence that he was inclined to slip back into his old ways.

---

[63] White, p. 103.

[64] İlkin and İnanç, *Planning in Turkey*, p. 46.

The 1960 budget betrayed signs of a return to inflationary investment in the showy projects characteristic of the earlier years. Indeed, by the time of the May 1960 coup that toppled the DP regime, the Turkish government had run through most of the aid package and was beginning once more to feel the pinch of economic stringency.[65]

Impact on the aid program

Naturally the aid program itself suffered from the friction between the American administrators in Turkey and the Turkish authorities. The clash of economic philosophies inevitably impaired efficiency in carrying out existing projects, and cooperation in elaborating new ones became more difficult. Nor was it possible to record much progress in bridging the differences in aim and attitude that separated U.S. and Turkish leaders. Ankara remained transfixed by the political implications of economic programs, while Washington was interested in a whole gamut of activities representing what American planners felt a developing society required. Hungry for American assistance, those in charge of the Turkish development effort were ready to accept U.S. proposals that did not entail obviously onerous conditions. In the words of one Turkish observer, "An unpopular program will find acceptance . . . if there is enough gravy for everyone." [66] As a result, some agreed projects meshed only superficially with what many of the Turks most intimately involved considered necessary.

Educational projects: a case study of aid problems

Perhaps the premier example of difficulties in the aid relationship is to be found in the educational assistance projects of the 1950s.[67] Education was a domain the Turkish elite generally considered the most sensitive area of national life; the educational process was viewed as the way to consolidate the Atatürk reforms. Clearly, the majority of Turkish educators felt no need of advice and assistance from abroad. Turkish universities were highly structured institutions with powerful

---

[65] White, pp. 105–6.
[66] Walter Adams and John Garraty, *Is the World Our Campus?* (East Lansing, Michigan, 1960), p. 26.
[67] Ibid., passim, analyzes the U.S. educational assistance program in great detail. See also Edwin J. Cohn, *Turkish Economic, Social, and Political Change* (New York, 1970), pp. 99–115.

vested interests in their prerogatives and privileges. Attitudes and practices would always remain resistant to change. In this milieu, success of an American-sponsored endeavor could come only when able and devoted people were engaged in a long-term effort, backed by a clearly formulated program that was accepted and understood by their Turkish counterparts. Such a constellation of favorable circumstances was inevitably rare. Even when it obtained, the going was by no means easy.

The U.S. government sponsored two major projects of higher education: the New York University program of public administration training and the University of Nebraska effort to assist in the creation of a land-grant college in eastern Turkey, Atatürk University. The first was a failure—worse, it left a bad taste among an important segment of the power elite. The second recorded somewhat more success, though it too fell short of accomplishing all the aims intended. There were three other noteworthy educational ventures during this period. One, funded mainly by the Ford Foundation, involved creation of a business school in Istanbul under the auspices of Harvard University; although this school managed to put down fairly solid roots, it alienated much of the Istanbul University community in the process. The English teacher training project run by Georgetown University was successful in teaching a number of Turks English, but few of these became teachers. Of all the American projects, the one that most successfully accomplished its aims was the Spring Garden program of technical training in automotive repair. By its very nature, however, the impact of this program on the political elite was limited.

The New York University project suffered from almost all imaginable defects. It was imposed on the University of Ankara's Political Science Faculty by the Ministry of Education after the arrangements had already been settled with the American institution. The Turkish faculty apparently acquiesced largely in hopes of lightening teaching loads and of securing travel to the United States for its members. From the outset there were no clearly agreed specific goals established. The Turkish educators did not even understand exactly what public administration implied in American usage. As for New York University, it treated the project as a stepchild from the first. Regular faculty members were conspicuously absent from its contingent. Although a handful of capable scholars were recruited from other institutions, their presence could not compensate for the run-of-the-mill mediocrities hired for the project; on occasion the latter seemed more concerned with making a financial killing than in work at the faculty. Instead of persuasive diplomacy in dealing with their counterparts, these Americans at times even indulged in crude threats to "terminate financial support" if their suggestions were not carried out.[68] Turnover among the American professors was rapid; there was not sufficient continuity to complete the promised public administration text adapted to Turkish conditions that was essential for any lasting impact. Overall, as the executive secretary of the project noted with perhaps some understatement, "with selfish motives on both sides . . . it is not surprising that the academic and idealistic objectives of the program were somewhat pushed into the background." [69] In the end, after seeing the quality of personnel decline, Ankara University terminated the project as a failure. Today, except for the legacy of disenchantment over the American aid motives and practices which were especially conspicuous at this institution, little trace of the New York University project survives.[70]

The Nebraska experiment encountered some of the same difficulties. The concept of creating an institution working on the principle of a land-grant university, i.e., "a mixture of pure and applied research directed toward . . . the dissemination of useful knowledge to the public through extension services" came from the American, not the Turkish side.[71] The law establishing Atatürk University did not accommodate this philosophy, but reflected the elitist attitudes of education that are so ingrained in the Turkish hierarchy of values. On the one hand, the project itself thus lacked clearly formulated objectives and during its decade of existence enjoyed little continuity of either Turkish or American leadership. On the other hand, the University of Nebraska did send significant numbers of its own faculty members to participate—

---

[68] Adams and Garraty, p. 67.

[69] Ibid., p. 26.

[70] NYU also worked with the Law Faculty at Ankara, toward the same ends and with generally similar results. The only lasting achievement of this aspect of the program was the start of publication of collections of legal decisions, something the Turks with their different legal tradition had not attempted in the past. A third, totally unrelated, activity directed by NYU, however, was an unqualified success. It was a technical project to devise an efficient Turkish typewriter keyboard and to train secretaries in its use. Need for this was readily apparent in Turkey and Turkish response to this well managed venture was enthusiastic.

[71] For a somewhat more sympathetic review of the University of Nebraska project, see Wayne E. Hanway, "An Evaluation of the University of Nebraska—AID Turkish University Program." Paper written in the Department of Political Science, University of Nebraska, September 1970, passim, especially p. 15.

and some of its best people at that. As a result, the American professors generally had the respect of their Turkish counterparts; some of the younger faculty members even absorbed something of the land-grant philosophy despite the legal and attitudinal obstacles of traditional Turkish practice. Today Atatürk University exists and is thriving in spite of its severe growing pains. Amid the controversies that swept over Turkish universities in the 1960s, American educational philosophy has come under serious fire, however, and Atatürk University in its approach owes little to advisers from the United States.

Education presented perhaps the most difficult challenge for American assistance, but similar problems cropped up in other areas. Under these circumstances it is not surprising that American aid failed signally in reducing Turkish dependence on outside help in the 1950s. Moreover, Turkey during this decade piled up additional foreign indebtedness, thus augmenting the debt service burden for coming years. Nor was there notable progress in overcoming structural imbalances within the Turkish economy or even in attracting sizable amounts of foreign investment. To be sure, much of the fault lay on the shoulders of the DP, which persisted so doggedly in its disastrous economic course. Yet America shared in guilt by association. However the blame may be apportioned, in the end it was the shortcomings of the 1950s that profoundly complicated Turkey's economic relations with the United States during the coming decade.

Success on wheels: the highway program

At the same time American aid did score some remarkable successes by any standards, notably in the highway program. These achievements were a tribute to the soundness of the individual programs involved and to the working-level relationships of some American advisers with their Turkish counterparts. The measure of accomplishment was also due to the determination of both Ankara and Washington to maintain a facade of normalcy in their economic cooperation. They tried to keep disputes in the development program more or less rigorously compartmentalized, and especially not to let them spill over to disconcert collaboration in the political or military realm.

Firm backing by Turkish authorities and their genuine sympathy with the aims of the U.S. aid administrators were important criteria for success. These conditions obtained more readily when assistance was used to create new institutions rather than to reform previously existing ones in which vested interests were sure to oppose change.

The most outstanding achievement associated with American assistance was the highway program.[72] Although originally initiated as part of the military aid extended under the Truman Doctrine, the highway administration was viewed almost from the first by both the Turks and the U.S. Bureau of Public Roads in a wider frame—as an agency that would provide the infrastructure for economic development. To accomplish this broad aim, a totally new general directorate of highways was set up with sufficient autonomy to be independent of control by the old-line ministries. After a decade of operation, it was able to dispense with American personnel and continue to work as perhaps the most efficient department in the Turkish government. Thanks to its efforts, Turkey has been endowed with an impressive road system, for the first time stretching to all corners of the country. To be sure, Menderes regarded this activity as an essential part of his promise to provide roads to the villages, hence politically a most valuable program. Yet he resisted the temptation to interfere in the operation of this directorate which, thanks to his favor, had the political muscle to carry out its projects as designed.[73] Only in recent years has the opposition criticized this program, and then merely with the reproach that the road network has made the costly railroad system redundant.[74]

Domestic Politics

U.S. involvement

Menderes' determination to use American aid to further his partisan purposes inevitably involved the United States in Turkish domestic politics. As early as the 1954 election campaign, the opposition had

---

[72] Robert S. Lehman, "Building Roads and a Highway Administration in Turkey," in Howard M. Teaf, Jr. and Peter G. Franck, *Hands across Frontiers* (Ithaca, 1955), pp. 363–409.

[73] Menderes was famous for his urban reconstruction, including construction of major arteries in Istanbul, Ankara, and other cities. Such road building was carried out in urban areas by the municipalities involved, not by the General Directorate of Highways. The city projects were fraught with complaints about the quality of workmanship, etc., whereas the work of the highway directorate enjoyed general approbation.

[74] Avcıoğlu, *Türkiye'nin Düzeni*, p. 277.

begun to voice irritation that economic assistance was protecting the DP from the results of its follies. "If Allah does not provide, America will," was a refrain among members of the opposition noted by one American observer at the time.[75] Washington's refusal to extend the large loan requested by the DP government, however, aroused mixed feelings in the mid-1950s. Patriotism in Turkey seemed to dictate pressing for this assistance; some critics of the Menderes administration thus felt constrained to urge the United States to approve the loan.[76] Even the opposition joined in bewailing the fact that the United States extended greater per capita support to Greece and more support in absolute terms to neutrals such as India. Yet as Washington periodically came through to relieve intense crises of foreign exchange, and particularly with the stabilization loan in 1958, members of the RPP expressed increasing annoyance that American aid served to bail out the Menderes government. The central point of this criticism was not that the United States provided assistance, but that the American government did not control its aid to prevent its use for political purposes. Ironically, therefore, what appeared to Washington as extreme pressure on the DP regime to eschew political exploitation by compelling the Menderes government to undertake the stabilization program was seen by the RPP leaders as critical support allowing Menderes to remain in power. Nor did the opposition's suspicion that the United States could not control its aid weaken as DP backsliding away from the stabilization measures became evident at the end of 1959.

During the DP decade, indeed, the United States was not able to project the image of impartiality in Turkey.[77] The American role as a purveyor of aid was only part of the reason. In addition, the DP leaders actively sought to foster the impression that they enjoyed special American favor. To bolster this contention, Menderes successfully pressed for invitations to the United States. He made two trips, and President Celâl Bayar made one; while President Dwight D. Eisenhower stopped for a brief but extravagantly celebrated visit on the way home from India,

[75] Robinson, "Impact of American Programs," p. 10; Welles Hangen, "Anti-American Feeling in Turkey Fomented by Opposition to Bayar," *New York Times,* February 9, 1954.

[76] See, for example, *Halkçı,* April 29, 30, 1955; *Cumhuriyet,* April 28, 1955. A. N. Karacan, in *Milliyet,* April 28, 1955, rejected the idea that Turkey's economic policy "should receive the supreme approval of the United States." He added that Turkey was "not an American colony."

[77] Ülman and Dekmejian, p. 774.

and Vice President Nixon called in during a round-the-world tour. The contrast of this high-level diplomatic intimacy with the paucity of even secondary-level visits during the İnönü era was all the more poignant in view of the infrequent contact between American officials and the opposition in Turkey. For in deference to Menderes' expressed sensitivity, relations between the U.S. embassy and the RPP leaders were significantly cut back, especially during the acrimonious years leading up to the stabilization program in 1958.[78] This snubbing of the opposition also contrasted sharply with the proverbial closeness of Menderes and U.S. Ambassador Fletcher Warren. It was all too easy for Turks to conclude on this basis that Washington in fact preferred to see a government of the stripe of Menderes' DP remain in power. This presumption was to become a permanent feature of the Turkish political landscape.

Among those who considered the Turkish leader an incipient dictator, the closeness between Menderes and the United States fed a certain disillusionment about Washington's motives in its overseas actions. Increasingly in Turkey the stage was being set to view America as a country concerned with protecting its own interests.[79] The altruism of American assistance came into question. Washington's willingness to maintain cordial relations with Francisco Franco of Spain and with Portugal's Premier Antonio de Oliveira Salazar as well as with Asian and South American autocrats—especially Ambassador Warren's friendship with Venezuelan President Marcos Pérez Jiménez—seemed to these Turkish critics to fall into a pattern of preference to deal with all-powerful leaders rather than to care about the fate of the people at large.[80] It was perhaps with this in mind that İnönü, speaking on foreign affairs in the name of his party in February 1960, appealed to the United States to make sure its relations went beyond the DP and

---

[78] Robinson, "Impact of American Programs," p. 10. Cf. Metin Toker, "Amerikalının Yanıldığı Nokta," *Akis,* February 1, 1958, p. 5; "Çirkin Amerikalı," *Akis,* September 8, 1959, p. 7.

[79] It was the right-wing Nation Party which led in questioning American motives. See, for example, Nurettin Ardıçoğlu's article of June 8, 1954, in *Millet,* which suggested that the main U.S. interest in Turkey might be "simply to control, without noise and complications, certain geo-political and strategic advantages in this key-point of the Middle East." Ardıçoğlu was tried *in camera* and sentenced for "activity liable to prejudice national interests" by publishing this criticism of the United States.

[80] This reproach was voiced by Özcan Ergüder in *Vatan,* January 25, 1959, and by Orhan Birgit in *Kim,* February 10, 1960.

were "from nation to nation." [81] So real was the RPP fear that America would turn a blind eye to the establishment of dictatorship in Turkey, that when in April 1960 the DP proposed setting up an investigating committee with vast powers to probe opposition sedition, prominent Republican Bülent Ecevit begged the United States not to be deceived by Menderes' claim that a totalitarian regime would serve American interests. [82]

The opposition's fears on this score were somewhat relieved when in mid-April 1960 Washington moved publicly to disassociate itself with Syngman Rhee's regime in Korea and to press him to reestablish political rights. Perhaps not a little wistfully, some RPP commentators hailed this American action as a "turning point" in U.S. postwar policy. They openly called upon Washington to exert similar pressure on non-democratic regimes among the NATO allies. [83] In this frame of mind, the opposition had high hopes that the NATO foreign ministers meeting in Istanbul at the start of May 1960 would act to induce Menderes to turn back from the bitterly repressive course that threatened to turn Turkey into a civil battleground. Ambassador Warren's sudden departure from Istanbul during the conference, reportedly to pay a call on Menderes in Ankara, was even read by some as a move to force the DP to back down, an interpretation that evoked an immediate denial by both USIS and the Turkish authorities. [84] While the opposition seemed for the moment unconcerned about the larger implications of inviting foreign intervention, NATO Secretary General Paul-Henri Spaak made clear at a press conference at the end of the Istanbul sessions that the allies were unwilling to embark on any concerted intrusion in the internal affairs of their partners. [85] Yet to the end, Menderes' opponents remained hopeful that the United States would follow the Korean precedent for intervention in Turkey.

The military takeover

On May 27, 1960, a small band of conspirators, enjoying wide support within the military establishment, seized the government in the name

---

[81] TBMM, *Zabıt Ceridesi,* devre XI, vol. 13, February 25, 1960, p. 498.

[82] *Ulus,* April 18, 1960.

[83] Coşkun Kırca in *Vatan,* April 27, 1960; Orhan Birgit in *Kim,* April 27, 1960.

[84] *Vatan,* May 4, 1960; *Yeni Sabah,* May 3, 1960.

[85] *Zafer,* May 5, 1960.

of preserving national unity. This was made possible by the political climate obtaining at that time.

By April 1960 the political scene in Turkey had reached the breaking point. Frustrated by the recalcitrant opposition, the DP administration ordered out the army to prevent RPP leader İnönü from traveling to Kayseri to investigate interparty violence. But the officers in charge of this operation failed to carry out their orders with resolution; İnönü walked through the troops deployed to block him and reached his destination. Further, three middle-grade officers resigned in protest against using the army for political purposes. Thenceforth, both the DP and the RPP turned to the soldiers as a court of last appeal in the political struggle, each party accusing the other of wooing the army as its political ally.

This process ineluctably drew the military establishment into the political arena. Officers disturbed at the injury to national unity inflicted by the political quarreling had long been plotting against this day. Declaration of martial law by the Menderes government in the aftermath of university student rioting at the end of April 1960 provided the aroused army even greater scope for action. And after War School cadets themselves made a protest march in sympathy with their university counterparts, the moment to strike could no longer be delayed. The conspirators swiftly rounded up the government leaders and the DP deputies. They declared a moratorium on political activity and ushered in a breathing spell from the fierce strife that had consumed all attention in the months before the move.

4

Aftermath of the 1960 Revolution

The period from the 1960 coup until the Cyprus crisis began in the closing days of 1963 formed a plateau in Turkish-American relations. The overthrow of the DP government, however surgically antiseptic it may have appeared in Turkey at the time, did not signify an immediate or complete break with the past. The patterns of politics in Turkey would prove resistant to change. Within a year and a half, a party in many respects the inheritor of the Menderes legacy would run strongly in elections; in five years it would be returned to office with a commanding majority. Likewise, trends in foreign policy would for some time continue to develop much in the mold of the past. Suspicions and doubts about the alliance sown in the Menderes era would grow, though largely below the surface. Perhaps they would mature less quickly than otherwise might have been the case, if only because minds were so intensely preoccupied with domestic affairs during the period of military rule and its immediate aftermath. In the eyes of most Turks these years were a time of good feeling toward the United States, one not generally marred, as the Menderes decade had been, by any compelling conviction that the Americans were playing favorites on the domestic scene. In short, the alliance was still popular, especially as a result of the heady mystique of President John F. Kennedy which took immediate root even among those most inclined to find fault with America.

The military junta—the so-called National Unity Committee—that now took over the Turkish government did not come to power with the intention of changing foreign policy. The soldiers had been impelled to revolt by the breakdown of the civilian political system and its descent into anarchy and disorder. In fact, at first they had little intent to make any basic changes. They generally assumed that by removing Menderes and his associates and by making minor constitutional adjustments to prevent abuses it would be possible to return swiftly to a civilian regime. Other matters had preoccupied them in the days before the coup, however, and the military conspirators had arrived in power without any firm consensus about what they would do and how long they would rule.

The realities of governing soon dispelled some illusions. It was not long before heated debate arose among the military rulers over their role and mission.[1] Some of them insisted that a civilian regime was inherently incapable of taking the politically unpopular reform decisions needed to galvanize Turkey into effective development activity. Others felt it a sacred obligation to return to a civilian system as soon as reasonably possible. Many apparently were torn by indecision: they followed no clear line of action. But it soon became obvious to all that the central task demanding the full attention of the junta was to decide the nature of the future regime in Turkey. Whatever bore on this issue would receive priority treatment; other business would be given as short shrift as possible. Foreign policy clearly fell into the latter category.

There was evidently no great dispute among the junta members concerning Turkey's role in the world. Their backgrounds having been in military affairs, in the main they accepted the prevailing view within the Turkish armed forces toward the cold war, and they appeared to have confidence that continuing the U.S. connection was in Turkey's ultimate interests. They thus quickly rebuffed Soviet overtures and did not accept Moscow's proffers of sizable amounts of economic assistance.

In this scheme of things, cooperation with the United States was of vital importance to the military rulers. Inheriting an almost empty treasury and uncertain as to the degree of Washington's attachment to the DP, the junta was concerned that American military and economic aid might be interrupted. Thus the conspirators took immediate steps to assure the United States that they were firmly committed to both NATO and CENTO. Early in the morning of the day they ousted Menderes, the military leaders sent a delegation to the American embassy to reaffirm their attachment to these pacts; in their first radio communique they broadcast a public message to the same effect.[2] But the

---

[1] For a detailed study of these debates, see Abdi İpekçi and Ömer Sami Coşar, "İhtilâlin İçyüzü: İkinci Bölüm: Birinci Milli Birlik Komitesi Devrinin Hikayesi," *Milliyet,* February 28–May 6, 1965.

[2] *Ulus,* May 28, 1960.

uneasiness of the new Turkish rulers in this regard was heightened when, three days after the coup, sources in the U.S. State Department commenting on the question of extending recognition to the new regime, announced to inquiring reporters that "merely carrying on our usual relations with Turkish government officials constitutes recognition. No other formal act . . . is considered necessary."[3] With release of 52 million Turkish lira ($5.8 million) from American local currency holdings a week later in accordance with an understanding made with the deposed government, and especially on receipt of a personal message from President Eisenhower made public in mid-June, their doubts about American cooperation began to lessen. It was clear from Eisenhower's letter, however, that the United States strongly desired Turkey's return to civilian rule at the earliest possible date. And to the end of its tenure, the junta was aware that Washington, which made no secret of its interest in the moderation of the military regime, had not changed its position.[4]

Resurgence of nationalism and the bilateral arrangements

The junta officers felt impelled to assert Turkey's national sovereign rights with greater vigor than they believed the DP had done. Some of the younger members, such as Captain Muzaffer Özdağ, betrayed suspicion of foreign activities in Turkey. In one speech Özdağ singled out foreign educational institutions—of which the most prominent exemplars were American—for special condemnation.[5] Orhan Erkanlı, another of the younger conspirators, even raised the specter that Turkey had become "an American colony," a charge that was vigorously rebutted by those press commentators who felt particular sympathy for the United States.[6] Although these sentiments were clearly more extreme than the

---

[3] *New York Times,* May 31, 1960.

[4] For the full text of Eisenhower's message, see *Ulus,* June 17, 1960. The United States let it be known openly that it disapproved of the death sentences carried out against Menderes and his ministers of finance and foreign affairs. *New York Times,* September 17, 1961.

[5] On Özdağ's views, see the commentary by Özcan Ergüder in *Vatan,* August 24, 1960.

[6] Ahmet Emin Yalman through editorials in *Vatan* led in opposing Erkanlı's views. See especially *Vatan,* September 30, 1960, where he wrote: "We may have many complaints about the Americans, but it would certainly be an injustice to say that they have been exploiting Turkey for their own interests and to claim . . . that they have transformed Turkey into an American colony. If the question of one country exploiting the other has arisen, it is we who have made America a sort of colony of ours for the sake of various interests and services."

consensus of the National Unity Committee, a strong sensitivity to national slights was shared by all. The issue which would reveal this attitude most prominently was that concerning the privileges and immunities of American personnel.

In pressing for changes in this area, the Committee had certain advantages over the DP leaders. The junta was not responsible for having negotiated the understandings that regulated the status of American forces in Turkey. Lacking full documentation on the promises and practices of the past, the military rulers had a plausible pretext to request changes to eliminate irritants. In particular, they could—and would— be far less accommodating than their DP predecessors in handling the matter of duty certification. Within months after seizing power, the Committee began exploring changes in the mode of determining duty status for American personnel.[7] By mid-November 1960, the junta had formed a special interministerial commission to draft a proposal in this regard and professed hope to be able to cut through the difficulties surrounding this tortured issue "in a day or two."[8] On this basis, the Turkish press confidently asserted that Turkish authorities would obtain the right to decide duty status.[9] But despite the enthusiasm of the Committee and firm support from prominent commentators who whipped up emotions by recalling the Morrison case, the Americans would not easily surrender this right, which they considered as basic to their worldwide position.

While events stood at this pass, an incident took place which would impart new urgency to the issue. In May 1961 a U.S. serviceman at the military installation at Sinop was accused of fatally shooting a Turkish guard. The circumstances surrounding this incident have never been satisfactorily explained.[10] Ballistic evidence and the testimony of American witnesses appeared to exonerate the soldier charged with the crime; Turkish testimony supported the accusation against him. Although some journalists sought to calm tempers, warning against blowing up the event out of proportion, the Committee personally intervened in the case to insist on additional investigation.[11] This effort, however, was unavailing; no agreed finding could be reached. Nonetheless, Turkish frustrations

---

[7] See Cemal Gürsel's press conference, *Ulus,* September 18, 1960.

[8] *Öncü,* November 16, 1960.

[9] *Yeni Gün,* November 18, 1960; *Ulus,* November 19, 1960.

[10] *New York Times,* May 19, June 4, 1961.

[11] *Vatan,* May 20, 1961.

were partly assuaged in July 1961 by reports that for the first time an American involved in an accident would be tried in a Turkish court. This did not represent any genuine breakthrough on the issue of duty certificates, for American officials ruled that the soldier was not on duty at the time of the shooting, but it did serve to take the heat off the issue in public opinion for the time being.[12]

Their interest in restricting the privileges and immunities of Americans did not mean that the military rulers intended a general assault on the complex of bilateral arrangements with the United States. Quite the contrary. The junta instead saw need to provide a legal mechanism that would meet the objections raised at the end of the 1950s to the effect that secret executive agreements were unconstitutional. To this end, the Constituent Assembly which elaborated the 1961 constitution agreed to permit several categories of exceptions to the requirement that international accords must be ratified by parliament. Of these, the most significant was the constitutional provision that "implementing agreements pursuant to an international agreement . . . do not require approval by the Turkish Grand National Assembly." [13] In commending this formulation, the Constituent Assembly committee that dealt with the issue noted specifically that this article would permit the government "to carry out some necessarily secret arrangements of the free world defense system which we joined of our own free desire and consent and in which we play a very important and honorable role." [14] This explanation elicited no objection from the assembled delegates, nor did they express any reservations that could form the basis for future assault on this reasoning.

Military housecleaning

The coup made changes in the Turkish military establishment inevitable. The conspirators desired a wholesale purge to clear out what they considered deadwood at the top, to end the "inflation of ranks," and to eliminate those whom they judged to be lukewarm about the new regime. Before undertaking this operation, the military rulers invited General Lauris Norstad, the supreme commander of NATO, to make a flying

---

[12] *Ulus,* July 1, 1961.

[13] Art. 65, Constitution of the Turkish Republic, promulgated July 9, 1961.

[14] TBMM, *Türkiye Cumhuriyeti Anayasa Tasarısı ve Anayasa Komisyonu Raporu* (5/7), March 9, 1961, pp. 30–31.

trip to Ankara to discuss Turkey's role in Allied defense plans and to enlist his assistance in making large-scale retirements possible with generous bonuses to reduce grievances. As the Turkish army was top-heavy with senior officers, the NATO Command did not view the junta's request as detrimental to the common defense effort. Norstad even promised to help secure the financial assistance necessary for the project.[15] On the heels of Norstad's visit at the end of July 1960, the Committee announced a program of radical reductions in senior-grade officers. Although this process was accompanied by retirement payments of unprecedented generosity, it left a residue of bitterness the junta had sought to avoid. The more than 4,000 field-grade and general officers retired in August 1960 soon became a powerful pressure group opposed to the regime.

Military efficiency naturally suffered from the radical upsets associated with the coup and the purge. On the working level, the officers were absorbed in political tasks; military functions were permitted to slide. Conspiratorial activity also distracted many from their normal professional responsibilities. Soon the officer corps was faced with the choice of lining up behind factions in the Committee or supporting generals seeking to reimpose the chain of command. During the period of military rule and beyond—until after the failure of coup attempts in 1962 and 1963—the preoccupation with politics rife in the military establishment kept the Turkish armed forces divided and unable to concentrate fully on the tasks of defense.

Return to civilian rule

These strains within the military increased pressures for a return to civilian rule. Both within the National Unity Committee and inside the officer corps at large, opposition to continuing military government grew. Respect for the parliamentary system had been deeply inculcated by Atatürk and his successors, and the senior generals in particular were dismayed by the disruption of discipline resulting from the deep involvement of the armed forces in daily politics during the era of the National Unity Committee. Thus, under strong urging from the RPP—whose leader, İnönü, as a former commanding general, enjoyed enormous prestige in the military establishment—the junta agreed to convene a

---

[15] İpekçi and Coşar, *Milliyet,* March 28, 1965, reported that the United States provided $12 million for this purpose. See also Avcıoğlu, *Türkiye'nin Düzeni,* p. 354.

Constituent Assembly in January 1961. This body prepared a constitution, which was adopted by referendum in August of the same year. And following elections in October, the soldiers allowed the civilian politicians to take office.

Because of the way it began its life, the Second Republic faced problems in assuring effective government. Voting had been held under a system of proportional representation designed to prevent any party from gaining an overwhelming parliamentary majority as Menderes had done during the previous decade. Moreover, four major parties contested the elections in 1961, though two of these, the Justice Party (JP) and the New Turkey Party (NTP), had then been in existence less than a year and had not had time to complete their organizations throughout Turkey. In these circumstances the RPP was able to gain a plurality in the lower house, but lacked the parliamentary strength to form a government unaided. For the ensuing four years, therefore, Turkey had to be governed by a series of coalition cabinets, headed for most of the period by İnönü, whose presence at the head of government was thought reassuring to the armed forces.

The first coalition saw the JP united with the RPP, an arrangement that offered the government the support of a large majority of the deputies. But within seven months this alignment foundered on the issue of amnesty for the *ancien régime,* a demand strongly voiced by the rank and file of the JP. The succeeding cabinet was composed of the RPP and two smaller centrist parties, the NTP and the Republican Peasants Nation Party (RPNP). Again unity of purpose was difficult to maintain, and in December 1963 the RPP established what was in effect a minority government with the cooperation of independents and dependent on a few votes from members of parties not represented in the cabinet. This unsteady structure was finally toppled during the budget debates in 1965, giving way to a coalition of the JP, the NTP, and the RPNP, led by the independent Suat Hayri Ürgüplü. It was under this last alignment that the fateful elections were held in October 1965 which returned the JP with a substantial majority, thus ending the procession of coalition expedients.

The Cuban missile crisis of 1962

The events surrounding the Cuban missile crisis of 1962 demonstrated the continuity in Turkish cooperation with the United States under the coalition governments.

At the end of 1957 the NATO ministers had agreed in principle to deploy medium range missiles with atomic warheads. The Menderes government had been almost alone in its enthusiasm for stationing missiles on Turkish territory. Indeed, only the United Kingdom and Italy agreed to accept them as well. Despite loud propaganda from Moscow strongly opposing its stand, the Ankara government prepared to receive Jupiter missiles, concluding a bilateral agreement to this effect in 1960. Although Foreign Minister Fatin Rüştü Zorlu had promised the parliament in January 1959 that he would inform it "when an agreement is to be concluded," the DP administration did not officially reveal these understandings.[16] Nonetheless, preparations to locate a squadron of Jupiters near Izmir went ahead. In view of the difficulties encountered in erecting the complicated launching equipment and the need to give specialized training to the Turkish troops involved, it was not until about July 1962 that the missiles were finally judged operational. By that time they were already considered obsolescent by American planners, though because of their location near the Soviet heartland they added measurably to the West's missile strength vis-à-vis the U.S.S.R.

The Jupiters became an important issue in Turkish-American relations when the Cuban missile crisis developed in the fall of 1962. As early as April 1961 President Kennedy had requested that the State Department negotiate removal of the missiles on the grounds that they were antiquated and their role could be better performed by Polaris submarines, which were then on the point of becoming available.[17] Foreign Minister Selim Sarper, however, had vigorously objected to letting the installations be removed at that juncture. One may conjecture that the Turkish military leaders, who always had a strong appetite for modern weaponry, believed that the Jupiters enhanced Turkey's military capabilities and thus added to Turkey's security against the U.S.S.R.

---

[16] *Zafer,* January 8, 1959. The exact date of the agreement with Turkey on the Jupiters has not been made public. But Secretary of Defense Robert McNamara told the House Committee on Armed Services that it was in 1960. See U.S. House, Committee on Armed Services, *Hearings on Military Posture . . .* (Washington, 1963), p. 283. For a critical Turkish view, see "Füzeler Gidiyor," *Yön,* January 30, 1963, p. 5.

[17] U.S., House, *Hearings on Military Posture . . .* 1963, p. 227; Max Frankel, "Mischief Seen in Offer of Bases Deal," *New York Times,* October 28, 1962. Robert F. Kennedy, *Thirteen Days* (New York, 1969), p. 94, leaves the impression that the original démarche with the Turks took place only some months before the Cuban confrontation. Ambassador Raymond Hare, who was in Ankara at the time, has confirmed the April 1961 date.

Besides, the missiles and associated equipment had been provided under the military aid program, hence were the property of the Turks. In any event, the newly installed civilian government in Ankara was in no position to insist on withdrawing missiles over the opposition of the Turkish armed forces. As a result, much to the chagrin of President Kennedy, the outbreak of the Cuban missile crisis found the squadron of Jupiters still in place near Izmir.

To the Kremlin, missiles in Cuba could be easily equated with missiles in Turkey. Thus when Kennedy faced Soviet Premier Nikita Khrushchev with demands to withdraw the medium range missiles surreptitiously introduced into Cuba, the Soviet leader on October 27, 1962, dusted off a well prepared counterproposal calling upon the United States to remove the Jupiters in Turkey in exchange.[18] This public bargaining over an issue that concerned them so intimately aroused some concern among the Turks, especially because of the implication that such missile bases would be first-priority targets in any war with the Soviets. Nevertheless, Prime Minister İnönü and his foreign minister immediately affirmed Turkey's support of the United States, come what might. President Kennedy, for his part, refused any public acceptance of a deal involving the Jupiters, though he did authorize his brother Robert to assure the Soviets that the Jupiters would soon be withdrawn once Soviet missiles had been removed from Cuba. In a confrontation of such immediacy, with time so obviously of the essence, the Turks perforce largely remained interested bystanders. At first the Ankara regime was not officially notified of the U.S. undertaking to pull out the Jupiters, and to its own audience staunchly denied that any "deals" were being made with the U.S.S.R. regarding missiles in Turkey.[19]

The play of the Cuban events left a deep imprint on Turkish-American relations. In the first place, it gave concrete form to creeping suspicions that the fate of the NATO allies might not be inextricably intertwined after all. As an astute observer had foreseen, "any effort to barter the symbols" of the U.S. commitment "for an advantage in the Caribbean [challenged] the principle of unanimity in the alliance and

---

[18] For the Khrushchev proposal, see *Bulletin,* November 12, 1962, pp. 741–43.

[19] As late as August 1963, İnönü still denied that any U.S.-Soviet "deal" had been involved. See A. Suat Bilge et al., *Olaylarla Türk Dış Politikası,* p. 352. By January 1970, however, İnönü was complaining that the United States and the U.S.S.R. had bargained over the Jupiter missiles without officially notifying Turkey of this fact. *Ulus,* January 23, 1970. See also Kennedy, pp. 94–95.

cast a long shadow over the United States promises to the allies." [20] To an important segment of the Turkish elite it appeared that Turkey had shared center stage with the United States in a confrontation in which the other NATO states, especially the Scandinavians, were mere spectators and which in no way directly concerned Turkish interests. The suddenness of the crisis also made impress on Turkish attitudes. Neither the Ankara government nor Turkish opinion was prepared for the sharp conflict generated by the Soviet move to place missiles in Cuba. This experience provided a vivid demonstration that the danger of war could arise without warning; this fear has become an essential underlay to the reactions of many in Turkey today. Moreover, these events formed the background against which Turks could come to believe for the first time that the mere possession of certain categories of weapons could make Turkey a primary target of Soviet ire, a line emphasized in the emerging left-wing press.[21] It was a complete reversal of the long-held view that increased military force meant increased security. As a result, sentiment in Turkey thereafter began to rise in favor of removing weapons systems which the Soviets considered especially dangerous, in order to decrease the likelihood that the country could be dragged into a conflict against her will.

Under these stimuli, the İnönü government now required little prodding by the United States to agree to the withdrawal of the Jupiter missiles. In April 1963 the allies exchanged notes agreeing to substitute Polaris submarines to cover targets previously assigned to the Jupiters. By the middle of that year, the missile installations had been entirely dismantled.[22]

The Turkish military establishment, however, was by no means willing to give up completely its role in the deterrent. On one hand, it continued to welcome the American strike aircraft, assigned to NATO and equipped with nuclear weapons, that were stationed in Turkey in accord with a tactical rotation agreement concluded in February 1957.[23] In the eyes of Turkish planners this force no doubt represented a useful trip-wire to assure U.S. and NATO involvement in the event of attack

---

[20] Max Frankel, *New York Times,* October 28, 1962.

[21] Doğan Avcıoğlu, "Füze Üsleri," *Yön,* October 31, 1962, p. 3.

[22] Bilge et al., pp. 351–52.

[23] *U.S. Security Agreements: Greece and Turkey,* p. 1864. See also "Füzeler Gidiyor," *Yön,* January 30, 1963, p. 5; Demirel's press conference of February 7, 1970, Appendix 5.

by the Soviet Union. It also served to demonstrate continuing American interest in Turkish defense and offered an additional argument for U.S. support to the Turkish military establishment. On the other hand, the Turkish General Staff was eager to modernize its own air force to enhance its military power vis-à-vis the U.S.S.R. The Turks therefore seized the opportunity to press Washington for additional modern aircraft to offset the value of the items removed in conjunction with the missiles.[24]

The United States agreed to a program of aircraft modernization in consideration for withdrawing the Jupiters. Nonetheless, it was clear that departure of the intermediate range missiles marked a significant shift in Turkey's strategic importance. With deployment by the United States of intercontinental ballistic missiles, backed up by Polaris submarines capable of launching strikes against all parts of the Soviet Union, the imperatives of nuclear deterrence no longer assigned so important a role to Turkey. Even the continuing presence of nuclear-armed strike aircraft—both Turkish and American—and the deployment of Turkish ground force units equipped with tactical atomic weapons could not conceal the fact that from a military point of view Turkey had now ceased to be a target of the most urgent priority in any cold war conflict. Moreover, the withdrawal of the Jupiters had removed a major irritant in Soviet relations with Turkey. No doubt this consideration helped to trigger a Soviet peace offensive calling for a wholesale relaxation of tensions between Turkey and the U.S.S.R.

Emergence of the left

If the 1960 coup did not mark a sharp divide in many areas of Turkish development, it did nonetheless unleash powerful leftist forces that would in time impart a distinctive cast to Turkish life. The coup plotters viewed themselves as the guardians of the Atatürk reforms; for all their diversity of view they displayed a strong reformist complexion reflecting a common concern with social issues—notably social justice. This attitude both stimulated and itself fed on a socialist movement which had revived and burgeoned thanks to the relatively free circulation of ideas fostered by the soldiers.

---

[24] Secretary of Defense McNamara's testimony before the House Committee on Armed Services, January 30, 1963, *Hearings on Military Posture* . . . 1963, p. 282.

At first the emerging left acted cautiously. Cloaking their appeals with the mantle of Kemalism, the socialists attempted to gain increased legitimacy by claiming Atatürk as one of their own.[25] Moreover, the early issues of the theoretical journal *Yön*, which made its appearance in December 1961 as an organ representing the views of these elements, provided a forum broad enough to accommodate a considerable range of opinion. Doctrinal considerations remained in the background, though from the start *Yön* radiated the belief that the intellectual elite would serve as the spark plug of social transformation. A tiny Turkish Labor Party, too, hesitantly began to seek support among the workers. Its task was all the more difficult as the masses still clung tenaciously to traditional values. By the time of the October 1961 elections this party had not yet sufficient local organization to participate in the contests.[26]

Gradually in the months that followed the return to civilian rule, the left picked up momentum and became more radical in tone. At first these circles were willing to concede that under certain conditions foreign aid could offer a potential contribution to industrial development; but with the passage of time U.S. interest in channeling assistance to the private sector was increasingly assailed and the left raised a call for greater independence from the West in foreign policy and for vigilance in preventing U.S. interference in Turkish affairs. Even before the end of 1962, *Yön* and other organs of like persuasion were alleging that America was working to destroy the left.[27] While some critics would moderate this claim on occasion—for example, *Yön* editor Doğan Avcıoğlu took heart at Washington's evident unconcern at the Baathi coup in Baghdad in February 1963—thenceforth the idea that the United States was its primary foreign foe would form a bedrock conviction of those on the extreme left of the political spectrum.[28]

The major political parties did not join in these attacks on the United States. The coalition governments were interested in tailoring their demands for assistance to the criteria most likely to receive favorable response from U.S. authorities. They also sought to resolve some

---

[25] Cf. Şükran Kurdakul, "Atatürk Sosyalist Değil midir?" *Ataç,* 1964, no. 2, pp. 21–23; Namık Zeki Aral, "A Fallacy: Was Atatürk a Socialist?" *Turkish Economic Review,* January 1964, pp. 10–13.

[26] The election law required a party to complete organization in fifteen provinces in order to qualify to offer candidates as a party.

[27] Mümtaz Soysal, "Birlikte Yaşama," *Yön,* November 28, 1962, p. 3.

[28] Doğan Avcıoğlu, "Amerika ve Arap Sosyalizmi," *Yön,* February 13, 1963, p. 3.

of the nagging problems relating to the sovereignty question, but without much success. Despite the conclusion of additional agreements regulating bilateral cooperation in 1962, difficulties remained. Some years after the event, the press was to publicize the incident in 1963 when American officers denied Third Army Commander General Refik Tulga entry to the Trabzon facility because he lacked explicit permission from the Turkish General Staff.[29] But for the most part these points of friction were veiled in secrecy and at the time did not affect the overall relationship.

Labor disputes

Other bilateral problems attracted more attention. For example, labor disputes involving the United States now began to come to the fore.

The labor movement in Turkey was gathering force. Long promised the right to strike by both the DP and the RPP in the period before 1960, the unions had not succeeded in getting this pledge redeemed. The 1960 coup revitalized the flagging union movement. Not only did the 1961 constitution legitimize the principle of the strike—a right finally conferred by law in mid-1963—but foreign labor advisers were permitted to come to Turkey, and unions were allowed to establish international affiliations for the first time.[30] Stimulated by representatives of American as well as European labor organizations, workers employed by the U.S. government and by American firms were early to be caught up in this atmosphere.

In one significant case, Turkish workers at İncirlik air base near Adana demanded increased benefits from the American Air Force. When U.S. authorities refused to meet their claims for holiday pay and overtime, the workers took their cause to court over American objections that the U.S. government could not be brought to trial. The Turkish court ruled in favor of the workers, leaving the United States to appeal in the name of Attorney General Robert Kennedy. Again the Turkish employees won.[31]

---

[29] Doğan Avcıoğlu, "Türk Ordusu ve Amerika, 1947–1969," *Devrim*, October 28, 1969, p. 3; Doğan Avcıoğlu, "The Turkish Army and the United States," *Outlook*, November 5, 1969, pp. 5–6.

[30] U.S. Department of Labor, *Labor Law and Practice in Turkey* (BLS Report no. 239, Washington, 1963), pp. 36, 56–57.

[31] See, for example, "Yargıtayın Önemli Bir Kararı," *Yön*, March 20, 1963, pp. 4–5.

Not only did this case earn bad publicity, especially in *Yön* and other organs of the left, but it impelled the United States Air Force to conclude an arrangement with a private U.S. contracting firm, the Tumpane Company, to act as employer for locally hired personnel. This expedient, which removed the U.S. government from the direct line of fire in labor disputes, was to undercut later arguments that workers should be prohibited from striking American activities on Turkish military bases. In those days, however, before the Cyprus crisis, the motivations for demands on American employers rested primarily on economic grounds, especially on the conviction that the U.S. government and American businesses had the money to pay better than the going Turkish wage scale. Political considerations were largely lacking in these confrontations.

Development assistance and the five-year plan

Economic relations between the United States and Turkey entered a new course during the early 1960s. On the Turkish side the main innovation centered around the creation of a mechanism for national development planning. This was an idea whose time had come in Turkey. National planning of a sort had been tried by the Turks starting in the 1930s; its utility was well enshrined in the Kemalist mythology. As early as 1951 the RPP had begun bitterly attacking the Menderes regime for its failure to draw up any comprehensive long-range plan. U.S. advisers, beginning with Max Thornburg, suggested that the Turkish government proceed along this path. Under these stimuli the military rulers moved without delay to announce the aims and strategy of a national plan for Turkey in July 1960; two months later the State Planning Organization was officially inaugurated. In short order it produced first a transitional plan for 1962, then a full-scale five-year plan for the years 1963 through 1967, and a fifteen-year perspective outlining the goals for a series of three successive five-year plans. These projections reflected many ideas that the United States had been supporting over the years concerning development without inflation. Their targets, calling for a 7 percent annual increase in Gross National Product and an end to concessionary aid in a decade, would initially be accepted by all of Turkey's allies as reasonable.[32] Indeed, these plans became the base for all subsequent economic assistance to Turkey.

---

[32] John White, *Pledged to Development,* p. 120.

The character of American economic aid to Turkey had been changing in the last years of the Eisenhower administration. Severe and growing balance of payments problems had led Washington to begin to shift increasingly from grant aid to loans by the end of the 1950s. At the same time, following the stabilization program of 1958, the United States had come to devote a higher proportion of its assistance to support for specific projects and less to underwriting a share of the Turkish balance of payments deficit. Among the noteworthy projects financed in this way was the Ereğli steel mill, to which in 1961 the United States loaned $130 million in its largest single commitment to a Turkish venture.

The Ereğli steel mill

The Ereğli project has been dogged with perhaps the worst problems to afflict the American aid effort in Turkey in the 1960s.[33] Turkish pride was heavily engaged in the urgent desire to have a second major steel mill; hence successive Turkish governments felt under great pressure to speed the venture along. It appears that the agreement was concluded before enough study had been given to the feasibility of the proposed plans. At any rate, some of the serious operational and economic difficulties encountered at Ereğli are clearly attributable to poor planning. For example, iron ore of sufficient quality to operate the mill efficiently has not yet been discovered in Turkey; the suitability of the product to the Turkish market is also open to question. As for the financing of the complex, it was done primarily through loans rather than through issuance of stock; thus the venture was saddled with a heavy debt service burden. Moreover, the amount of Turkish currency required for working capital to commence operations was initially seriously underestimated, leading to a succession of acute financial crises for the project. These problems apart, the venture from the start has labored under the difficulty that as a condition of U.S. assistance the Ankara government agreed not to own more than 49 percent of the enterprise. American insistence that the Ereğli mill be a private Turkish entity, though most of its financing came from U.S. and Turkish governmental sources, ran

---

[33] Among numerous critical Turkish assessments of the Ereğli steel mill, see "Ereğli-Çelik, Amerikalı Koppers Grubu ile Dâniş Koper'in Nasıl Çiftliği Haline Geldi?" *Yön*, December 25, 1964, p. 4; Doğan Avcıoğlu, "Ereğli-Çelik Dosyası Açılmalıdır," *Yön*, January 1, 1965, p. 3. For an American report questioning aspects of the Ereğli project, see U.S., AID, *Turkey: Ereğli Iron and Steel Works Incorporated* (Capital Assistance Paper, AID-DLC/P-567), June 1967.

against deeply rooted sentiment among the elite in Turkey that such an undertaking should be a state economic enterprise in the Kemalist tradition. This U.S. condition has provided fodder for continuing bitter attacks from Turkish leftists ever since. Moreover, from the moment that the agreement was concluded, the interest rate and the terms of participation of the American contractors, especially the Koppers Company, was assailed as prejudicial to Turkey's interests.[34]

Creating the consortium for aid to Turkey

A growing shift from foreign aid grants to loans, pursued worldwide, failed to relieve the balance of payments pressures on the United States in the late 1950s. Hence the Kennedy administration was determined to involve its European allies, especially West Germany, in sharing the burden of assistance to countries like Turkey. Negotiations to this end were speedily undertaken; before the end of 1961 the Germans had agreed to shoulder some of the load of military and economic aid to Turkey.[35]

The American move to enlist broader European participation in providing aid to Turkey came when Ankara itself was asking NATO for economic assistance. After "three wise men" had been sent to Turkey to inspect the situation in 1961, the Turkish request was transmitted to the Organization for Economic Cooperation and Development, which had guided the stabilization program of 1958.[36] From these beginnings, with strong American behind-the-scenes encouragement, an international consortium was assembled to coordinate aid to Turkey. But from the first, the consortium's mandate remained purposely vague, and many of the nine original members resisted submitting to any informal procedure to assess contributions. The Turks hoped that tying their request for aid to the requirements of their new development plans would lead to vastly increased foreign assistance. The United States, on the other hand, saw the consortium as a means to lower American contribution without decreasing the total foreign aid available to Turkey.

---

[34] *Ulus*, July 13, 20, 1961; *Öncü*, July 13, 20, 1961; *Kudret*, July 20, 1961; *Cumhuriyet*, January 10, 1961. İdris Küçükömer, "Ereğli Demir Çelik Kurumu ve Egemenliğimiz," *Yön*, October 9, 1964, p. 12.

[35] Charles Lam Markmann and Mark Sherwin, *John F. Kennedy: A Sense of Purpose* (New York, 1961), p. 109.

[36] White, pp. 108 ff.

Despite vigorous U.S. cooperation, the consortium approach was not immediately successful. Washington believed that in this venture it should follow tactics of "understating" its commitment in order to stimulate the other members to meet the projected deficit. While Washington actively worked to pursue the Turkish cause with its European allies, it pledged $66 million through the consortium in 1963. This represented a sharp cut in the level of American support, and naturally it offended the Turkish authorities—especially as the Europeans did not come forward to fill the gap.[37] Nor were the Turks happy with the consortium's emphasis on the funding of projects rather than on providing contributions to the general budget as had the United States in the past. When other consortium members failed to pledge sufficient amounts, the Turks were left to make up the shortfall with short-term financing from the International Monetary Fund and the European Monetary Agency.

It was on this uncertain note that the Cyprus crisis supervened to shake the U.S.-Turkish alliance to its core.

---

[37] White, p. 114. Cf. Doğan Avcıoğlu, "DPT 1964 Yılı Raporu," *Yön,* November 5, 1965, p. 9.

Part Three:
LOOSENING THE BONDS

5

Cyprus Crisis

The impact of the Cyprus issue in Turkey is both profound and complex. Mainland Turks have not always paid great attention to the fate of their island confreres; nor in fact is the Cypriot Turk ordinarily held in high esteem in Anatolia. But let the prospect arise as it did in the 1950s that this island, like almost all of those in the Aegean, might pass under Greek sovereignty, and the response in Turkey can be electric.[1] Even the uniting of Turkey and Greece in NATO could not dissipate the latent animosity born of the struggle to form the Greek state more than a century ago. When excited by sensational journalism, political intrigue, or government encouragement, support for the Turkish community on Cyprus can well up in Turkey with astonishing suddenness. Equally, government restraint, coupled with moderate press treatment and an absence of politically sponsored protests, can calm passions to a significant degree even when the rights of the Turkish community are involved. It is this manipulative aspect of the impact of the Cyprus issue on Turkey—the possibility of its containment within broad limits—that has been most misunderstood abroad. This misunderstanding contributed to the violence of the American reaction to Turkish moves in the Cyprus crisis.

The history of the 1950s conditioned foreign observers to take Turkish passions over Cyprus seriously. When agitation for uniting the island with Greece was first forcefully advanced in the early 1950s, it

---

[1] Some authorities claim that the Turks saw the attempt to link Cyprus with Greece as a step in reconstituting the defunct Byzantine Empire. See Ülman and Dekmejian, "Changing Patterns in Turkish Foreign Policy," *Orbis,* Fall 1967, p. 776.

led to the formation of the "Cyprus Is Turkish" Society in Turkey to oppose this possibility. Menderes took this group into his political calculations, seeing its activities as useful evidence of Turkish concern over the fate of the island. In 1955 a demonstration undoubtedly sanctioned by the DP for these purposes got out of control in Istanbul, and to a lesser extent in Izmir, leading to the destruction of much property, especially property belonging to Greek nationals or Turkish citizens of Greek descent. The virulence of this outpouring of emotion was well noted abroad;[2] less frequently remarked was the impressive ability of even a handful of Turkish troops to disperse demonstrators once they had clear instructions to do so.

Concerned lest their engagement in Cyprus disrupt Western alliances, Athens and Ankara, with active British assistance, agreed to a compromise in 1959: Cyprus would be independent; the Turkish community, which formed something under 20 percent of the island's population, would enjoy guaranteed political rights. With goodwill, this solution might perhaps have worked. But from the first, deep suspicion divided the communities on the island. They grew increasingly uncooperative with each other. A kind of separatism came into being which Archbishop Makarios, president of Cyprus, considered incompatible with his understanding of the agreements and which frustrated his efforts at unitary government. His proposal at the end of November 1963 to change the constitution to eliminate those privileges of the Turkish community which contributed to communal separation was masterfully timed. It passed with minimum notice in Turkey, where a severe cabinet crisis was threatening the country with political anarchy.[3] On the island, however, it aroused a storm as Turkish Cypriots sensed a grave threat to their existence. Under these circumstances, it took no more than a trivial incident on Cyprus to blow up in actual civil war between the communities. Once this happened, as it did on December 21, 1963, hopes of carrying out the 1959 agreements exploded with it.

---

[2] For example, see Frederic Sondern, Jr., "Istanbul's Night of Terror," *Reader's Digest,* May 1956, pp. 185–92.

[3] Only a few editorials on Cyprus appeared in the Turkish press during the first half of December 1963. These were surprisingly restrained. See, for example, Ahmet Şükrü Esmer, "Dış Politika: Makarios'un Marifeti," *Ulus,* December 11, 1963, which describes in notably noninflammatory terms Turkey's determination to oppose change in the status of Cyprus.

Turkish saber rattling, 1963

The urgent plight of the outnumbered Turkish Cypriots faced İnönü's recently constituted government with a need for immediate action. Preoccupied with internal matters, the procession of coalition cabinets in Ankara, like the public more generally in Turkey, had not prepared for this eventuality. The Turkish armed forces were neither trained, equipped, nor positioned to undertake a landing on Cyprus. Much as there were staunch advocates of an amphibious operation, the only feasible military option then open to the Turks was to make limited air strikes. Thus, when the Turkish minority seemed in danger of being overrun, the İnönü government sent four aircraft in token passes over the island on December 25, 1963, to underscore Turkey's determination to back up its beleaguered confreres. This maneuver was coupled with the dispatch of naval units from Istanbul to Mersin, the major Turkish port closest to Cyprus. But after the Cypriot representative at the United Nations accused the Turks of using tactics of intimidation, the Turkish ambassador assured the Security Council "officially and categorically that there are no Turkish ships sailing toward Cyprus, and that any ships which might have been seen in the area are sailing from one Turkish port to another." [4]

In taking these military steps, the Ankara authorities maintained they were acting solely to redress violations of the 1959 London-Zurich accords which had established the independent Republic of Cyprus. Among the provisions of those accords was one permitting the guarantor powers (Turkey, Greece, and the United Kingdom) to take individual action to redress violations if joint efforts proved unavailing.[5] And indeed, Ankara had been in urgent communication with both London and Athens to cooperate in stopping the attacks on the Turkish community for two days before the warning flight. Moreover, the small detachment of Turkish troops stationed on the island in conformity with

---

[4] U.N., Security Council, *Official Records,* (S/PV. 1085), December 27, 1963, p. 12. The Cypriot representative at the United Nations claimed that İnönü had informed the Turkish parliament that naval units were stationed off Cyprus "awaiting orders to act." Ibid., p. 3. The official record of parliamentary speeches by İnönü and Foreign Minister Erkin does not substantiate this allegation. T. C. Senatosu, *Tutanak Dergisi,* dönem 1, vol. 17, pp. 6–10 (session of December 26, 1963). However, Erkin on December 25, 1963, did announce the departure of the fleet for Mersin. *Cumhuriyet,* December 26, 1963.

[5] For the London-Zurich accords, see Great Britain, Secretary of State for the Colonies, *Cyprus,* Cmnd. 1093 (London, 1960).

the agreements cooperated with British and Greek forces in seeking to impose a cease-fire. Only when the aroused Greek Cypriot majority initially refused to heed the joint appeal of these powers did Ankara order its planes to fly over Cyprus—at the same time appealing to President Johnson and other Western heads of state to intervene to halt the bloodshed.[6] Thanks to these combined efforts, by the end of December something of a lull in the communal conflict had come about, with the Turkish Cypriots assembled for the most part in enclaves representing areas of the densest Turkish population.

For their sorties, the Turks used aircraft provided under NATO auspices and assigned to the NATO command. In fact, at that time the Turkish air force and the bulk of the ground force were thus equipped and assigned. The gendarmerie (except for its mobile brigades stationed in southeastern Turkey) was the only regularly constituted force of any dimension that was neither supplied by NATO nor committed to its operations. The gendarmerie, however, was not equipped for full-scale military action, far less for an amphibious landing.

It would be a matter of dispute whether the Turks were making a legitimate use of NATO-assigned planes by ordering them over Cyprus. According to the 1947 aid agreement, equipment furnished by the United States could not be used "for any purpose other than that for which the article . . . is furnished." [7] This vague formula could serve to justify whatever the Turks considered a necessary adjunct of their defense,[8] or it could be interpreted far more restrictively. Up to that time the question of defining the provision had not arisen. Even after the Turkish air action in December 1963, the United States did not immediately resolve its position on the issue; nor was Washington quick to issue any complaint to Turkey over the flights.

NATO peace-keeping

The next stage of the Cyprus crisis involved an intense search for some mechanism to dampen tensions on the island and prevent a resumption

---

[6] U.S., Department of State, *American Foreign Policy: Current Documents,* 1963 (Washington, 1967), pp. 470–77.

[7] See Appendix 1, Art. IV.

[8] This agreement carried no precise definition of the purpose of aid beyond the statement in its preamble that Turkey had requested "assistance which will enable Turkey to strengthen the security forces which Turkey requires for the protection of her freedom and independence."

of full-scale hostilities between the communities. For the danger that the Cyprus dispute could trigger war between Greece and Turkey was unmistakably evident after the Greek prime minister, at the start of January 1964, publicly warned that his country would forcefully counter any Turkish intervention.[9]

NATO offered a natural forum for Athens and Ankara to seek to coordinate an approach. But it was soon apparent that the Western alliance system could not effectively focus on local discord between its own members. The idea of a NATO peace-keeping force, which was broached almost at the very outset, was resisted bitterly by Cypriot President Makarios; it also ran into formidable obstacles posed by both the Greek and Turkish governments, whose views of the Cyprus problem remained far apart. Washington, wary of injecting itself into the forefront of the dispute, endeavored to persuade the parties concerned to accept such a NATO force.[10] Like all the members of the Atlantic alliance, however, the United States was reluctant to endorse any positive plan for the solution of the Cyprus dispute for fear of alienating either Greece or Turkey. While NATO Supreme Commander Lyman Lemnitzer came to Greece and Turkey at the end of January and again in June, and while Secretary General Dirk Stikker visited in the closing days of April and was given a "watching brief" in May, this activity could not conceal the alliance's impotence to deal with such an internally divisive problem, especially in view of the fact that a third party—Makarios—held the swing position.[11]

UNFICYP

Under the circumstances, the creation of the U.N. peace-keeping force in Cyprus (UNFICYP) seemed the most feasible way to deal with the periodic outbreaks of severe local fighting that continued to rock the island. Turkey was not enthusiastic about seeing the United Nations intervene in this way, probably because Ankara generally had little confidence in the ability of this international organ to act effectively to protect the Turkish Cypriot community, and perhaps also because it

---

[9] *New York Times,* January 2, 1964.

[10] Ankara's acceptance of this NATO force was announced following an all-night cabinet session prefaced by an urgent meeting with Ambassador Hare. See *New York Times,* February 1, 1964.

[11] Cf. Francis A. Beer, *Integration and Disintegration in NATO,* p. 17.

was felt that the presence of a U.N. force might ultimately inhibit Turkish freedom of action. It took an urgent mission by U.S. Under Secretary George Ball in February 1964 to induce Prime Minister İnönü to give the U.N. approach a trial.[12] Even then Ankara preferred to keep its own forces at the ready, holding naval maneuvers in the İskenderun area near Cyprus and keeping its air force on alert. In fact in March 1964, while the U.N. force was being assembled, Ankara again publicly threatened to intervene if attacks against the Turkish community did not stop; in mid-March 1964 the Turkish parliament granted İnönü specific authority to intervene on Cyprus.[13] Thus from the outset the Turkish government established for the record its lack of confidence in the U.N. operation.

Enter the United States

Continuing violence on the island and Ankara's repeated threats of armed intervention brought the United States to modify its conception of its role in the crisis. As late as the end of December 1963, Washington had told the Turkish government that it was "not a party to this issue." [14] But soon thereafter President Lyndon Johnson's advisers saw the need to convey forcefully their desire for a peaceful solution. American Ambassador Raymond Hare became a constant caller at the Turkish Foreign Office. In addition to Ball, who in February 1964 had touched base with all parties to the dispute, President Johnson sent Senator J. William Fulbright as his special envoy to assist in bridging the gap between Athens and Ankara.[15] Yet to the end Washington remained unwilling to take sides in the quarrel and was determined to stand squarely for peace and compromise, without accepting fully the arguments of either party. This stance satisfied neither Greece nor Turkey, and fed a growing clamor in both countries against the United States.

---

[12] İnönü had warned Ball that it might be necessary for Turkey to intervene to restore order. See İnönü's reply to President Johnson's letter, *Middle East Journal,* Summer 1966, pp. 308–9.

[13] For the Turkish threat to intervene, see *American Foreign Policy. Current Documents: 1964,* p. 569; *Milliyet,* March 17, 1964.

[14] See İnönü's reply to President Johnson's letter, *Middle East Journal,* Summer 1966, pp. 388–93.

[15] To some commentators, Fulbright's impartiality and discrimination were suspect. See İffet Aslan, "Gerçek Peşinde: Sohbet: Zengin Adamın Çilesi," *Ulus,* May 10, 1964.

All through this period Greece and Turkey alike were doing their utmost to paint the United States into their respective corners. Foreign Minister Feridun Cemal Erkin at the end of April 1964 interpreted President Johnson's call for order on Cyprus as an appeal to stop Greek Cypriot aggression against the Turkish community.[16] He also warned that the island could become the "Cuba of the Mediterranean," an argument obviously tailored to trigger a sympathetic response in the United States, if not to provide a justification for future Turkish intervention. For the Turks would now point to the growing closeness of Makarios with the Soviet Union as a harbinger of danger to the eastern Mediterranean. In this campaign, Ankara secured a special session of the NATO Council in May 1964. But still Turkey's NATO partners refused to take sides.

Turkish reaction

Disillusionment with the Western alliance mounted steadily in Turkey. Many Turks had an exaggerated notion of what could be done toward solving the Cyprus problem if Washington would only throw its weight into the balance. Of course they did not expect that the United States would try to force Turkey to give up its cause, but they assumed that Johnson could bring Nicosia and Athens into line if he chose. America's initial reluctance to become involved in the dispute and its subsequent neutrality stood in the eyes of these Turks as prima facie evidence that Washington did not want to help Turkey.[17] For those who had seen the connection with the United States as stretching across the gamut of human activity, it was painful to conclude that the relationship after all had its limits. This was a special disappointment because emotions over Cyprus had been inflamed to such heights. Reports of slaughter of women and children appeared frequently in the Turkish papers. Assailed at every hand by claims that the Greek Cypriots were carrying out "genocide" and attempting ultimate "annihilation" of the Turkish community, public opinion generally in Turkey could not comprehend why the United States was so flaccid in its backing of Turkey in this hour of need.[18] All the more poignant for the Turks

---

[16] *New York Times,* April 29, 30, 1964.
[17] See, for example, "Kıbrıs ve Yön," *Yön,* September 25, 1964, pp. 8–9.
[18] *Cumhuriyet,* February 15, 1964; *Ulus,* December 30, 1963; *New York Times,* December 25, 1963, February 14 and May 25, 1964.

was the comparison noted by many commentators between the unwillingness of Washington to espouse Ankara's cause in Cyprus and the steadfast support Turkey had shown America during the Korean conflict and especially through the dangerous days of the Cuban confrontation. Later in the summer, after the Tonkin Gulf incidents, Turkish journalists would ruefully contrast President Johnson's swift recourse to air strikes against North Vietnam with his consistent disapproval of Turkish military action against Cyprus.[19]

In the early stages of the crisis, there were few in Turkey who would go so far as to claim that Washington might actually favor the Greek side. It would take months of disappointment before the suspicion would begin to take root that America at heart supported the union of Cyprus with Greece. Through the spring of 1964 the main complaint was that by counseling peaceful means and by discouraging Turkish armed intervention, the United States was permitting a buildup of Greek Cypriot forces equipped with foreign arms which could be used to liquidate the Turkish community at will.[20] In other words, it was widely feared in Turkey that Washington's policy in fact was contributing substantially to Greek advantage in the communal conflict.

To invade or not to invade

Given the sentiment in Turkey, the pressures on İnönü's government to take action mounted rapidly. Strong elements in the Turkish military establishment apparently urged recourse to force. Later in the year General Cemal Tural, then chief of the Ground Forces, would openly indicate his sympathy for intervention in Cyprus by his presence at a student protest demonstration on this issue.[21] Other high-ranking officers too apparently were among the "hawks." Moves to reinforce and train the division based in İskenderun for use in Cyprus merely fed the emotional climate in the Turkish armed forces and lent conviction to hopes that the Turkish troops would carry out amphibious

19 Cihat Baban, "Tonkin Körfezi ve Kıbrıs," *Ulus,* August 7, 1964; İlhan Selçuk, "Pencere: Endişe . . . ve Esef!" *Cumhuriyet,* August 7, 1964; Ecvet Güresin, "Günün Notları: Serzeniş," *Cumhuriyet,* August 8, 1964.
20 *New York Times,* February 23, May 6, June 2, 1964.
21 *New York Times,* September 2, 1964; *Milliyet,* September 2, 1964.

operations. There were numerous vocal civilian proponents of military action as well, but of course they hardly bulked as large in policy making. The "doves" in Turkey, or at least the comparative moderates, were undoubtedly headed by İnönü himself; they probably included many of his lieutenants in the RPP. A number of these leaders had been critical of Menderes' efforts to whip up emotion over Cyprus in the 1950s, and had called for a less flamboyant—though no more concessive—policy. As for İnönü, he had shown himself throughout his career to be wary of foreign adventures. In fact, this caution had figured prominently in his break with Atatürk in 1937 [22] and his reluctance to embark on a course whose outcome was seriously in doubt had been amply demonstrated during the Second World War. His wariness had not decreased over the years. İnönü understood the game of world politics from long experience at the top of government. He could appreciate the complex problems that would inevitably accompany any Turkish landing on Cyprus; there is evidence that in the councils of war that took place at this time his was the voice to question whether Turkey was prepared to deal with the ultimate implications of intervention or even to carry out the operation itself. And he clearly recognized that the Americans would inevitably get wind of Turkish intentions before a landing could be accomplished.[23]

Yet it was not easy, even for a politician of İnönü's stature, to resist the demands to land troops in Cyprus. The civilian regime itself maintained but a precarious hold on power. Military uprisings in 1962 and 1963 had been put down, the last only after elements loyal to the government had opened fire. While the severe punishments meted out to the conspirators in the wake of the 1963 unsuccessful putsch had dampened further plotting in the military establishment, memories of past restiveness were still very fresh. İnönü's personal standing as a former general and military hero was widely considered a major factor enabling civilian government to continue. Yet there were obvious limits on how far his prestige could keep the war faction at heel. Indeed, it is clear from recitals after the event that İnönü did not feel himself able to take any categoric stand in opposition to the "hawks." [24]

---

[22] For a detailed discussion of this point, see Harris, "A Political History of Turkey," pp. 126–35.

[23] "Devlet Teşkilatımızdaki Amerikan Ajanları," *Yön,* July 15, 1966, p. 5; Doğan Avcıoğlu, *Türkiye'nin Düzeni,* p. 409.

[24] Doğan Avcıoğlu, *Türkiye'nin Düzeni,* p. 409.

Matters came to a head in June 1964, after the Cypriot parliament approved a bill establishing general conscription for the Greek Cypriot defense forces. As these units already enjoyed a huge margin of military superiority over those of the Turkish community, this step touched off a vigorous response inside the Ankara government. Although press treatment of the Cyprus issue at this critical juncture was by no means hysterical in tone [25]—Cyprus at the time was sharing the news spotlight with the approaching senatorial elections—İnönü apparently felt he could no longer hold back his armed forces. Active preparations for a landing on Cyprus began.

İnönü's intentions at this point cannot be ascertained with assurance. It seems probable, however, that even then he hoped that military intervention would not take place.[26] Perhaps he expected that when the Americans learned, as they inevitably would, that Turkish forces were massing in the south and embarking on naval vessels, they would exert pressure on the Greek and Greek Cypriot side to back down. Very likely he anticipated that Washington would once again issue a warning to Turkey to use only peaceful means to press its course—a warning that could strengthen his hand in resisting the hawks in the military establishment. What is certain is that İnönü, who appreciated the U.S. dilemma, never foresaw that when invasion appeared imminent Washington would react with a presidential communication of great harshness, calling into question the very bases of the alliance. He must have been especially surprised inasmuch as the current course of intensive diplomatic interchange had raised the prospect, as had analogous discussions in earlier months, that the Turks might stand down.

The Johnson letter

The American president and his senior advisers were so concerned lest a Turkish move against Cyprus precipitate war between Greece and Turkey that on June 5, 1964, they dispatched what came to be

---

[25] Only on June 5, 1964, in an apparent—perhaps deliberate—press leak, did the major responsible papers, *Milliyet* and *Akşam,* specifically warn that the landing of Turkish forces on the island was imminent.

[26] *Cumhuriyet,* June 24, 1964, carried a report by Fred J. Zusy from Washington noting the impression prevalent there that İnönü had not wanted a landing in Cyprus, and that he had let the news of the impending Turkish intervention leak out in hopes that the Americans would step in to settle the issue.

known as the "Johnson letter." [27] The operative sections of this message to İnönü warned that "your NATO allies have not had a chance to consider whether they have an obligation to protect Turkey against the Soviet Union if Turkey takes a step which results in Soviet intervention without the full consent and understanding of its NATO Allies." Further, Johnson cautioned, "I must tell you in all candor that the United States cannot agree to the use of any United States supplied military equipment for a Turkish intervention in Cyprus under present circumstances."

The Johnson letter created a sharp divide in the Turkish-American relationship. To the top-level advisers who participated in its drafting, the harshness of tone—reflecting shortness of time and also exasperation that the specter of Turkish intervention could not be laid to rest—seemed essential to head off Turkish action; however, a more conciliatory and less categoric approach probably would have accomplished Johnson's aim without abrading Turkish feelings so severely. It is further entirely possible that delivery of a formal written communication was unnecessary under the circumstances. In any event, the questioning of NATO support if the Cyprus dispute should lead to a Soviet attack against Turkey was undoubtedly a major error. It impelled İnönü to conclude that "there are as between us wide divergence of views as to the nature and basic principles of the North Atlantic Alliance." In the Turkish interpretation, the need for the NATO alliance to debate the issue of "whether aggression was provoked" and "whether they have an obligation to assist" would shake "the very foundation of the Alliance . . . and it would lose its meaning." These considerations led the Turks to begin a wide-ranging reevalution of the alliance and added to the fears about Turkish defense already stimulated by the shift of NATO strategy toward "flexible response." [28]

To make matters worse, somewhat distorted and tendentious versions of the Johnson message leaked into the Turkish press almost immediately, generating profound popular reaction.[29] İnönü's acceptance of the invitation to discuss the matter in depth in Washington did not stanch the flow of bitter feeling against the United States. Rather

---

[27] The text of this letter and İnönü's reply are in the *Midlle East Journal,* Summer 1966, pp. 386–93.

[28] Ibid. For the strategy of "flexible response," see below, pp. 149–51.

[29] See, for example, *Milliyet, Yeni Sabah, Akşam,* June 7, 8, 1964; "Durum: Türk-Amerikan Münasebetlerinde Dönüm Noktası," *Milliyet,* June 10, 1964.

his trip became a peg on which columnists of diverse points of view hung bitter reproaches against America. From that time forth, all Turkish governments would be on the defensive in regard to the American connection, and memories of the Johnson letter would color popular impressions of the United States for many years to come.

İnönü's Washington visit

İnönü's political position in Turkey was considerably compromised by the American démarche. His government did its best to put a favorable gloss on the U.S. role. Under Secretary George Ball, who was accounted in Turkey as the sole senior American policy maker who understood how to deal with Makarios, made another flying trip to Turkey in the days immediately following the Johnson letter to seek to salve Turkish feelings.[30] General Lemnitzer, too, traveled to Ankara at that time, to weigh in with the Turkish armed forces. In public statements Foreign Minister Erkin interpreted these visits as evidence that Washington would defend Turkish interests and play a very active role in achieving a settlement of the Cyprus dispute. But this line fell flat against the extensive press diatribes condemning the United States for having blocked Turkish intervention. The JP, which was heartened by a sweeping victory in the recent senatorial elections, sharply scored the İnönü government for its failures in the Cyprus issue. The cabinet survived the vote of confidence demanded by İnönü on the eve of his departure for Washington by the narrow margin of 200 to 194—but a sizable group of deputies deliberately refrained from attending the parliament that day.[31] It was therefore with the most tenuous backing that the Turkish prime minister set off for the United States toward the end of June 1964. He departed amid mounting public protest against America, which some foreign observers believed to have been at least partly inspired by the Ankara authorities themselves in order to strengthen their hand in negotiations.[32]

[30] *New York Times,* June 12, 1964.

[31] Millet Meclisi, *Tutanak Dergisi,* dönem 1, vol. 31, pp. 73–76. This record shows 42 deputies absent, of whom 19 were members of the JP and only 3 were from the RPP (one of the RPP deputies was counted absent because he was serving as presiding officer). See also *New York Times,* June 20, 1964.

[32] Some of the bitterest recriminations against America at this time came from the pen of Metin Toker, owner of *Akis,* one of Turkey's largest circulation magazines. See, for example, his "Aptal Dostu Olmaktansa . . .", *Akis,* June 12, 1964, p. 7; and "Türk-Amerikan Münasebetleri," *Akis,* June 19, 1964, p. 5.

İnönü's trip to Washington scored several successes in the short run. On the one hand, Johnson and İnönü in their final communiqué obliquely reaffirmed the validity of the London-Zurich accords, the cornerstone of the Turkish position.[33] This was a matter of surpassing concern to the Turks, for these agreements acknowledged Ankara's right to intervene in Cyprus. President Johnson's talks with İnönü were also portrayed to the Turkish public as successful in eliminating the "confusion" in Turkish-American relations. Metin Toker, İnönü's son-in-law and at that time one of Turkey's most influential journalists, accompanied the prime minister on the trip and widely disseminated the view that the personal contact between İnönü and Johnson had dispelled the "shadows which had fallen on relations between Turkey and America." [34] Finally, the Washington talks set the stage for an intensive U.S. effort to devise a solution through the mediation of Dean Acheson, who was recalled from private life to assist U.N. mediator Sakari S. Tuomioja in Geneva.

The Acheson plan

Pursuant to the understandings with İnönü and with Greek Prime Minister George Papandreou, who visited Johnson immediately after İnönü, Acheson undertook to meet with special representatives of Greece and Turkey in Geneva. His effort very nearly achieved success. Starting from the premise that no solution that excluded a physical Turkish presence on the island would be possible, Acheson attempted to provide for a Turkish sovereign area as well as for local autonomy for those of the Turkish community outside this area.[35] At the end of July 1964 he drew up a first version of his plan calling for the union of Cyprus with Greece in exchange for cession of the tiny island of Castellarizon to Turkey, a Turkish military base on Cyprus, and compensation for those Turkish Cypriots who wished to emigrate to Turkey.

But negotiations were disturbed when Makarios leaked Acheson's plan prematurely and with some distortions; the outbreak of severe

---

[33] The joint communiqué of June 23, 1964, noted that "the discussion [proceeded] from the present binding effects of existing treaties." *Bulletin,* July 13, 1964, p. 49.

[34] Metin Toker, "Bir Seyahatın Bilançosu," *Akis,* July 3, 1964.

[35] İnönü gave extensive accounts of these negotiations to the lower house on September 3, 8, 1964, and to the Senate on September 4, 1964. See Millet Meclisi, *Tutanak Dergisi,* dönem 1, vol. 32, pp. 274–80, 386–91; Senato, *Tutanak Dergisi,* 1964, vol. 21, pp. 575–82.

clashes on the north coast of Cyprus in August 1964 also disrupted the talks. To deal with the fighting, İnönü authorized air strikes modeled on the pattern of U.S. retaliation after the Tonkin Gulf incidents in Vietnam and designed to demonstrate that the United States had not deprived Turkey of its ability to take military action. Shocked by the Turkish response, the Greek Cypriots stood down, ushering in an era of comparative calm on the island.

The Geneva talks reconvened shortly thereafter, but the parties showed themselves to be farther apart than ever. Unable to deliver the obdurate Makarios, Athens could not steel itself to make available a sizable area or to grant Turkish sovereignty over any part of the island. Ankara for its part rejected any lease arrangement and insisted on sufficient land to absorb a Greek Cypriot first strike without losing a foothold on the island. In a last-ditch effort to save the negotiations, Acheson presented a final version of his plan on August 20, 1964, in effect meeting Ankara's desire for a larger space, but offering Turkey only a fifty-year military base. This compromise, however, was not acceptable to either Greece or Turkey and the Acheson mission came to a close.

Complaints against the United States

The failure of the Acheson mediation effort loosed a torrent of protest against America in Turkey.[36] Toward the end of August 1964, as it became clear that Washington would not espouse the Turkish cause, daily demonstrations took place in front of the American embassy in Ankara. For the first time, crowds of thousands chanted "Yankee Go Home!" and threw rocks at the building. While Turkish security forces prevented any large-scale destruction in Ankara, demonstrators in Izmir wrecked the American as well as the British and Soviet pavilions at the international fair. Students formed the backbone of most of these mobs, but what was remarkable was that officers of the Turkish armed forces and civilian adults also took part. These physical demonstrations were stimulated by inflammatory press reports blaming the United States for having let Turkey down once again.[37]

---

[36] See, for example, Çetin Altan, "Paşa ve Durmuş Ağa," *Milliyet,* August 28, 1964.

[37] *Cumhuriyet,* August 29, 1964. Among the signs carried by the demonstrators was one reading: "Henpecked Johnson, don't act under your Greek wife's influence. Use your own will power!" Ibid., September 2, 1964.

One new facet of the many complaints about American actions at this time was particularly prophetic of accusations that would be commonplace in years to come. A group of journalists following the lead of Metin Toker now charged the United States with attempting to intervene in Turkish domestic affairs to find a prime minister compliant with its wishes.[38] Toker accused the CIA of taking an opinion poll in an effort to discover a suitable replacement for İnönü and associated this alleged act with the visit of Lieutenant General Robert W. Porter, Jr., to Turkey. Porter, who had previously served as the U.S. military representative to CENTO in Ankara, returned in August 1964 for a brief visit during which he called on a number of high-ranking Turkish officers, including General Cevdet Sunay, then chief of the General Staff. The Turkish foreign minister immediately and categorically rejected any hint of impropriety in connection with Porter's actions; however, because of Toker's close family relationship with İnönü some inferred that the accusations might reflect the prime minister's views. *Yön* and leftist student organizations quickly echoed the allegation of American meddling in Turkish domestic politics, and despite the flimsiness of the evidence this theme was eventually repeated in more moderate circles as well.

The Turkish press also voiced considerable criticism of the U.S. embassy for "misleading" Washington through "erroneous" reporting on the sentiment in Turkey concerning Cyprus.[39] Turkish critics contended that it was such faulty information that had induced Washington to propose that Turkey accept a leased base arrangement on Cyprus; similarly, they held that irresponsible accusations by American officials had stimulated reports in the *New York Times* suggesting that the Turkish government had done little to halt protest demonstrations against the United States. And, of course, these more recent supposed lapses reminded some Turks that Johnson must have been misinformed about the temper of Turkey at the time he sent his June letter.

Taken together, these suspicions contributed to the view increasingly accepted by the Turkish public that the alliance was an instrument primarily to protect American interests and that U.S. interests diverged

---

38 *Hürriyet,* August 27–29; "Kıbrıs: 'Go Home!'" *Akis,* August 28, 1964, pp. 8–12; *Son Baskı,* August 28, 1964; Doğan Avcıoğlu, "Milliyetçilere Sesleniş," *Yön,* September 25, 1964, p. 3; "Müttefikiz, Peyk Değil," *Forum,* September 1, 1964, p. 2. See also Ülman and Dekmejian, p. 782.

39 *Milliyet,* September 1, 1964; *Cumhuriyet,* September 9, 1964.

sharply from those of Turkey.[40] From this point on, notwithstanding all the American efforts to achieve a workable compromise between its Greek and Turkish allies, it was commonly assumed by Turks at large that the United States was at heart in the Greek camp; some of the more extreme critics even affected to believe that Washington would stop at nothing in opposing Turkish desires. In short, the ground was by now well prepared for the growth of the belief that the alliance served the United States far better than it did Turkey.

Despite the mounting suspicions, the İnönü government clearly wanted to limit damage to Turkish-American relations. To free their hands for the air strikes in August 1964, the Ankara authorities withdrew units of their air force from formal jurisdiction of the NATO command in order to obviate objections of the sort Johnson had raised in his famous letter. After this operation had achieved its purposes, however, the Turks responded to appeals by General Lemnitzer and recommitted their air force to the NATO command. İnönü preserved a calm, almost detached tone in his lengthy public explanation of the Acheson talks and their failure. At the end of debates on Turkish foreign policy in September 1964, where some deputies had argued for a radical change in Turkey's course, he reiterated that his government was determined not to let the Cyprus imbroglio harm its NATO ties.[41]

The United States too, though unwilling to espouse the Turkish cause, sought to soothe passions in Turkey. To mitigate the fears provoked by the Johnson letter, an American embassy spokesman assured the Turkish press that "the United States will be beside Turkey if it is attacked by the U.S.S.R. while using its treaty rights on Cyprus."[42] And he repeated that the Sixth Fleet had not intervened to prevent a Turkish landing on the island. The AID chief in Ankara as well took pains to deny the rumor that economic assistance was being cut to punish Turkey for its Cyprus stand. The first deliveries of C-130 E cargo planes, which can easily be adapted for air drops of paratroops, also took place in the fall of 1964. Moreover, in December of the following year the United States even voted against a U.N. General

---

[40] See, for example, Cetin Özek, "Düşünenlerin Düşünceleri: Türkiye-Amerika-Nato," *Ulus,* September 13, 1964, for a forceful exposition of these views, recalling also the Morrison automobile accident as an illustration of inadmissible capitulatory privileges granted to Americans.

[41] *Cumhuriyet,* August 20, 1964; *Ulus,* September 9, 1964.

[42] *Milliyet,* September 24, 1964.

Assembly resolution favoring the Greek position, although there was evidence that Washington generally sympathized with the resolution.[43] But in the atmosphere of aroused nationalist sensitivities, these gestures had little evident impact on those outside the Ankara government.

Fortunately for the Turkish-American alliance, the failure of the Acheson mission coincided with a turn to moderation on the island. Armed clashes between the communities decreased in frequency and intensity. Ankara, for its part, contributed to the lowering of tension by delaying the regular rotation of the Turkish contingent that was to have taken place at the end of August 1964. While there was no softening on either side in determination to prevail in the long run, the Greek and Turkish communities gradually settled down to their own "cold war" confrontation. With this development, pressure from the Cyprus issue slowly relaxed in Turkey after 1964.

Renewed crisis

The Cyprus controversy, however, was far from settled. Pressures against the Turkish community on the island continued without much letup, though short of actual military conflict. In the ensuing years the Turkish enclaves were rigorously isolated. The introduction of supplies that might in any way appear strategic—from shoelaces to shovels—was subject to stringent restriction. To be sure, men and materiel were smuggled in small amounts from Turkey to stiffen the will of the Turkish community in these straitened circumstances. On the other hand, Athens found it easy to strengthen the position of the Greek Cypriots both by providing weapons and by infiltrating battalions of regular troops from Greece onto the island. Inevitably there were periodic alarums and excursions as local incidents tested the stability of the *modus vivendi* between the Cypriot communities; tension built especially in connection with the semiannual rotation of the Turkish contingent. It took constant efforts by the United States and other

---

[43] The U.N. resolution was passed 47 to 5, with 54 abstentions. U.N., General Assembly, *Official Records* (A/PV. 1402), December 18, 1965, p. 6. In addition to the United States and Turkey, CENTO partners Iran and Pakistan also voted against the resolution. However, Turkish commentators sharply attacked the United States for not assuring the support of other NATO states for Turkey's position. See, for example, Cihad Baban, "Antestezi Tesiri Yapan Müsbet Oy!" *Ulus,* December 19, 1965; Metin Toker, "Haftanın İçinden: Bir Fiyaskonun Anatomisi," *Akis,* December 25, 1965, p. 5; W. M. Dobell, "Division Over Cyprus," *International Journal,* Spring 1967, pp. 283–84.

interested powers in addition to those of the U.N. peace-keeping mission to prevent resumption of major hostilities.

A balance so precarious was indeed difficult to maintain over the longer term, particularly because it depended integrally on shifting alliances and alignments within the Greek Cypriot community and on the nature of the regimes in Athens and Ankara. Arrests of Greek officers in connection with activities of ASPIDA, a nebulous left-wing military plotting group that supposedly drew its membership principally from among the Greek forces in Cyprus, threatened to unhinge this delicate situation.[44] The military coup in Greece in April 1967 likewise had repercussions on the Cypriot scene. Hence it was not surprising that by mid-November 1967 major fighting had again broken out on the island, largely it would seem as a result of disarray within the Greek Cypriot camp.[45] But again the Turkish community was not able to hold its own or redress the loss of position it suffered.

Renewed conflict in Cyprus triggered many of the traditional responses in Turkey. The Ankara government felt it imperative to defend the interests of the Turkish community on the island; its problem was to devise a strategy that would accomplish this at least risk. Precedent favored making a convincing show of its determination to exercise its treaty rights to invade if necessary in order to compel a return to the status quo ante. Of course, essential to such a policy was the ability to carry through the threatened military operation if all else failed. Thus without delay the Ankara regime began to make the open preparations required. The commander of the Turkish Navy departed for İskenderun on the southern coast, and Turkish ships began putting to sea in the vicinity of Cyprus.[46]

The Vance mission, 1967

President Johnson dispatched Cyrus Vance as his personal representative to promote an immediate settlement of the renewed crisis, for again the United States was caught in an uneasy position between two allies. Though war between Greece and Turkey was as "unthinkable" in 1967

---

[44] ASPIDA was an organization involved in Greek domestic politics and had no direct relation to the Turkish community.

[45] Rivalry between General George Grivas and President Makarios may have played a major role in triggering this incident.

[46] *Cumhuriyet,* November 22, 1967.

as it had been in 1964 in Washington's eyes, it was obvious that the Turkish military operations could lead to forceful countermeasures on the part of Greece. To cope with this fearsome possibility, the United States had no alternative but to counsel peaceful negotiations, though mindful that this would be a bitter pill for Ankara under the circumstances.

The similarities of this course with that of 1964 were not lost on the Turkish audience. A number of highly vocal Turks were by now disposed to assume that American conduct would repeat itself, i.e., that Washington would exert itself energetically to block Turkish action. Thus rumors immediately flooded Ankara to the effect that the Sixth Fleet had interposed itself between Cyprus and Turkey. Denials by American spokesmen made little impression on Turkish public opinion; the Turkish press continued to assert that the American ships were positioned for action just as they were believed to have been in 1964.[47] Nor were American embassy denials of a story that the United States had again warned Turkey not to use NATO arms convincing to the inflamed public.[48] In this atmosphere, it was hardly surprising that students demonstrated before American installations in Turkey and prepared to march with placards denouncing NATO as a "device of U.S. imperialism." [49]

But events did not evolve in the pattern of the past. The colonels in Athens were not prisoners of their public opinion. Furthermore, they were extremely reluctant to compound their already considerable difficulties in NATO by conflict with Turkey. In short, Athens was prepared to compromise. Makarios as well was not eager to face a Turkish military move, particularly alone. As a result, through tireless shuttling between Athens, Ankara, and Nicosia, Vance was able to piece together an acceptable arrangement: Greece was to pull back the troops illegally stationed on the island; Turkey would do likewise. The opposing communal forces would also stand down.

While this expedient lowered the level of tension on Cyprus, it met a mixed reaction among the public in Turkey. The Turks had won no complete victory. To the more radical students, NATO seemed again to have snatched the prize from Turkey; several hundred who

---

[47] *Cumhuriyet,* November 18, 1967; *Hürriyet,* November 25, 1967.
[48] "Olayların Ardındaki Gerçek: Yalan mı, Doğru mu?" *Cumhuriyet,* November 27, 1967.
[49] *Ulus,* December 7, 1967.

shared this feeling demonstrated in Ankara. The majority, however, apparently subscribed to the view articulated by İnönü, who publicly declared Turkish gratitude to Vance.[50] Indeed, it was notable thereafter that in Turkey the Cyprus issue gradually receded into the background. The Vance mission, by its skillful diplomacy, had done much to salve the wounds of the past.

If tensions on the island remained manageable after the Vance mediation, this was in no small part because the aftermath of the 1967 crisis finally brought the communal leaders on Cyprus to begin talks to explore the possibility of arranging a settlement. These negotiations evidently have been difficult; they have continued at a more or less deliberate pace ever since. Both parties appear to have found them a useful mechanism for relieving pressures which might otherwise have led to hostilities. Yet despite apparent goodwill on the part of the negotiators, no solution has emerged in more than three years of quiet talks.

Since Nihat Erim—the Turkish negotiator in the Acheson mediation effort—became prime minister in March 1971, the Cyprus issue has attracted renewed attention in Ankara. Erim's public statements suggest concern over the prolonged communal stalemate and interest in imparting new momentum to the search for a solution. His government's more active policy, coupled with embarrassing incidents on the island and a more strident response by Makarios, again make clear the precariousness of the present *modus vivendi*. And obviously any renewed flareup on Cyprus would once more embroil the United States with its allies, Turkey and Greece.

---

[50] *Ulus,* December 8, 1967; *Cumhuriyet,* December 8, 1967.

6

The Rise of Anti-Americanism

The growth of anti-Americanism during the 1960s posed a serious challenge to the Turkish-American alliance. Differences in approach had marked Turkey's cooperation with the United States almost from the start. But it was not until after the acute stages of the Cyprus dispute that persistent public questioning of American motives began. This complex phenomenon drew its force not merely from the impact of conflicting policies over Cyprus. The changing international situation provided a milieu which permitted the luxury of quarrels between the allies; developments within Turkey contributed as well to the spread of antipathy toward the United States among the more vocal segments of the population. These factors, acting on and reinforcing one another, dictated both the rapid rise and the intensity of the anti-American feeling that has proved so embarrassing to the governments in Ankara and Washington. For the doubts and fears generated in Turkey relative to the United States had a palpable impact on the respective governments, significantly limiting their freedom to conduct relations with each other.

Thaw in the cold war

If the Turks felt free in the 1960s to vent their frustration over the course of the Cyprus dispute even at the risk of a breach with their Western allies, it was because the climate of the cold war was visibly shifting. A mood of détente was sweeping over Europe, and fears of armed attack rapidly evaporated in many influential circles in the West. Weary of remaining constantly on the alert, most of the NATO states were only too ready to let down their guard somewhat. Peaceful coexistence seemed at last to have come of age.

Until the departure of the Jupiters, the Turks lagged behind their allies in repairing relations with the U.S.S.R. To Ankara, overtures from Moscow seemed to carry a high price tag: the Turks probably felt that acceptance of any substantial Soviet offer might jeopardize continued NATO assistance. Nor for its part did the Kremlin stop harsh propaganda assailing the İnönü regime. Once the Jupiters were gone, however, the Soviets moderated their outpourings. In keeping with the general NATO-wide relaxation of tensions, the Turks then responded to Moscow's initiatives and in 1963 cautiously agreed to exchange visits of parliamentary delegations.

These halting steps toward rapprochement had not gone very far by the time the Cyprus crisis broke out at the end of 1963. Strangely, the Soviets at first took little advantage of the opportunities thus presented for wooing the Turks. The Kremlin professed the famous Johnson letter to be "a smokescreen, an attempt to give the United States an alibi just in case Cyprus is attacked"; Moscow proclaimed that the Turkish air strikes in August 1964 were "actually the handiwork of NATO at large." [1] But by the time of Khrushchev's sudden ouster early in October 1964, it had become generally recognized in the Kremlin that Turkey's troubles with the United States offered promising possibilities to divide the allies. Thus Khrushchev's successors in the CPSU leadership, Aleksei N. Kosygin and Leonid I. Brezhnev, made a modest gesture toward the Turkish position. They urged Foreign Minister Erkin to make his long-promised trip to Moscow and took the occasion of his visit to announce their recogntion that the Turkish community on Cyprus had a legal right to coexistence with the Greek.

The Turks responded with alacrity. In Ankara the Foreign Office accepted the Kremlin's position as tantamount to endorsement of the Turkish demand that Cyprus be an independent federated state. [2] An exchange of parliamentary delegations took place in short order, followed by visits of the respective prime ministers. Indeed, both the interim nonpartisan Prime Minister Suat Hayrı Ürgüplü and Justice Party successor, Süleyman Demirel, traveled to Moscow in the space of little more than two years. During the same period there was a decided

---

[1] Moscow radio, June 9, 1964; *New Times* (Moscow), August 26, 1964, p. 3.

[2] Feridun Cemal Erkin, *Les Relations Turco-Soviétiques,* p. 443.

shift in official propaganda on both sides. An era of good feeling between the two states appeared to be fast developing, in which many Turks ignored continued Soviet gestures toward Greece and Makarios and the buildup of Soviet naval units in the Mediterranean. Even the Soviet invasion of Czechoslovakia marred the rapprochement only briefly.

To some degree, of course, the enthusiasm with which the Turks took up their efforts to improve relations with the Soviet Union reflected the depths of their disappointment with U.S. policy toward Cyprus. But to view Turkey's relations with the U.S.S.R. as the mirror image of those with the United States—or vice versa—would be a profound mistake. As a matter of official policy, both the RPP and the JP regimes have unequivocally favored preserving close ties to the West in general and to the United States in particular; all recent Turkish governments have equally sought at the same time to "normalize" relations with the Soviet Union. Indeed, this dual effort has been the hallmark of the more independent foreign policy—the "foreign policy with a personality"—that Turkish regimes have now been pursuing for nearly a decade.

Of course the growing Soviet connection did impinge to some extent on Turkey's ties with the United States. The effects, however, were probably more fortuitous than deliberate. In continuing the course set by İnönü toward improving relations with the U.S.S.R., first Ürgüplü, then Demirel and Erim saw themselves as merely following the pattern already established by their NATO allies. Pique at the United States may have made Turkey more eager to embark on this tack, but rational calculation has ordered Ankara to hold to its path ever since. For relative rapprochement with the Soviets has offered successive Turkish governments the prospect not only of some economic assistance, but of increasing détente in the military confrontation, hence greater security as well. In this, Ankara has had no design to damage the association with Washington, nor has it met any strong objections from its NATO allies.

Yet the improvement of Turkish relations with the U.S.S.R. has worked indirectly to weaken the bases of the Turkish-American alliance and to diminish Turkey's strategic importance in the cold war. Détente with the Soviet Union has fostered the impression in Turkey, even outside leftist quarters, that the Kremlin no longer has a compelling interest in military operations against the Turks in a NATO conflict. In this context, Soviet offers of a guarantee not to use nuclear weapons against Turkey if there were none on Turkish territory, seemed reasonable to some leftist circles.[3] This state of mind played an important role in the debates within Turkey on the questions of national security and the proper military relationship with NATO.

Growth of radicalism

There were also numerous forces at work inside Turkey in the 1960s that would affect the climate of the alliance with the West. Perhaps foremost of these was the rising tide of radicalism. The 1960 military upheaval set in train a process of probing and experimentation that steadily broadened the range of permissible political activity. But it was not until the shock of Cyprus had torn a number of younger Turks from their accustomed moorings that the full consequences of this trend would manifest themselves.

The radical movement in Turkey was fed by a number of tributaries that converged in the beneficent atmosphere of the mid-1960s. First were the students who had emerged as a truly independent force out of the convulsions that precipitated Menderes' overthrow in 1960.[4] Though in fact the students played a relatively modest part in that drama, the attention and sympathy which their activities aroused led many to conclude that university youth wielded great political power—probably far more than in truth they actually did. After 1960, student organizations began to assume strong political coloration and to vie among themselves for leadership of this potentially important force. Quite naturally, activism soon proved the most effective tactic to mobilize support. It was not long before radicals of the left and the right had largely polarized the student body, overwhelming the silent center.[5]

---

[3] *Akşam,* February 17, 1966. For the evolving Turkish attitude toward NATO, see below, "No to NATO."

[4] Joseph S. Szyliowicz, "Students and Politics in Turkey," *Middle Eastern Studies,* May 1970, pp. 150–62. Leslie L. Roos, Jr., Noralou P. Roos, and Gary R. Field, "Students and Politics in Turkey," *Daedalus,* Winter 1968, pp. 184–203, concluded that student activism was subsiding, a judgment, however, not borne out by events.

[5] This process began first in such politically aware institutions in Istanbul and Ankara as the Political Science Faculty, the law faculties and the Middle East Technical University. Polarization developed more slowly in the liberal arts faculties, in Robert College, and in the newly organized Hacettepe University (whose creator was one of Turkey's foremost exponents of American educational philosophy). The outlying Atatürk University at Erzurum and the Aegean University at Izmir were slower still in being drawn into this process.

Trading on their claim to represent a sort of neo-Kemalism, the left wing apparently far outnumbered those on the other extreme. At first the issues of conflict centered on domestic politics. With the Cyprus crisis, however, foreign policy became a principal concern among university youth. Students of all persuasions took to the streets to protest the American role in blocking Turkish aspirations. Those on the left rapidly expanded their complaint, condemning Turkey's Western alliance as a whole. From their perspective, the Cyprus experience appeared to reaffirm the always tempting thesis that Western imperialism loomed as the greatest threat to Turkish independence. Egged on by a group of younger professors and instructors who promoted the view that Turkey's backwardness stemmed directly from Western designs to prevent modernization, the activists of the extreme left began systematic demands for Turkish withdrawal from NATO as well as an end to the special U.S. connection.[6] To those on the right, these prescriptions appeared much too far-reaching, if not Communist inspired. In this situation, Turkey's attachment to the United States and to NATO became one of the major touchstones in the struggle for dominance within the student movement. This struggle quickly passed from the stage of verbal insults to fisticuffs, and then to armed clashes in which some students even lost their lives and the normal functioning of the universities was seriously interrupted. Indeed, this disruption played a leading part in provoking the ultimatum of the generals on March 12, 1971, which brought down the Demirel government.

The press also played a major role in stimulating the radical current. In a milieu where sensationalism was a time-tested device for spurring circulation, journalists found the temptation to use inflammatory rhetoric hard to resist. Moreover, since a disproportionate number of newsmen were sympathetic to the Turkish Labor Party (TLP), its strident views got wide circulation. Embroidering on the theme that American imperialism was the root cause of trouble for Turkey, TLP protagonists stressed the notion that the United States derived far more from the alliance than did Turkey, that the alliance was dangerous for the Turks, that the United States was seeking to protect its position in Turkey through an alliance with local capitalists,

---

[6] For the teachings of these professors and others, see Aksoy, pp. 689–799. See also Sedat Özkol, *Geri Bıraktırılmış Türkiye* (Istanbul, 1969), passim, especially pp. 69–73.

and that the United States was an especial enemy of social justice. Over time and through constant repetition, such themes became accepted well beyond the narrow circles in which they were spawned.[7]

Labor was another force contributing to the radicalism of Turkish society. To be sure, the worker was for the most part still profoundly attached to the traditional, conservative ways of the agricultural population. His interests were not in the theoretical dogma which fascinated the aspiring intellectual elite. Bread-and-butter issues of wages and fringe benefits formed his main concern, and even here his expectations were not high. The right to strike was new, and the worker was always conscious that in an economy where unemployment and underemployment were rampant strikers could easily be replaced. Yet, nonetheless, he too was encouraged by elements of the educated elite and by his international labor connections to adopt an increasingly activist approach.[8]

The first strikes in Turkey had predominantly economic motives.[9] But as time wore on, some of the smaller labor unions—whose leaders were also personally at odds with those of the major national confederation (Türk-İş)—became enmeshed in radical political currents and added a new dimension to their agitation.[10] It was all too tempting for them, and for their political allies, to seek to arouse nationalist fervor against the United States as a means of bolstering union solidarity and of gathering public sympathy. Some of the bitterest strikes in Turkey, therefore, were directed either against American concerns or against contractors who supplied labor for U.S. installations.

---

[7] For example, a poll of workers conducted by a panel of professors in September 1969 showed 47 percent of the sample believed that America exploited Turkey and another 25 percent were undecided on this question. The poll also indicated that the higher the educational level of the respondents the more apt they were to hold negative views of the United States. *Milliyet,* October 1, 1969.

[8] The ICFTU representative, John Thalmayer, was one of the most prominent and active of these. He was expelled from Turkey in 1962 by the Ankara government for encouraging the Turkish unions to consider forceful tactics against American firms engaged in defense contracts. See also Adil Aşçıoğlu, "Niçin Grev," *Yön,* October 2, 1964, p. 13.

[9] Workers finally acquired the right to strike by Law No. 275, enacted by the Turkish parliament on July 15, 1963. There had, however, been some unauthorized strikes previously.

[10] These elements formed their own rival confederation, DİSK—Confederation of Revolutionary Workers Unions—in February 1967. Demonstrations in June 1970, protesting a law bill that seemed likely to militate against DİSK by leading to the exclusive recognition of Türk-İş, elicited imposition of martial law in Istanbul to restore order. On the radical union movement, see Yıldız Sertel, *Türkiye'de İleri Akımlar* (Istanbul, 1969), p. 145.

Under these stimuli the political contest itself showed a propensity toward radicalism. If the political struggle in the 1950s had generally focused on control of the center, by the mid-1960s the political spectrum had shifted to the left in significant degree. In the give and take of party shifting the TLP gained a voice in parliament even before the 1965 elections. Its achievement of winning fifteen seats in the lower house in those contests added momentum and stridency to the leftward movement. Under this challenge, the RPP itself shifted ground, defining its stance as "left of center." [11] It was not altogether easy to understand the differences between the point of view of the RPP and moderate socialism; indeed, the party continually groped toward a clearer exposition of its stance. On the right wing as well, the tiny Republican Peasants Nation Party, later to take the name of National Action Party,[12] led a procession of splinter groups that attempted to make the danger of communism a major stock in trade. In this situation the impetus to adopt more extremist positions was ever present, and the political contest came to concern itself ever more intensively with foreign policy.

The "American factor"

These circumstances drew the United States into the crossfire of domestic politics in Turkey at every hand and made America appear a major factor in Turkey's internal affairs. However cordial Ambassador Hare's personal relations with Prime Minister İnönü may have been, they could not dissipate the aura of public suspicion aroused during the Cyprus crisis that Washington was hostile to the RPP. The very play of events contributed to reinforcing these suspicions. For during the fall of 1964 the JP had made no secret of its intention to vote against the government's proposed budget; other minor parties too indicated they were reluctant to give approval to the İnönü administration on this issue. As a minority government, İnönü's cabinet thus faced considerable difficulties. When Ambassador Hare nonetheless at this moment paid a round of ceremonial visits to the opposition party

---

[11] C.H.P. Araştırma ve Yayın Bürosu, *C.H.P.'nin Rejim Konusundaki, Sosyal Konulardaki, Dış Politika ve Savunma Konularındaki Görüşleri* (Ankara, 1966), passim.

[12] After former National Unity Committee member Alparslan Türkeş became leader of this party, it sponsored formation of some paramilitary groups called "commandos," which its critics said were modeled after Hitler's storm troopers.

leaders, including for the first time Süleyman Demirel, the newly elected head of the JP, those seeking to confirm their suspicions of American motives found an easy explanation. They claimed that the United States was relaying orders to Demirel to bring down the İnönü government.[13] This interpretation received further impetus when the İnönü administration's budget was rejected in February 1965, whereupon İnönü withdrew. President Gürsel promptly tapped a neutral, Suat Hayrı Ürgüplü, to form a cabinet based mainly on the JP. Demirel's hasty appointment to the Senate and his inclusion as deputy prime minister redoubled speculation in the press.[14]

İnönü himself categorically rejected the insinuation of American involvement in the fall of his government. To the parliament on March 1, 1965, he stated:

> I will not agree that a shadow be cast on an honest and serious person because of a bad coincidence. In sum, at the time we relinquished our official duties we were in complete and mutual confidence with the American government and its Ambassador.[15]

Furthermore, the Republican Peasants Nation Party, which had been specifically accused of acting on orders from Washington, issued a firm denial that Ambassador Hare had made improper suggestions to its leaders. The counselor for public affairs of the U.S. embassy added his official disclaimer concerning Hare's alleged intervention in domestic political concerns. Despite these immediate and unambiguous repudiations, however, insinuations were rapidly cast into accusations; among the more extreme opposition accusation later hardened into belief that Washington was somehow involved in İnönü's overthrow.

That charges of this sort against the United States could find ready acceptance among a fair-sized audience of the Turkish elite stemmed in part from memories of the closeness of American officials to the Menderes regime. In part, too, it was a product of growing suspicion in Turkey about the motives of the United

---

[13] *Akis,* February 19, 1965, pp. 7–9; Ecvet Güresin, "Tehlikeli Nedenler," *Cumhuriyet,* February 15, 1965; Metin Toker, "İsmet Paşa ile 4 Buhranlı Yıl," *Milliyet,* February 16, 1969; Dana Adams Schmidt, "Turks' No. 2 Man Target of Attack," *New York Times,* February 28, 1965.

[14] Some circles accused Washington of dumping İnönü in exchange for a favorable petroleum law. See *Akis,* February 12, 1965, p. 11; İlhan Selçuk, "Pencere: Dolar Karşılığında Uşaklık mı?" *Cumhuriyet,* February 13, 1965.

[15] İnönü was speaking on the budget in the name of the RPP. Millet Meclisi, *Tutanak Dergisi,* dönem 1, vol. 37, p. 16.

States in its actions around the world. American intervention in the Dominican Republic and allegations of involvement in Indonesia and elsewhere had a notable impact in Turkey. Most important in this context was the expansion of U.S. activity in Southeast Asia. Vietnam was too far away for most Turks to feel that success or failure of the U.S. effort there would have any direct repercussions on their country. What many vocal Turks saw as significant about the American role in Vietnam was the parallel that could be drawn between Washington's willingness to commit vast resources to prop up a friendly regime in Saigon and the supposed U.S. preference for a JP government in Turkey. To many, not necessarily on the extreme left, the U.S. action in Vietnam made a mockery of the idea that America did not intervene in the internal affairs of other countries. It conjured up the specter of American military intervention to preserve the U.S. position in Turkey, a stake which was assumed to be much more valuable to Washington than was the Saigon regime. Hence the slogan "Turkey will not be a Vietnam" spoke believably to the Turkish elite in a way that even the gradual exodus of Americans from Turkey after 1967 could do little to counteract.[16] By the same token, Nixon's declaration of November 1969 that the United States would withdraw from Vietnam was received cynically by much of the Turkish press.[17]

Suspicion of American favoritism toward the JP figured prominently in the election campaign in the fall of 1965. Turkish newspaper readers were exposed to frequent articles embroidering on the theme that the United States was seeking to use "stooges in every field to capture Turkey from within." [18] More specifically, the widely read and radical Çetin Altan charged that America was conniving with the JP to carry out "American military intervention to suppress all the opposition and to come to power alone." According to Altan's calculations, "every

---

[16] This slogan was used during the Türk-İş demonstration in Ankara in November 1966. See *Cumhuriyet*, November 13, 1966. *Akis*, February 19, 1965, pp. 7–9, discussing American protests that the United States did not interfere in the internal affairs of other countries, wryly noted that "the Vietnam example is unknown to few in Turkey." Abdi İpekçi in *Milliyet*, May 4, 1965, argued that "Events since 1958—Lebanon, Vietnam, Panama, the Congo, the Dominican Republic—show that the United States is willing to intervene militarily." As for the TLP, its then President Aybar took part in Bertrand Russell's "War Crimes Trial" of President Johnson in November 1966.

[17] For example, see *Cumhuriyet*, November 5, 1969; and *Akşam*, November 5, 1969.

[18] *Akşam*, July 22, 1965.

vote cast for the JP will serve to turn Turkey entirely into an American colony." [19] Even the moderate RPP-oriented *Milliyet* reported that the State Department "will heave a deep sigh of relief in proportion to the size of the margin the JP achieves in the elections." [20] After the results had been tabulated, showing the JP winning with an impressive 56 percent of the vote, Metin Toker's influential *Akis* bitterly observed that there was considerable truth to the widely accepted belief that the returns were a victory for the United States.[21] On the extreme, Altan in analyzing the postelection scene accused the United States of sponsoring Kasım Gülek, one-time RPP secretary general, to block the emergent left-of-center trend and turn the party into a "capitalist opposition." [22]

Elections apart, the major opposition groups would evince continuing fears that the United States might be intervening in other areas of the political arena. For example, in debate over foreign policy late in 1965 the issue of the Johnson letter was again raised—the RPP arguing that America had prevented Turkey from acting in 1964, hence that Washington was responsible for the failure to prevail in Cyprus. The JP meanwhile accused İnönü of passing up an inviting opportunity, and thus leaving an almost insoluble legacy to successor governments. U.S. Ambassador Parker Hart, who arrived at this juncture to take up his post, was inadvertently drawn into the controversy. A reporter quoted him as denying that Washington had prevented İnönü from carrying out an amphibious operation against Cyprus and explaining that Johnson had merely "recommended" that Turkey desist. The ensuing controversy grew all the more heated as JP spokesmen sought to appeal to Hart's reported words to silence their RPP critics.[23] In the end, the press published an unofficial translation of the entire text of the Johnson letter. This forced the hand of the White House, which in coordination with the JP government released the corre-

---

[19] *Akşam,* September 6, 1965. Altan was making veiled reference to the Cooperation treaty of March 1959. The canard that the United States intended to use it to protect the JP now became a perennial charge. In the Senate, February 2, 1967, Demirel denied that this accord provided for American intervention in the event of an uprising.

[20] *Milliyet,* October 7, 1965.

[21] "Amerikanın Zaferi," *Akis,* October 16, 1965, p. 18.

[22] *Akşam,* November 20–22, 1965.

[23] *Milliyet,* January 4, 1966; *Cumhuriyet,* January 5, 1966; *Adalet,* January 6, 1966; "Teksaslı Başkanın Aslan Elçisi," *Akis,* January 8, 1966, p. 11. On March 4, 1966, *Cumhuriyet* carried Hart's clarification, noting that he had not mentioned the Johnson letter but had merely denied that the United States had stopped a Turkish invasion by interposing the Sixth Fleet.

spondence in January 1966. The resulting publicity revived recriminations against the United States among vocal segments of the population.[24]

The CIA

The atmosphere of suspicion concerning U.S. activities was conducive to the growth of the myth of CIA omnipresence and omnipotence on the world stage.[25] The image of this intelligence organization was undoubtedly colored by the spate of sensational accounts of its purported activities that appeared in the *Nation, Ramparts,* and the *New York Times* in the mid-1960s. Books such as *CIA: The Inside Story, The Invisible Government,* and even Allen Dulles' own account, *The Craft of Intelligence,* also had their impact.[26] To the large segment of the Turkish elite who tended to credit the conspiracy theory of history, these allegations of CIA involvement in fomenting coups, in suborning politicians, and in infiltrating international student and labor organizations merely reinforced the conviction that this agency must be actively working along similar lines in Turkey. Indeed, after the Johnson letter increasing numbers of vocal Turks came to view the CIA as a "McCarthyite" agency dedicated to hounding the left, branding liberals indiscriminately as Communists, and working to maintain the capitalist order throughout the world.[27] No doubt there was a measure of cynicism in efforts of those on the extreme left to make the CIA a scapegoat for their failure to block the JP, but underneath lay genuine deep-seated fears that the U.S. agency might in truth be able to manipulate Turkish society. Without question it was hard for many Turks to dismiss entirely *Yön's* warning that "the CIA is everywhere and the CIA can do everything." [28]

This suspicion infected the RPP, particularly the newly dominant wing which championed the view that the party was "left of center"

[24] See, for example, Bülent Ecevit, "Mektuplar," *Akis,* January 22, 1966, pp. 8–9. The newsmen responsible for publishing the Johnson letter in *Hürriyet,* January 13, 1966, were given six-month suspended sentences.

[25] Ülman and Dekmejian, "Changing Patterns in Turkish Foreign Policy," pp. 781–82.

[26] For reaction to these works among the critics of America, see "Amerikan İstihbarat Teşkilatının Marifetleri," *Yön,* February 19, 1965, p. 11; "CIA'nın Dünyada Genç Liderleri Satan Alma Planı, *Yön,* March 17, 1967, pp. 8–13.

[27] "C.I.A.'nin Yetkisindeki Türkiye ve Orta Doğu," *Yön,* August 6, 1965, p. 4.

[28] "Siyasi Notlar: C.I.A. Marifetleri," *Yön,* October 15, 1965, p. 5. A list of supposed CIA agents in Turkey was published in *Ant,* October 15, 1968, pp. 10–11. This list was drawn from the East German publication *Who's Who in CIA.*

in outlook. RPP Secretary General Bülent Ecevit, the spokesman of this persuasion, waxed especially eloquent in pointing out the evils of the CIA. In June 1966 he told his party's parliamentary caucus:

> In America it has been disclosed with what "dirty games" the American Central Intelligence Organization, the CIA, is involved affecting domestic politics in friendly and allied countries. It pours money into elections in order to bring those it wants into power and to unseat those it does not want; in some countries it even stuffs the polling boxes with false ballots. In order to prepare a pretext for smashing legal and democratic opposition, it has claimed that there was a great communist danger; or else, in order to prepare justification for armed American intervention, it has claimed that there was a danger of "unarmed and indirect aggression," and has organized demonstrations, sabotage, and even civil war. Even in America public opinion and some honest politicians have revolted at this situation. Thus President Johnson two days ago had to change the head of the CIA. The justification given was that this organization had become "an invisible Ministry of Foreign Affairs." [29]

But it was the TLP and those who vied with it for the leadership of the left who are the most concerned about the issue of the CIA in Turkey. Still none too sure of toleration by their own government, these elements saw themselves as the main target of American undercover activity. As early as September 1965, TLP President Mehmet Ali Aybar had appealed for "all political and nonpolitical organizations that reject foreign influence and domination in Turkey and all honorable patriots" to join "in a united front against Anglo-American imperialism." Several months later he committed his party to "struggle until no American is left in Turkey." This process reached its logical conclusion early in July 1966, when Aybar proclaimed a campaign of passive resistance to the United States—calling all Turks to sever relations with Americans in order to induce U.S. personnel to withdraw from Turkey.[30]

---

[29] *Ulus,* June 21, 1966.

[30] The proclamation of passive resistance came in reaction to the alleged American espionage documents publicized by Natural Senator Haydar Tunçkanat early in July 1966. See below, p. 138; *Milliyet,* July 11, 1966. For earlier TLP attacks against America, see Mehmet Ali Aybar, "Kıbrıs Tezimiz" (September 6, 1964, speech to the TLP General Executive Board meeting in Ankara), in his *Bağımsızlık Demokrasi Sosyalizm* (Istanbul, 1968), pp. 317–36; and his "İkili Anlaşmaların Feshi Bağımsızlığın İlk Şartıdır" (replies to questions from *Cumhuriyet,* October 17, 1964), ibid., pp. 337–43.

A Turkish view of the duty status issue:
Race prejudice in the service of anti-Americanism

"–yes sır, ıɢfal ettim ama vazife esnasındayım."

Cumhuriyet, February 19, 1966

"—Yes sir, I seduced her, but I was on duty."

Demonstrations against the Sixth Fleet

Wide World Photos

*"Dirty Imperialist. Don't forget
the blow by M[ustafa] Kemal [Atatürk]!"*

Wide World Photos

"Get out!"

A Turkish cartoon, depicting Octopus America
up to dirty tricks around the world

Milliyet, June 16, 1968

Destroying U.S. truck in front of
American military headquarters, Ankara, June 1969

Wide World Photos

Before the ban:
A field of poppies near Afyonkarahisar, 1971

Atatürk University in Erzurum:
American-assisted Turkish educational project

Photo by author

Crowd and folk dancers welcoming President Eisenhower before the American embassy, Ankara, December 1959

Photo by author

Rousing welcome to Apollo 11 astronauts in Ankara, October 1969

National Aeronautics and Space Administration

The U-2: Flights of these planes from
İncirlik air base were discontinued after May Day, 1960

United Press International Photo

American-equipped Turkish forces on review

Photo by author

U.S. satellite-tracking radar at Diyarbakır

United Press International

To be sure, the TLP leaders themselves were not entirely consistent in their behavior: in private some even continued to rent living quarters to Americans.[31] Nor did all those who sympathized with the party's point of view reject American overtures out of hand. For example, soon after his arrival in Istanbul as consul general, Douglas Heck attempted to reassure the TLP that it was not the object of American hostility. His public assurance that a more independent Turkish foreign policy would be accepted by Washington with good grace received mild approval in the newspaper *Akşam,* a journal normally highly critical of the United States.[32] Yet such was the general climate of suspicion of America among these elements that nothing could effectively disabuse the TLP of its supposition that it was a special target of CIA operations.

The left-wing press organs thus led in leveling against the CIA the most diverse charges of intervention in Turkey. For example, the American intelligence organization was charged with supporting the moderate Türk-İş labor confederation against its more extreme rivals.[33] Some even claimed that the CIA was providing funds to the Ford Foundation, which in Turkey was heavily involved in educational activity.[34] Another important target was the Peace Corps, which was accused of assigning volunteers to eastern Turkey in order to gather data for the CIA. The hue and cry over this issue eventually led to the end of the community development program run by the Peace Corps and the transfer of all its volunteers from the traditionally sensitive southeastern Turkish provinces.[35] Social science research also fell under this cloud. In the projects of U.S. researchers to investigate attitudes of Turkish villagers, government administrative personnel, workers in Germany, etc., some Turks affected to believe they could discern a coherent and malevolent design to develop the information necessary

---

[31] Aydınlık, "TIP Nereye Geldi," *Aydınlık Sosyalist Dergi,* November 1970, p. 2.

[32] *Akşam,* February 22, 1969. Cf. Ambassador Hart's farewell press statement, singling out the TLP as the sole party which had not observed a friendly attitude toward the United States. *Milliyet,* October 3, 1968.

[33] See, for example, *Akşam,* February 12, 1967. This article was based in part on a story from the *Washington Post,* May 23, 1966.

[34] "15 Mart: Banka Darbesi," *Ant,* March 21, 1967, p. 2.

[35] For early attacks on the Peace Corps, see "CIA," *Ant,* May 2, 1967, p. 5. Also see "The Peace Corps," chap. 8.

to perpetuate the JP in power.[36] The presence of American experts in government offices, such as the State Planning Organization, was condemned as another facet of this supposed conspiracy.[37]

More sensational, however, were exhibits produced by former National Unity Committee member Haydar Tunçkanat. In July 1966 he unveiled with great fanfare documents purporting to be reports from a Turkish agent to his chief in the CIA asking American cooperation in purging the bureaucracy and the military establishment of elements disloyal to the JP. The provenance of these documents was never publicly established. American authorities categorically denounced the documents as forgeries; and while the RPP, the ostensible target of these reports, cautiously demanded further study of the issue, it too recognized that the authenticity of the documents remained in doubt.[38] Subsequently Demirel, who had by then become prime minister, professed himself satisfied that the signature of the American allegedly involved was forged, and some journalists also pointed out serious technical flaws in the letters.[39] The issue then largely dropped from public sight. In the end, however, the Tunçkanat documents would gain a place in the Turkish national mythology as one more indication that the United States was tampering with Turkey's political fortunes.[40]

The Greek coup in April 1967 imparted fresh impetus to the CIA issue among left-wing commentators in Turkey. These circles

---

[36] See Edwin J. Cohn, "Middle East Studies Review: The Climate for Research in the Social Sciences in Turkey," *Middle East Journal*, Spring 1968, p. 208. *Yön*, for example, in its article, "Amerikanın Sözde Bilimsal Araştırmaları," July 30, 1965, linked Lieutenant General Porter's visit in August 1964, allegedly to "seek a prime minister," to findings of the village attitudinal poll run by AID in 1962 which showed the Turkish peasant to be in search of leadership. See also *Akşam*, August 10, 1966.

[37] *Meydan*, September 1, 1965.

[38] Some RPP journalists, e.g. Metin Toker, "Amerikalılar," *Akis*, July 16, 1966, p. 5, accepted Tunçkanat's revelations, explaining that the United States wanted a government of its own liking in Turkey, viz., the JP. Toker added that the CIA for its own interests was supporting the Turkish National Security Organization with money and equipment.

[39] *Son Havadis*, July 11, 1966; *Milliyet*, July 14, 19, 1966. Cüneyt Arcayürek in *Hürriyet*, July 20, 1966, gave perhaps the most detailed explanation of the flaws in the documents. Tunçkanat himself in his *Türk-Amerikan İlişkileri Üzerine Cumhuriyet Senatosunda Tabiî Senatör Haydar Tunçkanat Tarafından Açıklanan Çok Gizli Rapor!* strongly criticized *Hürriyet* (as well as *Adalet* and *Zafer*) for questioning the validity of his revelations.

[40] Ülman and Dekmejian, p. 782.

had long credited the American intelligence agency with an important role in supporting the king and the conservatives in Athens against the Papandreou government.[41] Immediately after the colonels took over in Greece, therefore, these journalists wasted no time in advancing the claim that the CIA was responsible for the military regime in Athens. Grandly disregarding all evidence of U.S. displeasure at the intrusion of the armed forces into politics in Greece, these Turkish critics dwelt on the "Prometheus Plan," which had supposedly ordered the military intervention. Terming it a NATO contingency plan, some Turks affected to believe there must be an analogous scheme for Turkey, and they demanded that the Ankara government investigate this matter carefully.[42]

Arrival of Ambassador Komer

Against this background, it was bold indeed for President Johnson to send one of his former special assistants, Robert Komer, as ambassador to Turkey at the end of November 1968. Komer's past service as a CIA analyst was a matter of public record. In addition, his immediately preceding assignment had been in Saigon, where he had been chief pacification adviser, an activity that was given a profoundly sinister interpretation by his Turkish critics. From the moment of his arrival, therefore, leftist student activists mounted protest demonstrations against what they decried as an attempt to carry out "a new Vietnam experiment" in Turkey.[43] These circles alleged that Komer had been sent to direct a CIA conspiracy to split the left.[44] In this atmosphere, when in January 1969 the new U.S. ambassador lunched at the Middle East Technical University on invitation of its rector, an incident ensued: a handful of radical students spotted his car parked on their campus

---

[41] *Akşam,* September 15, 1965.

[42] C. L. Sulzberger, "Foreign Affairs: Prometheus Unbound," *New York Times,* May 3, 1967, provided Turkish audiences with a description of the "Prometheus Plan." For early commentary on this report, see "Yunanistandaki Amerikan Plânı," *Yön,* May 5, 1967, p. 4; also "NATO 'nun Kara Listesi!" *Yön,* May 12, 1967, p. 5. As late as March 8, 1968, *Akşam* carried appeals to the Ankara regime to investigate similar NATO contingency plans for Turkey. For a lengthy analysis of the supposed American involvement in the Greek coup, see D.A. [Doğan Avcıoğlu], "Ortanın Solu ve Amerika," *Yön,* April 14, 1967, pp. 8–11.

[43] *Akşam,* November 30, 1968; *Cumhuriyet,* January 9, 1969; *Ant,* December 3, 1968, pp. 4–5; "Robert W. Komer Geldi," *Tüm,* December 11, 1968, pp. 7, 16.

[44] Kemal Bisalman, "Çiviler: Komer'e Açık Mektup," *Milliyet,* December 10, 1968.

and seized the opportunity to set it afire. Not only did this event lead to bitter clashes between right-wing "commandos" and leftist students; it also provoked a confrontation between police and students that obliged the university to shut down for a time. The cry immediately rose that the ambassador, knowing the students were bound to react to his presence at the university, had deliberately provided this opportunity in order to give the JP justification for introducing harsh and repressive legislation against the left.[45] And when a few days later the JP announced its decision to introduce a controversial bill to narrow the scope of constitutional rights, leftist circles took this coincidence as confirmation of their diagnosis.[46]

Under these circumstances, Komer faced an uphill battle to convince his detractors that he was not masterminding a complex CIA conspiracy. Student demonstrations frequently demanded his recall. But he did not pursue a passive course. Openly defending his previous service as an analyst for the CIA and his activities in Vietnam, he engaged in a running dialogue with his left-wing critics. He let it be known that he sympathized with certain of their criticisms and was taking steps to alleviate problems connected with the American presence in Turkey. To the widely voiced accusation that Turkey was becoming increasingly dependent on the United States, however, he took sharp exception, advancing statistics to buttress his case.[47] Although this tack brought him into direct confrontation with the RPP (which had begun to advance the claim that foreign capital was subjugating Turkey) and earned him continuing attacks in the press until his departure in May 1969, his forthrightness persuaded some of his critics that he was a worthy antagonist. A tiny minority of his erstwhile detractors even voiced the sentiment that however much of a mistake it might have been to send him in the first place, it was also a mistake to remove him so abruptly after only a few months.[48]

---

[45] In *Akşam*, January 8, 1969, İlhami Soysal wrote: "One can't help wondering if the simple incident at the Middle East Technical University is to be the excuse for starting in Turkey the methods of 'pacification = intimidation' Mr. Komer practised in Vietnam." For the supposed "plot" to pave the way for "fascist legislation," see *Cumhuriyet*, January 9, 1969.

[46] This bill was shelved in April 1969 in view of the wide opposition to it both in parliament and outside. See *Cumhuriyet*, April 18, 1969.

[47] *Milliyet*, April 18, May 4, 1969; *Yeni Gazete*, May 6, 1969. For the background of these charges, see Edwin J. Cohn, *Turkish Economic, Social and Political Change*, pp. 32–33.

[48] *Yeni Gazete*, April 8, 1969; *Ulus*, April 22, 1969.

"No to NATO"

Komer's arrival in Turkey coincided with the culmination of the campaign launched by the left to take Turkey out of NATO. The Atlantic alliance celebrated its twentieth anniversary in 1969. According to treaty, a member state could withdraw at any time thereafter on one year's notice. Already in the mid-1960s Gaullist France had taken steps to disengage from military cooperation; in 1967 the NATO command had been obliged to move from Paris to Brussels. Uncertainties over French intentions and the growing agitation of the left inside Turkey combined to provoke national debate over the issue of whether the Turks should remain in NATO. By 1968 student associations were staging frequent seminars and public meetings questioning the utility of Turkey's association with the West; legal scholars were inspecting the ramifications of withdrawal from the alliance; and the Turkish Labor Party was capitalizing on its access to the parliamentary forum to demand that Turkey leave NATO.[49]

Under this impetus, the major parties felt need to reinspect their positions. At the end of 1967, the RPP commissioned a special panel, chaired by Nihat Erim, to review this matter urgently and report to the party's top policy organ. Reflecting the temper of the time, the committee returned a report in the spring of 1968 weighing the pros and cons in great detail.[50] Among the twelve principal disadvantages of remaining in the Atlantic alliance, the report listed:

- The presence in Turkey of NATO and U.S. nuclear bases which made the country a target of possible Soviet nuclear attack;

- The possibility of Turkey's being dragged into war for matters of no concern to itself;

- Doubt that NATO would operate to defend Turkey in the event of attack;

- The curtailment of Turkey's freedom of action because of the commitment of forces to NATO and because of U.S. control over the use of equipment provided under the aid agreement;

---

[49] For a general review of this problem, see Ferenc A. Váli, *Bridge Across the Bosporus: The Foreign Policy of Turkey* (Baltimore, 1971), pp. 157–64.

[50] The panel began work in December 1967. Its 52-page secret report was summarized in *Milliyet* first on April 14, 1968, then at greater length on July 5, 1968. See also *Devrim,* October 28, 1969; November 18, 1969.

- The exacerbation of relations with the U.S.S.R. and the Arab world as a result of participation in NATO.

On the positive side, the committee found that NATO did contribute to Turkey's security and especially that it provided access to arms and assistance that could not be obtained otherwise at any price.

Balancing the advantages and the drawbacks, the report recommended that Turkey retain its NATO ties, but with substantial change. It called for a radical revision of the bilateral agreements in Turkey's favor through abrogation of agreements on the electronic intelligence network existing in Turkey and through repeal of any concessions granted to Americans in Turkey that went beyond privileges extended by European states to Americans in their countries. The panel advocated elimination of bases and installations that might make Turkey a nuclear target—for example, the U.S. strike aircraft at the İncirlik airbase—and asked for the complete "denuclearization" of Turkey to dispense not only with offensive or tactical nuclear weapons, but with atomic mines as well. To protect Turkey's regional interests, the committee requested a radical change in the country's military force structure to provide a "national" force independent of the Atlantic alliance. Finally, the report recommended that the headquarters of the Allied Forces Southeast Europe NATO command in Izmir be disbanded and its functions transferred to the South Europe command in Naples.

After nearly a week of heated sessions presided over by İnönü in July 1968, the RPP watered down the criticism of NATO practice in its formal policy position released to the public.[51] However, the party did insist on the urgency of alterations in the bilateral arrangements to gain more stringent control over the operations of foreign military personnel and installations. It also called for creation of a force independent of NATO to be used for Cyprus and in other contingencies. While rejecting the recommendations of the panel to remove all nuclear weapons from Turkey, the RPP senior policy body noted that some changes in regard to the disposition of nuclear arms were necessary in the interests of maintaining good relations with the U.S.S.R. as well as with the United States.

With its strong appeal for alterations in the NATO arrangement— a desire echoed by the minor parties of the right—the RPP policy state-

---

[51] *Milliyet,* July 10, 1968.

ment added momentum to the debate over the future shape of Turkey's ties with the Atlantic alliance. But this mood of disengagement was set back at least temporarily by the Soviet invasion of Czechoslovakia in August 1968. Even Mehmet Ali Aybar, head of the TLP, denounced this Soviet move as a revival of Stalinism; [52] indeed, reaction to it split the Turkish left more profoundly than ever before. Perhaps even longer lasting in its impact on Turkish attitudes toward NATO was the decision of France not to withdraw. The fall of French President Charles de Gaulle and the comparative moderation of his successors on the issue of the Atlantic alliance undermined the arguments of the Turkish radicals who had expected NATO simply to fall apart when its twenty-year term was over. Thus, by early 1969, the heat had gone out of the drive to take Turkey out of the alliance. A few extremists of course continued to harp on the theme of "No to NATO," but it was clear that this slogan had lost much of its earlier drawing power.

Post-Komer lull

Something of a lull in attention to the American factor followed Komer's departure. His successor, William J. Handley, was not "tarnished" by any prior association with intelligence activity. Moreover, he eschewed publicity and did not court confrontation with the left. With a less visible target, demonstrations against the United States abated.

Perhaps a more important reason for the comparative slackening of attacks against America was the growing preoccupation of the left in Turkey with its own internal difficulties. The Turkish Labor Party had never been a homogeneous body. Wracked by personality conflicts often cloaked in ideological guise, the TLP faced an open rupture in the aftermath of the Soviet invasion of Czechoslovakia. At its congress in November 1968, factional differences led to widespread defections. Efforts to patch up a solution at an extraordinary session at the end of December 1968 were none too successful. Right up to the elections in the fall of 1969, the extreme left remained fractured by bitter internal feuds; an alliance of convenience to support the TLP in the elections was pieced together only on the eve of these contests. Engulfed as they were in this intense political rivalry, these factions concentrated more on debating the fine points of socialist doctrine for

---

[52] *Milliyet,* August 22, 1968.

Turkey—e.g., the question of whether the Ottoman Empire had passed through a feudal period and whether there were feudal survivals in present-day Turkey—than on assailing the United States.[53]

Turn to violence

In the aftermath of the 1969 elections a new tendency became apparent in the ranks of the extreme left: a turn to violence. Shortly before the balloting the TLP's unofficial organ, *Ant*, had carried an article suggesting in scarcely veiled fashion that Ambassador Handley be kidnaped in Latin American style to trade for a left-wing hero in jail for ideological offenses. [54] Though amid the press of other concerns this insinuation failed to trigger any visible response, it was a sign of things to come.

The election results shattered the faith of many in the left that their cause could prevail by parliamentary means.[55] Changes in the election law restricting the scope of proportional representation had resulted in a dramatic fall in the number of minor party deputies in parliament. Further, such factors as the impact of the Soviet invasion of Czechoslovakia and the disarray of the left had contributed to a significant decrease in the percentage of the popular vote received by the TLP. Even the decline in the Justice Party vote, which left it vulnerable to the defection of its more conservative wing, was scant consolation to the left for its poor showing.

---

[53] Among the notable controversies were those between Muzaffer Erdost, who was then aligned with the faction led by Mihri Belli (whose previous conviction for engaging in Communist activity had kept him outside the TLP), and Ahmet Aras, who represented the party. Their dispute over the nature of feudalism in eastern Anatolia was touched off by the publication of a lengthy study of this question by İsmail Beşikçi, *Doğuda Değişim ve Yapısal Sorunlar* (Ankara, 1969). See *Ant*, May 13, 20, June 17, August 26, 2, 1969; *Aydınlık*, June 1969, pp. 117–126. Erdost carried on similar polemics with *Emek*. See *Türk Solu*, May 27, June 3, 10, 1969.

Another bitter controversy was triggered by publication of İdris Küçükömer, *Düzenin Yabancılaşması* (Istanbul, 1969), analyzing the causes of backwardness in the modern Turkish regime. See *Aydınlık*, July 1969, pp. 218–38; *Ant*, July 22, 29, August 5, 1969; *Türk Solu*, April 29, 1969, pp. 2–3. For the polemics surrounding "revisionism," see *Türk Solu*, August 12, 19, 1969.

[54] Selma Ashworth, "Biz de mi Amerikan Elçisini Dağa Kaçıralım?" *Ant*, September 30, 1969, p. 11.

[55] Michael P. Hyland, "Crisis at the Polls: Turkey's 1969 Elections," *Middle East Journal*, Winter 1970, pp. 1–16, gives an early—and overly reassuring—appraisal of the outcome of these contests.

Once it was clear that the possibilities for the left to participate in the regularly constituted institutions of government had narrowed, the "out-of-parliament" opposition was faced with the need to work out new tactics. Some of those who had lost hope in the democratic process as an avenue to power appeared attracted by the idea of extraparliamentary action. The appearance of the new weekly *Devrim* ("Revolution") at the end of 1969, representing a highly nationalistic and authoritarian approach, was perhaps symptomatic of this probing for a new direction. At the same time, the tide of translations of Latin American revolutionary literature—from Che Guevara's *Diary of a Guerrilla* to Carlos Marighella's *Minimanual of the Urban Guerrilla*— rose rapidly, as did attention to the ascendant Arab fedayeen movement based in nearby Syria and Jordan. By mid-1970 the press in Turkey was already carrying reports of Turkish young people training in Arab guerrilla camps.[56]

The fruits of this process soon made themselves apparent. A small band of student extremists, said to be associated with the Revolutionary Youth Organization (known in its Turkish abbreviation as Dev Genç), began a wave of politically motivated violence directed heavily against U.S. activities and personnel in Turkey. Starting with the shooting of two policemen outside the American embassy in December 1970, these terrorists the following month kidnaped and held briefly an American sergeant on guard duty at a U.S. installation on the outskirts of Ankara. On March 4, 1971, an even more daring kidnaping took place: a group calling itself "the People's Liberation Army" abducted four American airmen. In a statement to the press, these guerrillas declared their aim was "to clear the country of Americans and all foreign enemies. . . . It is our most sacred duty to revolt against a handful of traitors who are sucking our blood and the United States which supports them." [57]

Although the kidnaped airmen were subsequently released unharmed, the shock of this incident provided final impetus to the generals who had shown growing impatience with the deterioration of law and order in Turkey. On March 12, 1971, the force commanders issued

---

[56] *Cumhuriyet,* February 4, 1970, reported the arrest in Diyarbakır of a group of guerrillas trained by the Arab fedayeen organization al-Fatah. Cüneyt Arcayürek published a lengthy account of the activities and intentions of these guerrillas in *Hürriyet,* March 11–17, 1970.

[57] *Cumhuriyet,* March 5, 1971.

an ultimatum in effect obliging the Demirel government to resign. After intensive consultations, President Cevdet Sunay then named as prime minister Nihat Erim, a respected and experienced politician who resigned from the RPP to accept this post.

Enter Erim

Erim imposed martial law; and when the terrorists, undeterred, kidnaped and murdered the Israeli consul general in May 1971,[58] the authorities launched an intensive manhunt which eventually netted most of those accused of complicity in guerrilla activity. In addition, the government rounded up a number of professors, journalists, and politicians whom it suspected of having—however indirectly—inspired these guerrillas. At the same time, the martial law command closed leftist periodicals and banned the sale or possession of many of the more extreme pamphlets and books. Finally, by court order the TLP was disbanded in July 1971; its members were prohibited from joining any other political organization for five years.[59]

These moves, though designed in the first instance to combat anarchy and terrorism, nonetheless served effectively to silence many of America's most virulent critics. Even those who were not taken into custody by the martial law authorities found their access to press outlets curtailed. Thus it was that while U.S. Vice President Spiro Agnew aroused little enthusiasm among the general public when he visited Turkey in October 1971, he also encountered no significant criticism from those opposition circles which had heaped derision on his nomination three years before.

Of course not all public criticism of Turkey's Western alliance was ended. Some of the left-of-center faction in the RPP—notably the party's secretary general, Bülent Ecevit—interpreted the selection of Erim as an attack not against Demirel or the democratic system but against their wing of the RPP. Ecevit, who resigned from his party post in protest of Erim's appointment, declared that the new prime minister's program "was prepared first of all with the aim of satisfying foreign

---

[58] The choice of an Israeli official as a target may have been related to the influences of the Arab fedayeen on the guerrillas.

[59] *Akşam,* July 21, 1971. The Constitutional Court ruled that the TLP had violated art. 89 of the Political Parties Law and art. 57 of the Constitution.

capitalist states, NATO, and the Common Market." [60] Under the circumstances, however, such charges were muted. With the specter of further military intervention ever present in the event the opposition frustrated effective government, there was little incentive to harp loudly on this theme.

[60] Ecevit's speech to the RPP caucus, *Milliyet,* April 4, 1971. Retired Admiral Sezai Orkunt had been dropped from consideration for a cabinet post in the first Erim government after he was charged with being a "socialist" and a "thoroughgoing enemy of the Americans." See Abdi İpekçi, "Durum: Yanılmışız," *Milliyet,* March 25, 1971.

7

Problems of Military Cooperation

NATO strategy underwent a significant shift during the 1960s. After the Soviets developed first nuclear, then thermonuclear weapons, the concept of massive retaliation began to appear outmoded. The Kennedy administration lost no time in arguing for a new doctrine to meet the changed circumstances of the confrontation with the U.S.S.R. Instead of planning to meet any level of aggression with all-out attack, the NATO Council in May 1961 acceded to U.S. urgings to explore a strategy of "flexible response." The new concept envisaged graduated replies to Soviet aggression, offering NATO the option of responding by forces armed with conventional weapons without immediately proceeding to a nuclear engagement. In addition, this strategy provided for selectivity in targeting to permit counterforce or damage-limiting ripostes outside of population centers.

Within the alliance the American initiative to abandon the earlier doctrine of massive retaliation aroused strong opposition from the first. It was difficult to formulate the new strategy in precise terms. Even after numerous efforts to clarify the issues, ambiguities remained as to when the allies were committed to employ nuclear weapons and whether the process of escalation once begun could be halted short of general war. These uncertainties fed discontent among the European members, who on the one hand perhaps resented American preponderance in the alliance and on the other were increasingly concerned lest the United States leave them in the lurch as a result of the new flexible response doctrine. French President Charles de Gaulle led in resisting the American proposals. And it was not until December 1967, after he withdrew French forces from the alliance, that the Defense Planning Committee gave final approval to this strategy.

Although Turkey officially supported the U.S. position in NATO forums, senior Turkish military officers nourished doubts about the new approach. Some saw in the notion of graduated reaction a design to localize conflict. Concerned lest this strategy imply a difference between the "wings" and the "center," they feared that their allies might not join in a nonnuclear conflict that did not appear to threaten more widely shared NATO interests. This raised the specter for Turkish military planners—and for their civilian colleagues as well—that their partners in the alliance might not consider a localized attack from Soviet forces on Turkey as necessitating military response. Yet unable to offer any alternative in its stead, the Turkish leaders saw no option but to go along with the new strategy.[1]

Among the expedients devised by the United States to allay the fears of its NATO allies was the so-called ACE Mobile Force attached to the NATO European command. This conventionally equipped token unit was organized as a fire-fighting body ready for immediate deployment in threatened areas. It was obviously intended more as a trip-wire to assure that all NATO members took part in a conflict than as an impressive deterrent in itself. From the first, some of Turkey's civilian politicians expressed doubts about the ability of this mixed-manned unit to respond with conventional weapons in timely fashion to an attack on eastern Turkey. Opposition leader İnönü repeatedly warned against being confident that this force would serve Turkish requirements in the event of hostilities.[2]

Turkish concerns were heightened as Washington displayed growing interest in reducing American troop strength in Europe. In 1968, under mounting congressional pressure, President Johnson's administration cut U.S. support forces in West Germany by about 10 percent. In the same year, to relieve fears of its European members that they would be left exposed to Soviet military threats, NATO proposed negotiations with the Warsaw Pact for mutual and balanced force reductions. The U.S.S.R. and its allies, however, were slow to respond and these proposals became involved to a degree in the glacial progress of strategic arms limitation talks between Washington and Moscow.

---

[1] See Abdi İpekçi's interview with retired Admiral Sezai Orkunt, "Esnek Savunma ve Biz," *Milliyet,* June 1, 1970. Orkunt was assigned to the NATO Standing Group from 1958 to 1964.

[2] *Tercuman,* December 12, 1967. For İnönü's views, see *Hürriyet,* January 7, 1960.

The concept of mutual and balanced force reductions did not arouse enthusiasm among Turkish leaders. Ever mindful of Turkey's proximity to the Soviet Union, the Ankara government was insistent that there be no arrangement with the U.S.S.R. that would permit Moscow to transfer to the Turkish border Soviet troops withdrawn from the central front in Europe. And despite repeated reassurances from Washington that neither the strategic arms limitation talks nor the NATO mutual force reduction proposals would damage Turkey's interests, the Ankara authorities remained uneasy over the negotiations with Moscow. This concern was further fueled by news of mounting pressures within the U.S. Congress to reduce American military personnel in Europe without waiting for a negotiated agreement with the U.S.S.R. Hence, when in November 1971 the U.S. Senate only narrowly overturned the decision of its Appropriations Committee to demand the withdrawal of 60,000 American troops from Germany, Turkish officials made no secret of their apprehension that such unilateral cuts in U.S. forces would harm NATO.[3]

Control of nuclear weapons

Closely related to the strategic problems of the 1960s was the issue of the control of nuclear weapons committed to the NATO alliance. The U.S. monopoly of nuclear arms had long agitated the European members of NATO, and by 1960 de Gaulle felt impelled to seek his own *force de frappe*. To cope with the discontent among the remaining non-nuclear members of the alliance, the United States in 1963 gave urgent priority to the idea of forming a ship-borne Multilateral Force (MLF) equipped with Polaris missiles and charged with responding to nuclear attack. The Turks took part in the Working Group set up to prepare a draft charter for the MLF and even designated a contingent to serve on the USS *Claude V. Ricketts* as part of this venture. Under the impact of the Johnson letter and the start of rapprochement with Moscow, however, Ankara shifted position and refused to participate in the MLF, noting that a number of other NATO countries were not taking part.[4]

---

[3] Cüneyt Arcayürek, "Türkiye, NATO Yardımının Artırılmasını İsteyecek," *Hürriyet,* December 8, 1971; *Milliyet,* November 24, and December 25, 1971.
[4] *Pulse,* January 18, 1965, quoting a Ministry of Foreign Affairs press release. This source revealed that the decision not to participate in the MLF had been taken almost three months earlier. *Milliyet,* October 14, 1964, carried a report from sources in the Turkish Foreign Office claiming that financial considerations were discouraging Turkey from joining in the MLF.

Yet the rejection of the MLF did not signify that the Turks were uninterested in nuclear matters. To counter the possibility that their allies might not take military action in a Turkish confrontation that did not spread beyond Turkey, many Turks saw a need for Ankara to play an increased role in the planning and decision for the use of nuclear weapons. Already by the start of 1966, the RPP was showing great sensitivity to this question. In an official statement, the party called for Turkey to get full command and control of all nuclear arms on Turkish territory.[5] As a step in this direction, the Turkish General Staff insisted that Turkey be allocated one of the revolving seats in the Nuclear Planning Group established by NATO in December 1966.[6] Ankara thereafter pressed strongly to retain this place in order to advance its interests in the matter of nuclear armaments.

For the Turks, the idea of deploying atomic demolition munitions for defensive purposes appeared to offer a promising approach to the thorny nuclear issue. No sooner had Turkey been admitted to the Nuclear Planning Group than Foreign Minister İhsan Sabri Çağlayangil declared in London that Turkey needed these "passive nuclear devices."[7] He requested that NATO study the question of placing nuclear mines in the rugged and thinly populated areas of eastern Turkey as a deterrent against Soviet attack. The Turkish military planners evidently hoped that the United States might be willing to relax the system of dual control imposed on the use of all nuclear weapons committed to the alliance because the munitions in question were devices that could be used only on Turkish territory, hence could have no offensive capability. Undoubtedly the Turkish General Staff regarded nuclear mines as a last resort against the contingency that the NATO alliance for any reason should fail to commit military force to Turkey's defense in the event of a Soviet attack.

The Turkish interest in nuclear demolition munitions posed evident difficulties for Washington. U.S. legislation allowed no distinction between mines to be laid on one's own territory and nuclear arms

---

[5] *C.H.P.'nin ... Görüşleri,* pp. 79, 83. As early as June 1, 1965, the pro-RPP *Milliyet* complained that Turkish command authority over nuclear weapons was very restricted.

[6] M. Ali Kışlalı, "Görüşler: Türkiyenin Savunması ve NATO," *Devrim,* December 30, 1969, p. 6; *Yeni Gazete,* December 19, 1966.

[7] *Hürriyet,* December 19, 1966.

capable of offensive use. But in order to explore the Turkish request further, the United States in April 1967 asked the Turkish General Staff to present a detailed deployment plan as the basis for discussions. In the process of preparing a response, the Turkish leaders soon recognized that the legal limits imposed on Washington precluded any effective surrender of U.S. control. And by the end of 1967, Ankara's ardor for atomic demolition munitions had cooled perceptibly. Moreover, domestic opposition to the idea of detonating nuclear mines within Turkey rose when it was noted that explosion of such devices would necessitate extensive evacuation of population and livestock from the border areas.[8]

Although in May 1969 it was publicly revealed that Turkey had withdrawn its request for NATO study of this issue, Turkish military planners—like those of their European allies—continued to press for some flexibility in the American stance on control of nuclear weapons. In this context, the NATO decision in December 1969 to provide more specific guidelines for the use of tactical nuclear arms was interpreted by some in Turkey as a constructive step toward meeting the needs of the nonnuclear powers.[9] But it was clear that the issue of nuclear weapons continued to trouble the alliance. Particularly the politicians of the left persisted in demanding that no nuclear weapons should be permitted in the country that were not directly under Turkish control.

Military aid levels

Flexible response implied bolstering the ability of all NATO states to absorb initial blows by heavily armored Soviet bloc forces without surrendering large tracts of territory. And in Turkey's case in particular, the move toward the new NATO strategy led to renewed emphasis on defending as far forward as possible—"at the border," according to the defense minister.[10] Such a defense in Turkey's case would require a considerable increase in the mobility of the Turkish armed forces so

[8] Kışlalı, op. cit., n. 6; Ferenc Váli, *Bridge Across the Bosporus,* p. 122; *Cumhuriyet,* October 6, 1970.

[9] M. Ali Kışlalı, "Tactical Nuclear Weapons and Turkey," *Outlook,* December 17, 1969, p. 6. Admiral Orkunt, on the other hand, decried this decision as a defeat for Turkey. *Milliyet,* December 3, 1969.

[10] See Senato, *Tutanak Dergisi,* 1969, vol. 50–3, p. 543, for the reply of Defense Minister Ahmet Topaloğlu, January 31, 1969, to a question on NATO defense policy by Haydar Tunçkanat. See Váli, p. 120, for a somewhat different interpretation of this debate.

that they could operate in advance of their traditional defensive lines.[11] In turn this would entail ambitious modernization of the existing Turkish military establishment, an endeavor demanding a level of resources far superior to that provided Turkey in the past. While a forward deployment strategy was naturally attractive to the senior generals, their efforts to press for foreign aid in the amounts necessary for this objective inevitably generated strains in the military relationship with America. For the Turks ever sought greater assistance than the U.S. Congress was willing to authorize in meeting the requirements of the forward defense posture (see Table 1).

Turkey's appetite for military modernization was further stimulated by a growing sentiment in favor of creating a so-called National Force without delay. The experience of Cyprus had been read by a number of influential Turks as demonstration of the need for military units independent of NATO to serve Turkey's regional interests. Domestic fundraising drives were launched by the press and other groups to build landing craft and the like as well as to purchase naval equipment from foreign sources.[12] By 1967 the Turkish General Staff had seen fit to adopt a long-term plan to create a modest domestic armament industry, and under this plan Chief of the Air Force General Muhsin Batur in 1970 began enlisting contributions for a fund to build aircraft in Turkey.[13] Even in its early stages this activity squeezed indigenous resources, thereby whetting Turkish desires to have NATO pick up a larger share of the regular military expenses.

By 1966 it was apparent that the divergence between Turkish expectations and the availability of U.S. military aid was reaching crisis

---

[11] Gen. Cemal Tural, then chief of the Turkish General Staff, explained that the desired mobility was to come through receiving M-48 tanks and M-113 armored personnel carriers (*Cumhuriyet,* February 9, 1965). For other equipment that the Turks wished in this connection, see *Cumhuriyet,* March 2, 1966.

[12] The lack of U.S. support—especially to the Turkish navy—was criticized by the Turkish press in connection with the findings of a study by Lieutenant General Charles H. Bonesteel on Turkish and Greek forces. Denials by American officials that U.S. aid had upset the balance between these forces were rejected by Turkish journalists. See *Cumhuriyet,* April 29, 30, 1965. Even Demirel complained that, because Turkey had not received sufficient military aid from the United States and NATO for the past four or five years, it was necessary to build landing craft in Turkish shipyards. *Cumhuriyet,* May 5, 1965. See also *Hürriyet,* May 7, 1965.

[13] *Milliyet,* December 24, 25, 26, 1971. Batur, who opened his fund drive on June 1, 1970, revealed that at the end of 1971 he had raised 120 million Turkish lira (about $8.6 million) and expected to have received 1 billion Turkish lira (about $71.4 million) within five years.

Table 1
U.S. MILITARY ASSISTANCE TO TURKEY, 1948-1971
(dollars in millions)

Fiscal Years	Authorized Program [a]	Deliveries or Expenditures [b]	Excess Defense Articles [c]	Military Sales
1948	100.0	68.8		
1949	95.0	83.5		
1950	102.0	7.3	7.1	
1951	150.0	43.1		
1952	240.0	102.0		
1953	175.0	151.8		
1954	235.8	238.2		
1955	87.7	178.2		
1956	98.5	191.3		
1957	152.3	152.4	19.5	
1958	136.8	249.4		
1959	141.0	196.3		
1960	90.5	92.6		
1961	180.3	85.9		
1962	179.3	156.4	1.6	
1963	166.0	172.2	2.6	
1964	115.1	101.6	2.0	
1965	96.7	118.4	4.4	*
1966	115.1	100.5	12.9	.5
1967	133.3	118.5	25.7	.3
1968	96.3	130.9	13.4	.4
1969	100.5	108.8	27.7	.4
1970	92.2	116.6	33.6	3.4
1971	99.6			
Totals	3,232.0	2,964.7	150.5	5.2

a Figures for 1949-1952 are from Richard D. Robinson, "Impact of American Programs," p. 24. Cumulative totals do not reflect the sum of annual commitments as programs were changed retroactively in some instances.

b Figures for 1950 and 1951 do not appear to reflect earlier programs, hence may understate deliveries.

c Surplus equipment delivered to the Turks, who paid only transportation costs. The value shown here is 33 percent of the original acquisition value.

* Less than $50,000. In years prior to 1966 a total of $200,000 worth of military equipment was sold to the Turks.

Source: U.S. Department of Defense, *Military Assistance and Foreign Military Sales Facts,* March 1971; AID, *U.S. Overseas Loans and Grants and Assistance from International Organizations* (Special Report Prepared for the House Foreign Affairs Committee), May 14, 1971 (and earlier editions).

proportions. The opposition had sharply criticized NATO for not bearing a fair share of Turkey's military burden; the RPP offered figures to show that something on the order of a sixfold increase in NATO support was due Turkey.[14] Other estimates placed the cost of rapid reequipment of the entire Turkish armed forces to meet NATO standards at about $1 billion a year for two or three years.[15]

In the interests of heading off a collision, Assistant Secretary of Defense John McNaughton traveled to Ankara at the end of February 1966 to propose to the Turkish military leaders that Turkey concentrate primarily on modernizing its ground forces. He recommended that little attention be paid to the air force and still less to the navy. To compensate for the deficiencies which this plan would entail in the air force and navy, McNaughton promised that the U.S. Sixth Fleet would provide close naval support and that U.S. air squadrons would be committed to move to Turkey in time of crisis. McNaughton estimated that his package would require some $670 million in foreign assistance to Turkey over a five-year period, a target figure which he indicated the Johnson administration would seek to provide, subject, naturally, to congressional approval.[16]

Constructive as this approach to the Turkish dilemma seemed to Washington, it had obvious defects from the point of view of the Turkish General Staff. The basic philosophy of the McNaughton proposals was to make a rational allocation of limited resources to achieve the strongest possible defense force. But the famous Johnson letter had cast doubt in Turkish minds concerning the operation of the alliance, generating concern even regarding the effectiveness of NATO in the event of confrontation with the Soviet Union. As a result, a proposal entailing heavier reliance on NATO reinforcement for basic defense was likely to be exceedingly unpalatable to any Turkish regime. Where Cyprus was concerned, of course, it was out of the question for Turkish military planners to consider relying on external forces to operate on Turkey's behalf. The Turkish press voiced its strong dissatisfaction that the Ameri-

---

[14] *C.H.P.'nin ... Görüşleri,* pp. 83–87. This position had been foreshadowed while the RPP government was in office. See the statement of Defense Minister İlhami Sancar, who estimated it would take 38 billion Turkish lira (then about $4.2 billion) to bring Turkish forces up to NATO standards. *Hürriyet,* December 23, 1964.

[15] *Hürriyet,* April 1, 1966; *Pulse,* May 8, 1965.

[16] *Milliyet,* August 16, 1966; *Hürriyet,* April 1, 1966; *Cumhuriyet,* September 18, 1966. For Foreign Minister Çağlayangil's own account, see *Akşam,* May 4, 1966.

can plans did not envisage building up Turkey's naval force, especially as many journalists accepted the dubious claim that Washington had deliberately fostered Greek naval superiority.[17] At the same time, the Turkish military leaders found the level of military aid suggested by McNaughton—$134 million a year—not generous when compared to greater sums provided in the past. Moreover, the allocation of this aid so unequally among the services was undoubtedly a divisive factor in the Turkish military establishment.

Turkish military authorities made no secret of their unhappiness with McNaughton's suggestions.[18] In further bargaining they sought to increase the amount of equipment by insisting on price reductions in the items to be supplied. On the other hand, they pressed very strongly for satisfaction of the air force goals and sent the commander of the navy to Washington in September 1966 to argue his service's case, invoking the need to bring Turkish forces up to the NATO goals which the Turks themselves had been instrumental in formulating.[19]

Faced with this Turkish insistence and not wishing to foul the atmosphere for the comprehensive renegotiation of all outstanding bilateral accords which Ankara had requested in the spring of 1966, Washington backed down somewhat. Indeed, the possibility of some shifts in allocation between the services had been envisaged by McNaughton. In addition, by granting lower price tags on some equipment it would be possible to meet many of the requirements for the air force; even the navy managed to extract a commitment for a speedup in the delivery of two destroyers which McNaughton had promised, though it still did not fare as well as the other services.[20]

Despite the fact that the Turkish government finally accepted McNaughton's general approach as a base on which to plan for U.S. aid, this formula by no means solved the problem of the modernization of the Turkish forces. For their part, the Turkish military planners con-

---

[17] *Yeni Gazete,* March 2, 1966; *Hürriyet,* April 1, 1966; *Ulus,* June 27, 1966. Despite efforts of U.S. officials to publicize statistics showing that Turkey received by far the greater aid, Turkish commentators recurrently ventilated the myth that U.S. assistance favored Greece.

[18] See, for example, *Hürriyet,* April 1, 1966.

[19] *Milliyet,* August 16, 1966. In another context, the defense minister openly acknowledged that "force goals for Turkey are set by the Turkish General Staff and then put on record by NATO. NATO never interferes with national armies and force goals established by the General Staff." *Cumhuriyet,* December 29, 1967.

[20] *Cumhuriyet,* September 22, 1966.

tinued to press for further modifications aimed at creating balanced forces capable of all types of military operations. They used to advantage the fact that there was now a precisely established dollar value of foreign assistance necessary to accomplish the McNaughton design for Turkey's military modernization. For when Washington, under pressure of its involvement in Vietnam, failed to meet the $134 million figure in years following the first, the U.S. shortfall was given publicity in Turkey.[21] On the other hand, American efforts to ease the pain by telling Turkey that it was still the second largest recipient of U.S. military aid merely elicited derision from critics who pointed out that Vietnam was not included in this calculation.[22] Moreover, although the United States began providing gratis large amounts of equipment surplus to its inventory, so that in effect total aid almost met the McNaughton levels, this program was also derided in the Turkish press: articles appeared claiming that the United States was outfitting the Turkish military establishment with castoff scrap.[23] In this situation it was obvious that the Pentagon was somewhat on the defensive.

The atmosphere of détente that had led the NATO powers to ratify the Harmel study in December 1967, calling the Allies to seek improved relations with the U.S.S.R., and the subsequent NATO offer of mutual force reductions to the Warsaw Pact in June 1968 had to some extent undercut Turkey's arguments for increased arms. When the Soviets undertook military occupation of Czechoslovakia in August 1968, however, military cooperation among the members of the Atlantic alliance assumed new importance. To meet this challenge, the NATO Defense Planning Committee decreed among other things the organization of a multinational "Naval On-Call Force" to cruise the Mediterranean in time of crisis. From the first, Ankara showed great interest in this force—although it will be recalled that Turkey had withdrawn its contingent from the earlier MLF experiment, the USS *Claude V. Ricketts,* and had announced its decision not to participate in this mixed-manned nuclear venture.[24] The impress of Czechoslovakia had changed all that. Besides, the need for a modern warship to assign to this "on-call" force provided additional justification for insisting that the United States provide more

---

[21] *Akşam,* March 8, 1968; *Cumhuriyet,* March 9, 1968. See also *Outlook,* September 30, 1970, p. 5.

[22] *Cumhuriyet,* March 9, 1968.

[23] *Yeni Gazete,* July 30, 1969, also January 30, 1970.

[24] *Pulse,* January 18, 1965.

naval support. In fact, as it turned out, the Turkish navy conditioned its ability to join the NATO "on-call" force on the acquisition of a suitable ship.[25]

This was a propitious moment to press for additional naval equipment. As a result of a reduction in authorized active duty ship strength in the U.S. Navy, Washington had surplus ships on its hands and thus became receptive to plans for a broad modernization of the Turkish fleet. In the fall of 1969, three additional destroyers were sold to the Turks at nominal cost. When, after refitting, the vessels were actually delivered the following August, the Turkish navy appeared to have largely met its most urgent requirements. Following U.S. Secretary of Defense Melvin Laird's visit in October 1970, it was announced that Turkey would receive additional submarines; there was even talk of the modernization of the entire Turkish Black Sea submarine fleet.[26] For all intents and purposes, therefore, the unbalanced force concept of the McNaughton approach was dead.

The struggle against the McNaughton proposals left an imprint on U.S.-Turkish relations. The outcome encouraged many in the Turkish armed forces to believe that their insistence on balanced forces had been right all the time. Some Turks interpreted the results as an indication that the United States would back down when faced with continuing pressure. But the demise of the McNaughton approach did not mark any real agreement on the scope of military cooperation or on the strategy to be followed. It left outstanding goals that would entail expensive demands for maintenance and operation in future years. Instead of a legacy of contentment, therefore, the abandonment of the McNaughton posture seemed likely to encourage attitudes that would work against smooth military cooperation in future.

These differing approaches to Turkish military support appeared all the more troublesome in light of the progressive reluctance of the U.S. Congress to fund foreign military aid. Even the withdrawal of the bulk of American forces from Vietnam did not incline U.S. congressmen to liberality elsewhere. When the Nixon administration's bill authorizing foreign military assistance encountered stiff resistance in Congress toward the end of 1971, it became obvious there might be a sharp cut in the level of aid to Turkey. In December 1971 Defense

---

[25] *Bayram Gazetesi,* March 1, 1969.

[26] On the result of the Laird visit, see *The Evening Star* (Washington), October 23, 1970.

Minister Ferit Melen informed parliament that the Turkish military establishment would not receive more than $55 million from the United States in the coming year.[27] Although he indicated that assistance from other NATO allies would make up a part of the shortfall below previous American aid levels, it was clear the Turkish armed forces were facing the prospect of increasing reliance on their own resources to support their ambitious military programs.

The 1969 Defense Cooperation Agreement (DCA)

The give and take over U.S. military aid to Turkey took place against the backdrop of negotiations for a Defense Cooperation Agreement to comprehend multitudinous bilateral accords. By the mid-1960s pressures to reopen a full-scale dialogue on the arrangements for Turkish-American military cooperation had become irresistible. In the spring of 1965, the left-wing opposition began to raise the refrain that the United States was in "occupation" of "35 million square meters" of Turkish territory, a theme that reached a crescendo after the Demirel government took office in October 1965.[28] Out of power, the RPP too felt free to express doubts about U.S. motives. On the heels of the elections, İnönü's party, which had lost heavily, demanded a closed session to debate Turkey's bilateral understandings with the United States.[29] During the budget debate in February 1966, RPP spokesmen called upon the government to bring all foreign "facilities and bases under full control."[30] In this situation, and under the stimulus of Soviet protests over the crash of a U.S. reconnaissance aircraft in the Black Sea in December 1965, the Demirel cabinet in the spring of 1966 asked Washington to open negotiations to review and bring up to date existing bilateral military arrangements.

From the outset it was clear that the Turkish civilian authorities intended not so much to reduce the scope of American activity in Turkey as to tie up loose ends and put the bilateral relationship with the United States in a more easily defensible framework. To this end, they sought essentially a thoroughgoing reaffirmation of Turkish sovereignty and

---

[27] *Pulse,* December 24, 1971.

[28] *Cumhuriyet,* May 1, November 8, 1965; *Hürriyet,* November 9, 1965; *Vatan,* October 19, 1965.

[29] *Milliyet,* November 10, 1965.

[30] *C.H.P.'nin . . . Görüşleri,* p. 79.

control over every facet of military cooperation with the United States. In this context, to obviate recurrent criticism that some American activities in Turkey fell outside the bounds of NATO, the Ankara authorities wished the agreement to state specifically that all joint defense cooperation would take place pursuant to the NATO Pact and within the limits of NATO commitments. To parry attacks against the vagueness of previous verbal understandings, the Turkish side wanted to establish for the record its right to have full and detailed knowledge before granting permission for any American activity. Initially, moreover—again harking back to the Johnson letter—the Demirel government desired categoric guarantees that the United States would support Turkey against attack from any quarter for any reason.[31]

From Washington's point of view, however, the Turks were pressing for more extensive authority over the scope and extent of U.S. military activities than other NATO countries enjoyed. In regard to the status of American forces, the United States was insistent that arrangements concluded with the Turks accord with general NATO practices and with outstanding multilateral NATO agreements. By the same token, the Pentagon felt it important to preserve rights to import supplies necessary for the morale of its troops and to operate certain services—such as the armed forces radio stations—which were sometimes heavily criticized in the Turkish press but were the normal accouterment of American military facilities elsewhere around the world. More important, however, was Washington's unwillingness to agree to an open-ended defense commitment that appeared to go considerably beyond the NATO alliance.[32]

Although in ultimate intentions the civilian leadership on both sides was not far apart, the pace of negotiations proved excruciatingly slow. Obviously both parties found it difficult to hurry the process, despite frequent predictions by Turkish officials that the negotiations would soon be over.[33] It was not even easy, given the diverse nature of the understandings in question, to assemble a complete set of the agreements. Evidently one complicating factor was the wholesale change associated with the 1960 military takeover, which had removed not only files but

---

[31] *Hürriyet,* April 1, 1966. See also Appendix 5: Prime Minister Demirel's press conference, February 7, 1970.

[32] *Cumhuriyet,* October 17, 1966; *Milliyet,* October 3, 1968.

[33] *Haber,* April 1, 1967, reported a Foreign Ministry statement that delays in the negotiations were not due to any U.S. unwillingness to negotiate, but reflected "technical" problems. *Cumhuriyet,* March 31, 1967, and other papers had charged the United States with delaying tactics.

also many of the people personally involved in the earlier stages of the relationship. The status of verbal understandings was another knotty problem. Moreover, the need to reconcile the views of various components of the Turkish government lengthened the process. Hence it was some months before the Turkish side could compile the necessary information to draft proposals setting forth their maximum position.[34]

Naturally, the negotiations, which began in earnest only in the spring of 1967, could not be entirely divorced from other aspects of the relationship. The sharp reduction in the stated level of U.S. military aid revealed in March 1968 had a visible impact on Turkish attitudes.[35] Hoping to preclude a repetition of this discouraging development, Ankara sought from Washington an explicit pledge to extend aid for Turkey's defense efforts, subject, of course, to congressional approval. The growing belief in Turkey that the United States was deriving more benefit from the alliance than Turkey seemed to be confirmed in the Turkish understanding of the findings of the Wood-McClintock report on the continuing value of overseas bases. Some commentators thus urged that Ankara exploit the worth of these facilities to pry additional aid from America.[36] Yet, however attractive this course might have seemed, it was not a dominant theme in the negotiations. The final agreement called for Turkey to provide joint installations without receiving rent or other compensation. Obviously the Ankara government felt an overriding concern to demonstrate that the United States did not operate these facilities as a sovereign lessee, but rather shared them with Turkey for mutually beneficial purposes.[37]

---

[34] For Foreign Minister Çağlayangil's explanation to the Senate regarding these delays, see "İkili Anlaşmalardan Bazıları Kayboldu," *Cumhuriyet*, February 2, 1969.

[35] *Akşam*, March 8, 1968, claimed that military aid for 1968 would total merely $60 million. In fact, thanks to a last-minute reallocation of defense funds, the Turks would get $96.3 million; see *Outlook*, September 30, 1970, p. 5. Cohn, *Turkish Economic, Social, and Political Change*, p. 151, suggested that the aid reduction also would cause particular problems for the JP government's "accommodation with the military leaders."

[36] "Amerika Türkiyedeki Üsleri Koruyacak," *Milliyet*, April 16, 1969; *Yeni İstanbul*, April 16, 1969. William Beecher, "Experts Analyze World Strategy," *New York Times*, October 25, 1968, summarizes some of the findings of the Wood-McClintock report.

[37] However, the Turkish press revealed that Washington would share operating expenses if Turkish personnel formed a significant proportion of a base complement. Where the Turkish contingent was negligible, the United States would pay all the operating costs. See *Cumhuriyet*, January 27, 1970.

Another important consideration was Turkey's desire to gain specific acknowledgment of its right to abrogate the bilateral cooperation arrangements on short notice. It was logical that, as an accord governing the application of the NATO agreement, the Defense Cooperation Agreement remain valid for the duration of NATO; and thus it would be. However, to emphasize their continuing sovereignty, the Turks insisted that the DCA affirm their right at any time to initiate negotiations looking toward abrogation of the bilateral understandings. This issue reflected the growing public suspicion of NATO and the apprehension that Turkey's continued participation might be a danger for the country in certain circumstances. And in his public explanation of this aspect of the DCA, Demirel rejected claims that Turkey would be committed to carry out the terms of this understanding for four and a half years after deciding to denounce them, arguing that the maximum period could be no longer than two and a half years.[38]

Negotiations over these matters would drag on until mid-1969 before a final accord could be reached. Both sides were more impressed with the complexities of their task than with the urgency of public pressure. Other considerations also supervened. For example, the absence of a U.S. ambassador during the summer and early fall of 1968 slowed the process somewhat, mainly by removing for a time any obvious necessity to record progress toward a solution during the transition period. Indeed, this was a time when the basic points of divergence in the negotiations had finally been sufficiently defined to make it clear that further progress would require decisions by the top levels of government. But during Ambassador Komer's brief tour, with an election in prospect in Turkey, both sides recognized a new urgency for agreement. By the time Ambassador Handley arrived, the last stumbling blocks had been removed; two days after he presented his credentials he was able to sign the Defense Cooperation Agreement.

This long course of negotiations was in itself corrosive, not only of military relationships but of the public image of the alliance as well. It provided a constant target for extremist critics, whose attacks were under the circumstances difficult for either the Turkish authorities or the United States to rebut effectively. As the talks dragged on, American motives became increasingly suspect to a number of Turks. The RPP took a strong public stand in favor of the speedy conclusion of these

---

[38] See Appendix 5. For the opposite point of view, see "İkili Anlaşmalar," *Devrim,* October 21, 1969.

negotiations. In the press, the United States was frequently given the entire blame for the delay. Some alleged that Washington wanted the stalemate to continue in order to slow other NATO countries from following Turkey's lead; it was also claimed that the United States had ulterior designs for operations in the Middle East which it could carry out thanks only to the imprecision in the existing arrangements.[39]

Signature of the bilateral Defense Cooperation Agreement on July 3, 1969, partially stanched, but did not completely eliminate, the flow of criticism of military arrangements with the United States. The text of the understanding itself was held secret by the Demirel government on grounds that there was no constitutional requirement to bring it before the parliament. This reticence irritated the RPP; its parliamentary faction called for a full-dress debate on the agreement, alleging that secrecy would merely breed suspicions about its contents.[40] The smaller opposition parties likewise demanded a chance to debate the accord, the TLP being especially bitter in its claims that these arrangements would be "totally null and void" unless ratified by parliament.[41] Yet preoccupied as they were with other issues relating to the upcoming elections, the main opposition parties did not pursue foreign policy with any urgency during their campaigning. Instead, the issue of parliamentary approval was largely deferred until after the October elections. Then, in January 1970, Demirel gave an extensive briefing to both houses of parliament in closed session, followed by a lengthy explanation to the press.[42]

This procedure did not entirely satisfy the RPP. Only somewhat mollified by the extensiveness of this briefing—itself unusual in Turkish experience—the main opposition party reiterated the need for parliamentary ratification of the understandings. The left, of course, was far more categoric in its condemnation of what it saw as the Demirel government's end run around parliament. Even though attention was distracted from the issue of bilateral military cooperation soon afterward by the defection of an important faction of the JP which brought down

---

[39] *Cumhuriyet,* January 29, 1968. Cf. Hıfzı Oğuz Bekata, *Türkiye'nin Bugünkü Görünüşü* (Ankara, 1969), pp. 80–82.

[40] *Milliyet,* July 4, 1969; *Ulus,* July 19, 1969.

[41] *Akşam,* July 14, 1969. Cf. Doğan Avcıoğlu, "The Question of Bilateral Treaties and NATO," *Outlook,* February 25, 1970, pp. 7–8, who alleged that "it is upon the formal request of the United States that the government has refrained from bringing to Parliament the said Basic Agreement, in spite of the Constitution's stipulations in this respect."

[42] See Appendix 5.

the Demirel cabinet in February 1970, time would show that the strains, though eased, were not entirely relieved by conclusion of this accord.[43] The Defense Cooperation Agreement was to be supplemented by individual accords to govern each activity or facility. According to the July 1969 understanding, this arduous exercise was to be completed within one year from the signing of the treaty. But so complex was the task of working out the details of the many necessary undertakings that the process spilled over beyond the target date. Indeed, it appears that some of the contentious issues that were accommodated in the covering agreement may again be troubling the negotiations at the technical level. This time, however, except for a brief flurry over a potentially nasty incident involving an American noncommissioned officer who held a Turkish soldier at gunpoint at Murted air base outside Ankara,[44] public opinion has not been engaged in the controversies.

Restrictions on American freedom of action

Additional complications of considerable importance have been injected by the retrenchment of American activity and the cutback in the number of Americans assigned to duty in Turkey in recent years. It is often said that the United States moved to reduce its stake in Turkey before being asked—at least officially—by the Ankara authorities. On the surface, this claim appears justified. But in another dimension, it cannot be denied that the Turkish government had already begun to restrict the scope of American activity before the U.S. defense establishment took the initiative to consolidate its facilities and withdraw personnel.

The accidental crash of the American reconnaissance plane in the Black Sea in December 1965 had important repercussions in the direction of limiting American freedom of action in Turkey. The mishap occurred while the plane was flying a routine mission over international waters in the Black Sea. Washington immediately suspended further reconnaissance flights. And after the Kremlin vigorously protested to the United States over what it termed a "dangerous provocation" in the

---

43 *Ulus,* February 11, March 11, 1970; *Milliyet,* March 11, 1970; *Pulse,* February 11, 1970.

44 *Milliyet* (and other papers), January 21, 1970, reported that a U.S. sergeant had kept a Turkish NCO at gunpoint in an incident that developed while the two men were working on aircraft in a "quick reaction alert" area. The RPP immediately raised the matter in parliament. However, the issue dropped from sight after Demirel explained to the press on January 24, 1970, that this was an isolated occurrence and was being investigated. See "Incident at Murted," *Outlook,* January 28, 1970, p. 9.

Black Sea and the Soviet press complained that Turkey was letting its territory be used for purposes that "endangered peace," the Demirel government asked Washington to stop all such reconnaissance activities until the question could be thoroughly reviewed. Accordingly these flights were discontinued.[45]

It was not only concern about the sensibilities of the Soviet Union that led the Demirel government to restrict American activity. Eager to court Arab votes in respect of Cyprus in the United Nations, the JP was equally unwilling to see Turkish territory again used as a staging area for operations in the Middle East. The six-day Arab-Israeli war in June 1967 touched off a new paroxysm of concern lest the Americans mount military intervention in that conflict from bases in Turkey. This concern did not abate despite Foreign Minister Çağlayangil's categoric assurances that the United States could not utilize the bases without explicit permission, and despite denial from the Foreign Office that the United States was sending troops.[46] All opposition parties joined in demanding that the government publicly proclaim to its allies that they could not use Turkish facilities in connection with the Middle East conflict.[47] It was obvious that under such heavy domestic pressure the Demirel government would have been hard put to sanction any such American operation.

This position emerged even more clearly during the Lebanese disturbances of October 1969. At that time Demirel felt obliged to state directly and openly that Turkey would not let its territory be used for intervention in Lebanon, enunciating the principle that joint bases could not serve for operations to interfere in the "internal affairs" of another country.[48] That this would remain the Turkish government's official position seemed clear; indeed, as late as September 1970, during the Palestinian commando insurrection in Jordan, the Turkish Foreign Ministry was obliged to deny rumors that U.S. troops were massing at the İncirlik air base.[49]

---

[45] *Akşam,* January 7, 1966; *Cumhuriyet,* April 28, 1966. *Hürriyet,* April 1, 1966, announced the ban on reconnaissance flights from Turkey. See also Appendix 5.

[46] *Cumhuriyet,* June 7, 1967.

[47] Ibid., June 8, 1967. *Zafer,* June 15, 1967, carried a denial by the Foreign Ministry of claims circulating in Turkey that American F-104 aircraft with Israeli markings had taken part in the conflict.

[48] "İncirlik Üssüne İzin Yok," *Milliyet,* October 31, 1969.

[49] *Daily News* (Ankara), September 24, 1970. These rumors were triggered by the arrival of four refugee evacuation transports at İncirlik. These U.S. planes, however, were not flown to Jordan.

Cutbacks in U.S. personnel

Starting in 1968, the United States undertook a worldwide reduction in overseas personnel. It had long been recognized, both within the U.S. government and outside, that the numbers of American military personnel in Turkey and their location placed a heavy burden on the alliance. Yet bad as the problems had been in the 1950s, they did not then lead to any major reordering of the size or nature of the American presence. Instead, the population of U.S. citizens continued to increase as projects such as the radar complex at Diyarbakır were expanded.[50] After the friction generated by the Cyprus convulsion had begun unmistakably to affect the atmosphere, the upward course of the American population in Turkey did not immediately reverse. As a concession to aroused feelings in Turkey, however, U.S. officials did shift such obvious irritants as the Post Exchange and the American school to relatively isolated locations within a Turkish military area on the edge of Ankara, for example, in hopes of easing the painful problems of community relations. But it was primarily pressures of economy, notably the adverse U.S. balance of payments, rather than events within Turkey, that were ultimately responsible for the start of the exodus of Americans.

The gradual decline in the numbers of U.S. officials and their dependents, from a high of about 24,000 in 1968 to about 16,000 by the end of 1970, was accompanied by a reduction in activity and function. Starting in mid-1968, when the important "site 23" complex outside Ankara was turned over for the exclusive use of the Turkish military, the United States has been steadily reducing and consolidating its operations in Turkey.[51] Two of the three major facilities on the Black Sea coast have been put entirely in the hands of the Turks. Outside of headquarters in Ankara and the NATO regional command in Izmir, American military personnel now remain in sizable numbers only in Karamürsel near İzmit, at Sinop on the Black Sea, at Diyarbakır in southeastern Turkey, and at İncirlik air base near Adana.[52]

[50] *Milliyet,* July 2, 1968; "Amerika'nın Yeni Taktığı," *Ant,* March 4, 1969, p. 5.
[51] *Cumhuriyet,* June 15, 1968; *New York Times,* June 8, August 9, 1968. See also Appendix 5: Demirel's press conference, February 7, 1970; and *U.S. Security Agreements: Greece and Turkey,* p. 1831.
[52] See Appendix 5. Metin Toker, in an article entitled "Batı İttifakı İçinde Türkiye'nin Savunması," *Hürriyet,* December 12, 1971, reported that at the end of 1971 there were American military personnel serving in 27 locations in Turkey. His data showed 1,852 military personnel in the Karamürsel region, 926 in Izmir, 878 in Ankara, 759 in Sinop, 422 in Istanbul, and 222 in Diyarbakır.

These changes have meant that in some instances the remaining facilities have slightly grown in size or perhaps added some functions to take over essential activities of those installations which were closed. But these shifts have not deflected the general trend toward cutting back U.S. activity in Turkey. Of course, reduction in American operations has inevitably had the effect of eroding further the U.S. strategic stake in this country, thus in effect working in parallel with the other forces bearing on Turkey.

The duty status issue

Reductions in the numbers of Americans contributed to some easing of pressures affecting relations between the U.S. and Turkish communities. Also reinforcing this trend was a change in the system for certifying duty status. Alongside and intimately involved with the bilateral negotiations of 1966-1969 had come intensive efforts to iron out difficulties in the application of the NATO Status of Forces Agreement. This facet of the alliance had been under study by the Turkish authorities concerned ever since the 1959 Morrison accident case. In the early 1960s more or less regular discussions of the question had begun between the Turkish government and the American embassy, revolving around the Turkish right to reject duty certificates. Finally, in September 1968, a formula was agreed specifying explicit procedures to be followed by the Turkish General Staff if it should desire to contest the certification of the American military authorities.

This agreement was not published in the Official Gazette until July 1969, following conflicting interpretations of its force by the Demirel government and some of the opposition press. In briefing parliament, Foreign Minister Çağlayangil argued that the Turkish General Staff had gained the right to reject American duty certificates.[53] But as *Milliyet* pointed out, although the accord did specifically authorize the General Staff to raise objections and to delay surrendering accused American personnel to U.S. authorities, Washington's political representatives con-

---

[53] Çağlayangil reportedly briefed the Budget Committee to this effect. See *Milliyet*, January 7, 1969. He softened this position somewhat in subsequent appearances before parliament. To the Senate, on February 2, 1969, he explained that in the event of irreconcilable differences between the Turkish General Staff and the head of the U.S. military mission over the duty status of an accused, the question would become a "political matter." See Senato, *Tutanak Dergisi*, 1969, vol. 51–1, p. 40.

tinued to "have the final say" in the matter.[54] How this accord would work in practice could become evident only when tested in some contentious case. It was clear, however, that the new agreement did serve to strengthen the image of the Demirel government on this sensitive issue.

Fleet visits

Against the signs that some problems in the bilateral military cooperation might be lessening, there was no doubt that others were generating more and more heat with the passage of time.

Visits of the U.S. Sixth Fleet figured prominently among the destructive strains on the alliance in the closing years of the 1960s. Until then, though the novelty of ship calls had inevitably worn off over the years, American vessels had been generally well received in Turkish ports. In November 1962 Turkey agreed to new rules established by NATO governing clearance procedures for fleet visits.[55] Not until June 1967, in the wake of the Arab-Israeli war, did radical student organizations in Istanbul foment the first major protest demonstration against Sixth Fleet calls.[56] By that time the erroneous impression had crystallized into an unshakable conviction among many in Turkey that President Johnson had interposed the Sixth Fleet to prevent any possible Turkish landing on Cyprus in 1964.[57] As a result, any American naval vessel had come to be regarded, especially by the Turkish left, as a personification of imperialism. Moreover, in their efforts to raise all manner of embarrassing issues—from the U.S. role in Vietnam to the race question in America—leftist elements found it attractive to harp on the theme that American sailors visited Turkey solely for "sexual discharge and satisfaction." [58] Under the influence of this agitation, students in Izmir had joined in active demonstrations against the American Navy by

---

[54] *Milliyet,* January 18, 1969. For the text of this agreement and of the "agreed minute" thereto, see Appendix 4.

[55] Çağlayangil's statement to the lower house, December 22, 1969. Millet Meclisi, *Tutanak Dergisi,* dönem 3, vol. 1, p. 594.

[56] *Milliyet,* June 24, 1967; *Ulus,* June 25, 1967. A visit to Izmir at this time, however, did not arouse much protest.

[57] Even Foreign Minister Çağlayangil told the lower house on December 22, 1969, that "Intervention by the Sixth Fleet in Cyprus affairs took place" during the earlier (i.e., 1964) crisis. Millet Meclisi, *Tutanak Dergisi,* dönem 3, vol. 1, p. 595.

[58] *Cumhuriyet,* October 7, 1967; *Milliyet,* October 7, 1967. *U.S. Security Agreements: Greece and Turkey,* p. 1831.

October 1967.[59] Thereafter, major Sixth Fleet visits to either Istanbul or Izmir almost invariably encountered harassment. Even during the wave of emotion against the Soviet invasion of Czechoslovakia in August 1968 a few students found time to take to the streets against the presence of U.S. warships at Izmir.

The course of the demonstrations against the Sixth Fleet was inextricably intertwined with the general course of student protest then developing in Turkey. As confrontations between students and the constituted authorities grew increasingly bitter, it became ever more difficult for the Ankara government to prevent physical clashes. Police intrusions into university campuses to arrest suspects raised tempers to the boiling point. In the same spirit, the level of violence of protest against the Sixth Fleet mounted steadily during 1968 and early 1969. It culminated in a fierce clash between "commandos" of the right and leftist student organizations which took place during an American ship visit to Istanbul in February 1969. This melee, punctuated by fatal stabbings, was dubbed "Bloody Sunday" by the leftist press.[60] The Sixth Fleet's connection with this turn of events might be only indirect, as Prime Minister Demirel pointed out. Nonetheless, the responsibility of the United States for the altercation became firmly fixed in the minds of many of the elite in Turkey.[61] As a result, even some of those who did not object to American ships coming per se, began to doubt whether port calls were worth the turmoil associated with them. The Ankara authorities obviously found this an awkward issue, for as Foreign Minister Çağlayangil made clear, however distasteful the prospect of continued disorders might be, the Ankara government considered it inappropriate to request an ally to stop sending its ships on friendly calls.[62]

The impact of the February violence at Istanbul was not lost on the United States. Thereafter, the pace of American ship calls in Turkey was reduced significantly, and no major units put in at Turkish ports until after the elections in the fall of 1969. Sixth Fleet vessels did take

---

[59] *Cumhuriyet,* October 14, 1967.

[60] See *Cumhuriyet,* February 19, 1969; *Ant,* February 25, 1969, passim; *U.S. Security Agreements: Greece and Turkey,* p. 1832.

[61] *Milliyet,* February 19, 1969. Demirel traced these events to the student disorders of June 1968, and claimed that the opposition, by its refusal to condemn the students, was encouraging illegality.

[62] Çağlayangil argued that for Ankara to cancel U.S. fleet visits would be "the start of governing this state from the street." *Milliyet,* February 2, 1969. See also *U.S. Security Agreements: Greece and Turkey,* p. 1833.

part in one visit to Izmir in December 1969—the only large-scale visit of that year—and evoked the predictable student reaction.[63] On the other hand, U.S. warships since 1969 have frequently called singly at small ports, principally on Turkey's southern coast. This expedient has dampened hostile reaction because the localities visited do not have the volatile university student population that has sparked demonstrations elsewhere. In 1971 the Erim government imposed martial constraints which have since precluded hostile displays against U.S. naval vessels in Istanbul or Izmir, but it appears all too likely that if these security measures were to be lifted visits to those cities would occasion renewed protest. In short, port calls in Turkey by the Sixth Fleet have become chancy affairs. They no longer serve to display the strength of the alliance, but rather add to divisiveness within Turkish society, embarrass the Turkish government, and focus discontent against the United States.

Passage through the Straits

Another naval problem between the Allies in the 1960s—though one that had relatively little impact on public opinion in Turkey—concerned the regime of the Turkish Straits. In line with U.S. desire to demonstrate its right to freedom of the seas, Washington had been regularly sending warships through the Straits into the Black Sea. The United States was not a signatory of the Montreux Convention, yet in fact it accepted the Turkish position that this instrument governed all passage through these waters.

Postwar advances in naval ordnance complicated interpretation of the Montreux agreement: there was no clear guidance for the treatment of certain new categories of weapons, particularly missiles. Washington took the view that destroyers equipped with antiaircraft missiles but otherwise meeting the restrictions on tonnage and caliber of armament specified in the convention, should be allowed to pass into the Black Sea.

---

[63] Some quarters professed to see "positive evidence that some of the students were paid by the Communists in order to protest Turkey's continued participation in NATO." Charges of this nature were not pressed by the Izmir authorities, however, and clearly no such impetus from abroad would have been required to trigger student demonstrations under the circumstances. See *Report by Subcommittee of the House Committee on Armed Services Following a Visit to Spain, Italy, Libya, Turkey, and Iran, January 2–17, 1970, on the Military and Political Problems in Spain, Italy, Libya, Turkey and Iran* (Washington, February 1970), pp. 5709–11.

In fact, American ships armed with missiles were permitted to enter the Black Sea until as late as January 1966.[64]

By September 1966, however, Ankara had shifted its interpretation of the limitations imposed by the Montreux agreement. The Turks no longer were disposed to accept the American contention that antiaircraft missiles did not fall under the category of arms limited by the convention. In part, this new stance represented the growing Turkish anxiety not to ~ive offense to the Soviets, who had complained loudly at the visits of .S. naval vessels. In part, too, it represented a desire to study this contentious issue carefully before ruling on its merits. In any event, Washington withdrew its request for the destroyer *Pratt* to pass through the Straits in September 1966.[65] Since then the United States has requested permission to send only ships not carrying missiles. The question still awaits a definitive solution.[66]

---

[64] The guided missile frigate *Yarnell* was admitted to the Black Sea on January 13, 1966, with little notice in the Turkish press. See *Cumhuriyet*, January 11, 1966.

[65] *Milliyet*, September 4, 6, 9, 1966; Harry N. Howard, "The Turkish Straits after World War II: Problems and Prospects," *Balkan Studies*, 1970, p. 57.

[66] Some observers have seen an additional potential problem for the United States in the Soviet mode of requesting clearance for dates to transit the Straits. Soviet requests for blocks of dates on occasion appear to preempt passage of naval vessels. For a discussion of this question, see "Sealing off the Black Sea," *East Europe*, March 1971, p. 11.

8

Development Assistance Problems

The sharpness of the political and military problems of the alliance tended to overshadow friction in the economic realm in the post-Menderes period. But in this sector, too, difficulties were rising.

By 1964, the Turkish economy appeared to be returning to all too familiar patterns. Inflationary pressures mounted. The relief accorded by the 1958 stabilization program had largely run its course. Debt repayment loomed as a major obstacle ahead; already Turkey's balance-of-payments position had deteriorated to an alarming extent. Despite efforts aimed at expansion, exports remained relatively immobile; nor in its first two years of life had the international consortium for aid to Turkey managed to alleviate these strains. Failure to receive sufficient foreign assistance was a heavy blow to the First Five-Year Plan. It faced the Turks with the unpalatable possibility of having to cut back the development plan, to slow economic growth, and to reorder their economic priorities in a most painful way. This prospect, coming as it did when the political dislocations generated by the Cyprus crisis were reaching their height, threatened to impart dangerous momentum to the forces impelling Turkey away from its Western alliance.

Meanwhile, Washington was going through its own process of revisionism. The intensity of the cold war was visibly receding. With it went some of the urgency in providing both economic and military assistance. This atmosphere inspired American policy makers to devise new strategies with which to approach and motivate an increasingly reluctant Congress. Economic aid to Turkey seemed particularly in need of a new face. As a political program to sweeten the alliance and impart a sense of dynamism and motion, economic assistance had served well.

But the pattern of recurrent financial crisis in Turkey undermined any confidence that, in terms of its stated goals, the economic aid program had been a success. Their disappointment led AID officials in Washington to ask Congress to provide a higher level of funds for a limited period, in effect to authorize a last-ditch effort to galvanize Turkey into a measure of self-sustaining growth sufficient to dispense with continuing grants or concessionary loans by the early 1970s. They believed that only in this way could the economic aid program be judged successful and then be terminated without damage to the Turkish economy. To direct such an enterprise, a dynamic administrator, James Grant, was dispatched to Ankara in 1964 as AID director.

As part of the new approach, a determined campaign was mounted to put new life into the consortium and to broaden its membership, particularly by the inclusion of the World Bank. The consortium staff itself had recognized the major deficiencies of its performance in the past and was already thinking along similar lines.[1] In this propitious atmosphere, the United States took the lead in proposing a comprehensive debt rollover; to demonstrate its good faith, Washington was even prepared to assist in the settlement of outstanding commercial arrears, an operation normally quite against its principles. The United States also stood ready to increase its contribution, hoping thereby to induce other consortium members to follow suit.

In tandem with the American effort, the World Bank exerted its influence to impel the consortium members to reschedule Turkey's indebtedness; indeed, it made debt rollover the prerequisite for World Bank participation in the overall venture. Such forceful stimulation brought the consortium to respond, although the Turks themselves took remarkably little initiative at first in pressing for large-scale debt relief. The European members now fell into line. After rather intricate talks, in which American desire to impose conditions binding future Turkish performance almost led Ankara to break off negotiations, a new schedule of repayments was drawn up to level out installments through 1973.[2] Consortium contributions also rose significantly in 1966–1967; even more significantly, these were years of unusually abundant wheat crops. Together these developments again relieved the pinch of foreign exchange pressures, permitting Turkish gross national product to rise by as much

---

[1] John White, *Pledged to Development,* pp. 140 ff.
[2] Ibid., p. 151.

174

as 9.2 percent during 1966 and nearly that much again in the following year.

Increased assistance was only one facet of the new AID approach. There was also to be more active involvement in encouraging the Turkish government to plan effective use of resources and to be resolute in carrying out the reforms called for in the five-year plans. On one hand, this involved an effort by the United States to extend an increasing proportion of its assistance in the form of loans for projects that could be reviewed in terms of economic feasibility. On the other hand, Ankara officials, quite understandably, pressed Washington to provide general budgetary support in order to permit greater flexibility, and to keep authority to allocate aid in Turkish hands. The conflict in approach was never clearly resolved; it formed a recurrent source of discord between the allies as each year's economic assistance program came up for debate.

At the same time, Washington's strategy suggested close connection with the State Planning Organization and efforts through the consortium to review the Second Five-Year Plan, which was to run from 1968 to 1972. Here, too, possibilities for friction abounded. Not only were there the normal complement of problems associated with national sensitivity, but the State Planning Organization itself was undergoing considerable uncertainty at this point. In September 1962 the entire senior staff of this institution had resigned in protest over the failure of the İnönü coalitions to carry out land reform and associated measures. The new staff worked in closer harmony with the İnönü governments; but with the advent of the JP administration at the end of 1965 the future of planning itself initially appeared in doubt. It was feared in some opposition circles in Ankara that Demirel, although personally not opposed to the planning organization in principle, would not be willing to accord it sufficient authority and freedom of action to continue in the reformist tradition which had up to then motivated successive planning organization staffs.[3] Indeed, it soon became clear that with the JP in power the initiative in planning would shift somewhat more into the hands of the politicians.

The United States sought through the consortium to influence the Second Five-Year Plan. Judging from the poor performance in the first two years of the first plan, Washington was inclined to believe that the target of a 7 percent development rate was unrealistic; hence, the

---

[3] *Cumhuriyet,* November 18, 1965.

Americans advocated a reduction in investment and a rearrangement of priorities to reduce the foreign exchange component of the Turkish development effort. This position in its essence would be repeated in the report on the Second Five-Year Plan prepared in December 1967 under the supervision of Kenneth Berrill, the noted Cambridge economist, at the behest of the international consortium of donors.[4]

The notion of cutting back the five-year plans was of course distasteful to the Ankara government and it offered the left a new point of attack. Critics soon drew the conclusion that the United States aimed to turn Turkey into an agricultural country that would be the "cereal depot" for Europe [5]—this despite the fact that Turkey had since 1953 regularly been a net importer of cereals. The emphasis on the private sector that the opposition perceived in American assistance also elicited criticism. The consortium was accused of trying to get Turkey to liberalize the movement of capital in order to facilitate the economic domination of Turkey by the West. Thus, although the consortium was a useful device for concerting foreign aid, it carried with it a baggage of suspicion that could not be entirely overcome. Nor was the United States able to persuade the Demirel government to take all the corrective action necessary to prevent inflationary pressures from again threatening economic stability.

At issue here was a basic and fundamental question. Turkish economic activity had since the 1930s been directed at making Turkey self-sufficient industrially. Tariff walls had been erected, allowing the growth of hot-house industry which operated at high cost in world terms, hence could not compete in a free trade atmosphere. U.S. aid had bolstered Turkey in its efforts toward import substitution in the 1950s. Increasingly in the 1960s, however, Turkey's allies had come to see the creation of inefficient, noncompetitive plants as a major drag on Turkish advance. The remedy in U.S. eyes was to open these artificially protected industries to competition and the play of market forces. A major thrust of the American aid program in the 1960s, therefore, was to assist Turkey in moving away from the protectionist frame of reference, to

---

[4] *Cumhuriyet,* December 25, 1965; *Yeni Gazete,* May 23, 1968. For Berrill's report of May 1964 to the consortium, see White, pp. 133–36.

[5] *Cumhuriyet,* March 24, 1966; *Hürriyet,* January 6, 1966. Also see "Orta Doğu' nun Hububat Ambarı Türkiye!" *Yön,* March 17, 1967, p. 5. Charges that Washington wished Turkey to remain an agricultural economy were also voiced by leftist circles in Ambassador Komer's day. See "Komer'in Yeni Bir Küstahlığı!" *Ant,* February 18, 1969, p. 12.

increase exports, to promote tourism as a source of foreign exchange, and to reform the inefficient state economic enterprises which bulked so large in the Turkish industrial sector.[6]

To Westerners the economic case for this prescription has always seemed convincing. But to many of the Turkish elite it is a highly suspect formula. Where assembly plans have been set up with foreign capital as an efficient way to reduce foreign exchange costs—truck and jeep assembly plants, for example, which were originally intended to contribute to Turkey's defense requirements—those of leftist views have seen a scheme to gain an assured monopoly of parts imports. In efforts to increase agricultural yield by introducing a high-producing Mexican lowland wheat, these elements have perceived a plot to tie up resources in fertilizer and distract Turkey from industrialization. Suggestions for reform of the state economic enterprises have been portrayed as anti-etatist and excessive in their advocacy of private enterprise.[7]

Timetable for economic disengagement

Integral to the new U.S. aid policy was the idea that American assistance should have a definite terminal date. This notion was first broached in low key by Stuart Van Dyke, chief of the American aid mission in the early 1960s. But insistent efforts to prepare Turkish public opinion for the eventual end of the program began only in the spring of 1965, when AID Director Grant indicated publicly that Turkey would soon be able to dispense with concessionary support from abroad. In this context he made it clear that the American economic aid program aimed to cease by 1973, a theme which he constantly repeated during the remaining years of his tour in Ankara.[8] His message was entirely consistent with the stated aims of the fifteen-year perspective development program, which envisaged the end of concessional assistance on completion of the Second Five-Year Plan. But by giving the target date such prominence and by linking the course of American assistance to it, Grant had imparted a quite new emphasis to this goal.

Neither the Turkish government nor public opinion leaders in Turkey seem to have been quick to grasp all the implications of Grant's words. After all it was technicians who had set the target, and it was

---

[6] *Milliyet*, May 25, 1967; *Yeni Gazete*, May 23, 1967.

[7] *Akşam*, July 14, 1969; Doğan Avcıoğlu, *Türkiye'nin Düzeni*, pp. 402 ff.

[8] *Son Havadis*, December 10, 1965; *Cumhuriyet*, December 12, 1966.

pleasant to bask in the possibility that it might come true. But that Washington would predicate its policy on this cutoff date was probably not entirely anticipated, at least not at the outset. Indeed, it appears that the 1973 term was set "because 10 years seemed a reasonable period for the continuance of aid, neither so long as to be unduly dispiriting nor so short as to give rise to skepticism." [9] Despite the fact that the 1967 Berrill report to the consortium took sharp issue with these calculations, challenging the notion that Turkey's balance-of-payments deficit would be manageable without continuing help, the goal of ending the American assistance program in the 1970s would remain part of U.S. aid strategy thereafter.[10]

The interest of the United States in terminating its economic assistance program by the mid-1970s was not taken seriously by most of its vocal critics. They seemed to believe that America benefited much more than Turkey did from the aid extended, and that there was little prospect that Washington would voluntarily withdraw from such a lucrative venture.[11] The editors of *Yön* explicitly charged that American assistance was turning Turkey into a colony and a market for the West; moreover, they contrasted this effect with that of Soviet aid, which they maintained ran parallel to Turkish desires for industrial development.[12] Another facet of attack was the charge that in providing wheat and other commodities to Turkey for local currency, the United States was building up funds to be used for subversion or to assist American firms to establish themselves in Turkey without making any dollar investments.[13] In short, the refrain was being voiced by mid-1965 that American aid was aid with strings, often subtle and invisible to be sure, but nonetheless dangerous for Turkey's economic independence. As an indication of

---

[9] John White, p. 122. Grant initiated a study of the Turkish economy directed at discovering whether or not this target was reasonable. This work concluded that the Turkish projections were feasible.

[10] *U.S. Security Agreements: Greece and Turkey,* p. 1865; *Yeni Gazete,* May 23, 1968; *Milliyet,* April 21, 1969.

[11] Even the organ of the RPP reflected this view. See *Ulus,* June 24, 1965.

[12] Doğan Avcıoğlu, "Demagojiye Paydos!" *Yön,* August 13, 1965, p. 3.

[13] Doğan Avcıoğlu, "Sam Amca'nın Türkiyedeki Hazinesi," *Yön,* April 23, 1965, p. 3. Avcıoğlu criticized especially the extension of local currency loans under the provision of Congressman Harold Cooley's 1957 amendment to Public Law 480. "Cooley loans," however, were relatively limited in size and from 1958 to 1966 a total of only $57.4 million was loaned under this program. Since 1966 no new commitments have been made.

the prevalence of these views, the RPP itself in its election manifesto in 1965 would call the government to reject "foreign aid with strings." [14]

Benevolent neglect

The American aid program took another sharp turn in 1968, a turn leading to a policy of benevolent neglect. By this time pressures within the United States for economic retrenchment had prevailed over the argument that Washington should mount a final assault to bring Turkey to self-sufficiency. The compelling force of America's own balance-of-payments squeeze was fostering cuts in assistance worldwide. It would have taken an exceptional case to withstand these pressures. Turkey's was not. To be sure, the Turks had met their physical objectives in most impressive fashion, but to the Berrill team and to others a more telling point was that the industry thus established could not compete in the world market. Berrill's findings had called attention to the inevitable misallocation of resources in such a system, where domestic demand was the sole criterion for investment. From this, the conclusion emerged that Turkey was trying to do too much too fast and that it had not moved very far along the way to attaining the sought-after self-sufficiency. In these circumstances, Washington's inclination was to let Turkey's development rate decline rather than to extend additional aid.[15]

As the American contribution through the consortium fell in 1968 to little more than half of its previous level, the European states took up some of the slack. West Germany in particular emerged as a major aid donor. Nonetheless, the total assistance pledged by the consortium declined significantly from its previous figure—i.e., from some $206.6 million in 1967 to $155.7 million in 1968.

In part, this fall represented the unwillingness of the consortium to cushion the effects of Turkey's failure to redress its own economic difficulties.[16] The value of the lira on the international market had declined to a point where remedial action had again become necessary. In 1967 the Demirel government had instituted a special exchange rate for tourists in hopes of preventing diversion of hard currency into the black market. Ankara also had set an attractive conversion rate for remittances from the several hundred thousand workers who had

[14] *Ulus,* September 18, 1965.
[15] *Yeni Gazete,* May 23, 1968; *Milliyet,* April 21, 1969.
[16] *Cumhuriyet,* July 24, 1970.

streamed to Germany (and in lesser numbers to other parts of Europe) during the 1960s to escape the unemployment and underemployment rampant in Anatolia. These steps could not offset the deleterious effects of a temporary drop in the flow of remittances caused by the slowdown in the German economy in 1967 and 1968. Yet, despite the slump, earnings remitted amounted to nearly $100 million a year, a sum roughly equal to one-third of the existing balance-of-payments deficit.[17]

The 1970 devaluation

Starting early in 1967 foreign lenders began calling insistently for devaluation as the only solution to the balance-of-payments problem and the growing liquidity crisis inside Turkey.[18] By mid-1968 this pressure, from the consortium and the World Bank as well as from the European Monetary Agency and the International Monetary Fund, had grown to significant proportions.

The Demirel government resisted devaluation tenaciously. In 1967 the JP administration had raised indirect taxes to drain off excess purchasing power and slow domestic inflation; the cabinet had performed creditably within the limitations of the philosophy of the Five-Year Plan. Having carried out what in the beginning all had agreed was an acceptable program, the Demirel regime argued—not without some justice—that the consortium's performance was the chief factor in the drop in foreign exchange reserves that necessitated reimposition of import controls. Moreover, the JP leaders rejected the contentions of the consortium donors that devaluation would stimulate exports, noting that Turkey's principal products sold abroad were agricultural and subject to quotas in the European market. Finally, the Ankara government pointed out that devaluation would significantly raise the value of existing foreign debt.[19]

These protests did little to convince the consortium. The international monetary agencies were persuaded by the logic of the argument that Turkey's protectionist economic policies, especially its low exchange rate, were promoting inefficient, noncompetitive industry. Hence the consortium did not provide the relief that could have obviated the need for devaluation. Instead, it offered enough aid to keep Turkey

---

[17] *Yeni Istanbul,* July 10, 1970; *Pulse,* August 3, 1970.

[18] *Milliyet,* May 25, 1967.

[19] *Cumhuriyet,* August 16, 1968.

from drastic crisis but not enough to disguise the increasingly difficult position of Turkey's foreign trade.

If Demirel resisted devaluation and the package of associated measures, this course was dictated by political necessity. Elections were set for October 1969. It is understandable that he would not agree to provide the opposition a natural issue by taking such a major step before the ballots were in. Yet both business circles and the press recognized that Turkey would sooner or later find devaluation impossible to avoid—and in particular that segment of the business community which was affected by the import restrictions was ready to see the operation completed. Shortly after the elections a new complication arose when the Demirel government's budget was rejected in a revolt within the JP. The defection at that time of enough members to remove Demirel's assured majority threatened governmental stability and weakened his hand generally in dealing with contentious issues. Nonetheless, the urgency of the liquidity crisis into which Turkey had plunged after 1968 left no attractive alternatives. In August 1970 the Turkish government announced that the value of the lira had been reduced to fifteen to the dollar.[20]

The devaluation passed with a minimum of disruption in Turkish-American relations. The United States, while ardently favoring the measure, had not been in the forefront of the campaign to convince the Demirel government of its necessity. Indeed, the solidarity of all the Western powers on the issue made it difficult to attach responsibility to any one party. Washington did come forth with an additional loan of $25 million to ease the strains of the transition period. Thus, although the opposition, as might easily have been expected, unanimously condemned the government for devaluing—or coming to the position where devaluation was inevitable—the U.S. role was not singled out for particular disapproval.

Overall, the change in the Turkish exchange rate proved beneficial for Turkey. The government made an effort to limit price rises on the domestic market to keep exports competitive. But the major gain was a huge jump in remittances from Turkish workers in West Germany. From an annual rate of less than $200 million, revenue from this source

---

[20] *Milliyet,* August 11, 1970. The previous rate had been nine to the dollar, but worker remittances and tourist transactions had enjoyed the rate of twelve to the dollar. In December 1971 the Turkish government announced a revaluation of the lira to fourteen to the dollar in connection with the general adjustment of the dollar in relation to European currencies.

mounted to nearly $500 million in 1971, an amount far overshadowing the input of American resources for Turkey's economic development (see Table 2).

Table 2

U.S. ECONOMIC ASSISTANCE TO TURKEY, 1946-1971

(dollars in millions)

Fiscal Years	Obligations and loan authorizations		
	Loans	Grants	Total
1946-48	44.5	—	44.5
1949	33.8	—	33.8
1950	40.0	31.9	71.9
1951	—	49.8	49.8
1952	11.2	58.4	69.6
1953	—	58.6	58.6
1954	—	78.7	78.7
1955	25.5	83.8	109.3
1956	25.0	104.3	129.3
1957	25.1	62.3	87.4
1958	23.2	90.4	113.6
1959	97.2	107.0	204.2
1960	26.5	99.0	125.5
1961	131.0	89.8	220.8
1962	102.5	81.6	184.2
1963	100.0	61.9	161.9
1964	150.2	18.1	168.3
1965	180.3	11.4	191.6
1966	144.9	14.8	159.6
1967	137.4	14.2	151.6
1968	52.5	17.6	70.0
1969	58.5	28.1	86.6
1970	71.0	16.3	87.3
1971	79.4	9.6	89.0
Totals*	1,519.3	1,208.4	2,727.7

*Cumulative totals do not reflect the sum of the annual commitments, as programs were changed retroactively in some instances.

Source: AID, Office of Statistics and Reports, Bureau for Program and Policy Coordination, *U.S. Overseas Loans and Grants and Assistance from International Organizations* (Special Report Prepared for the House Foreign Affairs Committee), May 14, 1971 and earlier editions.

The European Communities

One of the main considerations that impelled the Ankara government to devalue and to dismantle some of its elaborate control mechanisms was its relationship with the European Economic Community (which in 1967 joined in the so-called European Communities). In 1963, a year after Greece's success in securing associate status in this association, the İnönü government had negotiated a similar arrangement with the Community. According to the terms of association, Turkey had five years in which to prepare for the start of a transition period looking toward eventual attainment of full membership. In the event that the Turkish economy appeared unready to enter transition status at this time, a second five-year preparation period was envisaged.

By the end of the original five-year term, attitudes in Turkey had undergone substantial change. The RPP, which had been the leading force in forging the commitment to Community membership in 1963, began to have second thoughts about the implications of economic incorporation into Europe. This change of heart was particularly visible in the statements of Bülent Ecevit, whose position as the acknowledged second in command of the party had been confirmed after Turhan Feyzioğlu, his principal rival, led his faction out to form the Reliance Party in 1968. Ecevit now publicly questioned whether Turkish industry could survive economic association with Europe and warned that Turkey might become merely another market for the highly industrialized countries of the West.[21] After considerable internal dispute, the party did endorse seeking full membership in the European Communities, but asked that Turkey exercise the right to delay the start of the transition period for at least an additional five years.[22] The TLP and those of more or less similar view had taken a stand of categoric opposition to the idea of intimate economic ties with Europe from the start. They saw a link with the free enterprise system of Europe as bolstering their opponents inside Turkey, hence threatening their political future.[23] They charged that economic association with the Western powers would soon lead Turkey to be swallowed up as a colony.

In view of this opposition, the Demirel government moved warily in negotiating the terms of the transition period. The Ankara authorities

---

[21] *Akşam,* January 31, 1970.
[22] *Ulus,* March 13, 1970; *Milliyet,* July 27, 1970. See also Besim Üstünel, statements in *Milliyet,* July 29, 1970.
[23] Behice Boran, *Türkiye ve Sosyalizm Sorunları,* p. 320.

felt it imperative to extract significant concessions to ease the strains of adjustment. It was obvious to all that Turkish industry by and large was not competitive with that in Europe and that protective tariff walls would have to be dismantled slowly if the Turkish economy was not to suffer painful shocks. In the end, a twenty-two-year transition was agreed. The terms announced in July 1970 afforded considerable protection to Turkish industry, while freeing Turkey's agricultural produce from both quotas and tariffs at an early date. Moreover, the Turks were to receive a $195 million loan on relatively favorable terms, and restrictions on the freedom of movement of Turkish labor in Europe were to be lifted.[24]

Turkey's membership in the European Communities accorded with U.S. policy and over the long run would be a most important step in assuring the permanence of healthy relations between the two states. Yet, immediately, the prospect of membership in this European association raised problems for which there were no ready and easy answers.

Of these, perhaps the question most in the public mind concerned the ultimate fate of the Ereğli steel mill in the environment of association with Europe. When RPP spokesman Besim Üstünel brought up this matter in debates following the announcement of the terms of the transition period, he was answered by the government with the explanation that iron, steel, and coal matters were outside the scope of the European Economic Community and that the term of agreement in no wise affected operation of the Turkish steel industry.[25] Nonetheless, it seems indisputable that this complex will be affected, at least indirectly, by the general economic environment resulting from economic association with Europe and in particular by imports of finished products permitted under this arrangement. An ambitious project of expansion to increase Ereğli's efficiency is already in its early stages. But the plant will have difficulty in competing effectively with European manufacturers at the postdevaluation exchange rates without cheaper sources of ore than are likely to be found in Turkey. Indeed, press reports allege that after completion of a third steel mill scheduled for construction by the Soviets, presently known higher grade ore bodies will be exhausted within two decades.[26] For the nearer term, when a sintering

---

[24] *Milliyet,* July 29, 1970; *Pulse,* July 24, 1970.
[25] *Milliyet,* July 29, 1970.
[26] *Cumhuriyet,* April 30, 1970.

plant completed early in 1972 begins its operations to concentrate lower quality ore, these problems will be masked to some extent. It will also be some time before integration into Europe has proceeded far enough to raise with full force the issue of Ereğli's production.

Strikes and labor disputes

Labor disputes have had a significant disruptive impact on the Turkish-American relationship in the past few years. The expedient of substituting the Tumpane Company as the employer for all workers locally hired for U.S. military activities provided more flexibility in labor relations, but it did not by any means eliminate serious problems. In 1964, in the wake of disappointment over Cyprus, the Turkish workers at American cold storage facilities in Istanbul and Izmir went on strike. They were joined by Turkish civilian personnel at other installations around Turkey, who claimed that the Tumpane Company was not living up to the requirements of Turkish laws. The Turkish government refused to consider this strike injurious to Turkish national security (although at about the same time it did prohibit a general dock strike on these grounds). Only when a wage board was set up to consider grievances was the strike finally brought to an end.[27]

A more explosive strike took place at the İncirlik air base in the fall of 1967, just before the revival of the Cyprus crisis brought Vance to Ankara. The strikers, who were seeking fringe benefits as well as a large raise, were rapidly roused to an ugly mood and a bitter confrontation with Americans at İncirlik ensued. The United States was subjected to a barrage of inflammatory accusations in the press. Such a widely circulated periodical as *Akis* carried on its cover a picture of an American soldier with a guard dog blown up beyond life size to suggest that vicious animals had been used to cow Turkish laborers.[28] After a week of growing bitterness, the cabinet ordered the strike postponed on grounds of national security, as a NATO exercise was to be held at this base at the start of October.[29] But the cabinet decree was overturned by the courts, and the strike was resumed even while the NATO maneuver was in mid-course. Under this pressure, the Tumpane Company backed down somewhat and a new wage contract was signed.

---

[27] *Milliyet,* September 19, 22, October 3, 21, 1964.

[28] *Akis,* October 7, 1967.

[29] "İşçiler: Bir Grevin Hikayesi," ibid., pp. 6–12; *Cumhuriyet,* September 29, 30, 1967.

A third major labor dispute took place at American facilities in Izmir and İncirlik in May 1969. Strikers seeking overtime pay and "social rights" again prevented the supply of goods and services necessary to keep the İncirlik base in operation.[30] The resulting suspension of air controller service during this strike affected civil air transport to Adana, evoking scathing denunciations by prominent political figures to the effect that by these measures the United States was putting pressure on the Demirel government to intervene.[31] Again the strike was settled only after agreement on a substantial raise was concluded.

These experiences, with their extensive publicity, confirmed in the minds of the Americans involved the need to have more protection against strikes that could hamper normal operations. This consideration figured in the negotiation of the Defense Cooperation Agreement: indeed, as the secretary general of the Foreign Office made clear during the May 1969 strike, signature of the agreement was threatened with delay at the last moment while the United States sought additional assurances against disruption of this kind.[32]

Another problem of labor relations stemmed from the U.S. effort to cut back its operations in Turkey. As part of this endeavor, not only were Americans withdrawn but the number of Turkish laborers needed by the Tumpane Company was decreased in rough proportion. Termination settlements proved a contentious issue—although the prospect of hastening the American departure always had something of a dampening effect. In the end, America received unfavorable publicity both for mistreating the Turkish labor force while it was in Turkey and for its settlements with the workers on its departure.[33]

The reason for this resentment was not any deep-seated antiforeign streak awaiting the opportunity to break forth, nor was it particularly the stimulation of the political radicals outside the labor movement; rather it was that the United States was viewed as inexhaustibly wealthy, hence easily able to afford the sums that would alleviate the penury of its Turkish work force. Moreover, bitterness was engendered by Washington's decision to work through the Tumpane Company, a concern which had gained the reputation of driving a hard bargain

---

[30] *Milliyet,* May 23, 1969; *Cumhuriyet,* April 9, 1969.
[31] *Milliyet,* May 30, 1969; Abdi İpekçi, "Bu Ne Haysiyetsizlik?" *Milliyet,* May 29, 1969.
[32] *Yeni Gazete,* May 29, 1969; *Milliyet,* May 29, 1969.
[33] *Milliyet,* May 15, 1970.

with its many Turkish employees for the benefit of its American owners.[34] However extravagant the union demands might have been when viewed against the prevailing local wage scale, they nonetheless paled by comparison with what the least-paid American worker would have received. There was, therefore, much haggling about small sums and about some labor practices long settled in the United States (e.g., sick leave and uniform allowance). While the unions did not win every encounter, they did prevail on many points, some of which in retrospect do not seem to have been worth contesting at the price of national animosity. In short, with a somewhat more flexible American stance it should have been possible to eliminate much of the friction.

Similarly, American private firms found themselves under particular labor pressure. Some of it was undoubtedly politically inspired, with the design of supporting protest over Cyprus or the more nebulous charge that American capitalists were exploiting Turkey. Political demonstrations not directly of concern to workers idled plants and even caused physical damage. And the police and other security forces did not always appear as avid to protect American plants from occupation or destruction as U.S. businessmen desired. The level of hostility to American business has risen perceptibly in the past few years as foreign capital has become the butt of attack not only from the TLP but from the RPP as well. Members of these parties have charged that foreign capital dominates the economy, despite the fact that foreign investment in Turkey is tiny in comparison to that in many other less developed countries, and minuscule in comparison to Turkey's own investments.

Pressures within the society at large found reflection in governmental treatment of American private enterprise at the end of the 1960s. Bureaucratic obstacles had always been rather formidable in Turkey; the operation of customs in particular had been a trying hurdle for all who would do business in Turkey. But by the fall of 1969 the Turkish government appeared to be launching a campaign to tighten restrictions on foreign concerns, paying special attention to penalizing firms that had not fully lived up to their commitments.[35] This more rigorous enforcement of existing legislation was complemented by new laws imposing additional conditions; for example, assembly plants were

---

[34] See *Akis,* October 7, 1967, pp. 7–8.

[35] *Milliyet,* November 15, 1969.

obliged to boost significantly the proportion of Turkish-made parts in their products. These regulations worked particular hardship on the automobile assembly industry, which was caught in a severe price squeeze after the devaluation when the government clamped a low ceiling on price increases—although taxes as well as the costs of parts and labor rose enormously. This situation even aroused the sympathy of those who were normally critical of the "assembly industry." [36] Obviously it was a delicate balance to strike: to assuage the demands of the public and at the same time continue to attract foreign investment which the JP government, at least, valued highly.

Erim's regime betrayed somewhat more nationalistic fervor than its JP predecessor. Atilla Karaosmanoğlu, then deputy prime minister for economic affairs, made a point of publicizing figures purporting to show that during the past few years the Turkish economy had received no contribution from foreign capital, indeed that there had been a net outflow of capital.[37] On this basis, the Erim government pledged that henceforth Turks must own a controlling majority in new enterprises set up with foreign funds; there was even a strong hint that the Ankara authorities hoped previously existing firms would move to vest majority ownership in Turkish hands. Additional restrictions were also placed on the export-import trade, adding to the tribulations of some foreign investors. While these measures were aimed at foreign investment in general, of course, the prominent position of U.S. firms meant that the burden fell heavily on Americans.

The Peace Corps

With every new area of involvement in Turkey naturally there came new problems. The Peace Corps proved no exception. Unlike most other American programs, the Peace Corps had come to Turkey not in response to evident Turkish need or request, but primarily as an outgrowth of domestic politics in the United States. Starting in 1961, American negotiators had undertaken a concerted effort to persuade the Ankara regime to accept the volunteers as an adjunct to the technical assistance program. Because granting immunities and freedom to work in villages in the restricted zone in eastern Turkey required waiving

---

[36] Abdi İpekçi, "Otomotiv Sanayiinde Zorunluğu Bir Ayırım," *Milliyet,* October 7, 1970.
[37] *Milliyet,* April 14, 1971.

some regulations, the exchange of notes effecting the accord on the Peace Corps did not take place until the end of August 1962; nearly three years more went by before the parliament got around to ratifying the agreement.[38]

The Peace Corps program did not arouse much interest or concern at first. Only a trickle of volunteers came in 1962, but their numbers swelled in the next three years. By the end of 1965 there were nearly 600 scattered throughout Turkey, engaged primarily in two activities: English teaching and village development. During the parliamentary debates early in 1965 preceding ratification of the agreement authorizing Peace Corps activity in Turkey, only a handful of deputies expressed reservations; their fears centered on (1) the possibility that volunteers might have designs to carry out missionary activity; (2) the proposed immunities and privileges of Peace Corps personnel; and particularly (3) the long delay in bringing this accord to vote.[39] The dominant theme of these debates was praise for the unselfishness of the volunteers and gratitude that they would come to share the rigors of rural Turkish life for minuscule remuneration.

The Peace Corps immunity from public criticism did not last long. The influx of volunteers and their spread to the sensitive areas of eastern Turkey, the strains of foreign involvement in the inherently difficult and delicate task of village development, and the rising tide of disenchantment with Americans in general, all led to a flood of attack by the end of 1965. A poll conducted by the leftist periodical *Kim* in December of that year showed the reputation of the corps already tarnished, with the view gaining prominence that "no good will come from the Peace [Corps] volunteers."[40] The following year was marked by a continuing drumfire of criticism against the volunteers. Student organizations joined in the clamor, adding demands for the dismissal of the Peace Corps to their growing roster of complaints. So intense

---

38 Müslim Özbalkan, *Gizli Belgelerle Barış Gönüllüleri* (Istanbul, 1970), pp. 125 ff. The Peace Corps agreement was ratified by the Turkish parliament on April 2, 1965. For the agreement, see Peace Corps Program, TIAS 5193, August 27, 1962.

39 Millet Meclisi, *Tutanak Dergisi,* dönem 1, vol. 34–2, pp. 661–65 (session of January 14, 1965). For statistics on the Peace Corps volunteers, see Özbalkan, pp. 150, 162, 163.

40 Barış Gönüllülerinden Hayır Gelmez," *Kim,* December 7–13, 1965, pp. 8–9. See also Özbalkan, p. 153. An earlier attack on the Peace Corps appeared in *Yön,* April 17, 1963, when the program was just getting under way, but even this organ was relatively mild in its criticism until 1965.

did this opposition campaign become, with allegations that the volunteers were seeking information about the Kurds for the CIA, that the Foreign Ministry anounced termination of the village development program at the end of 1966. In this atmosphere, the local Peace Corps director could do little to convince his detractors. Even his press conference to answer charges of espionage and religious exploitation leveled against the corps was unavailing.[41] With the end of the village development program, however, the intensity of attack tapered off for a time.

The English teaching activities of the volunteers also presented problems. To those most suspicious of the United States, American educational activity had for some time loomed as "intellectual exploitation" or "cultural imperialism." The charge was raised that the program was part of Washington's plan to make educated Turks accept the United States and its approach to the world through the influence of language on Turkish thought processes.[42]

This sinister judgment reflected the intensifying political activism of Turkish teachers and their educational associations. No doubt some of the antipathy derived from teachers' resentment at what they considered foreign interlopers arriving on the scene, sometimes with exaggerated notions of their role in inculcating American teaching methods. Some Turkish teachers may have seen the volunteers as competitors for jobs; other may have been embarrassed by their own lack of proficiency in English relative to the standards set by their Peace Corps colleagues. Fear and suspicion of the program were also whetted by self-criticism from the volunteers themselves, some of which found its way into the Turkish press.[43]

Against this background, hostility toward the volunteer English teachers grew steadily. On November 25, 1969, the Council of Professors of the Political Science Faculty in Ankara unanimously approved a report prepared by Professor Fehmi Yavuz condemning the Peace Corps for serving the United States to the detriment of Turkish interests. This report, noting that the corps did not perform unique functions, recommended that the program be ended. In December

---

[41] Joe Alex Morris, Jr., "Turkish Press Badgers Peace Corps, Levels Spy Charges," *Washington Post,* December 23, 1966.

[42] Özbalkan, pp. 196–210.

[43] For example, Peace Corps volunteer Jonathan Pool, in a letter to the editor, "Yabancı Dil Sömürücülüğü," *Yön,* October 8, 1965, p. 2, castigated the English teaching program as "linguistic imperialism," and advocated Esperanto in its stead!

1969, Turkish secondary school teachers who were boycotting classes to demand improved working conditions and higher salaries also insisted that all Peace Corps volunteers be withdrawn from Turkey.[44] Under the pressure of university student demonstrations in 1969 and 1970, it became physically dangerous for volunteers to teach in programs connected with Hacettepe and the Middle East Technical universities in Ankara.

Members of the Peace Corps themselves were dismayed by the antipathy their presence had aroused; a number resigned to avoid being a disruptive force in the already upset Turkish educational establishment. The universities, too, had second thoughts about continuing to use volunteers as English teachers. Faced with these developments, the Peace Corps administration offered its personnel the option of leaving Turkey before completion of their tours. By the fall of 1970 the volunteers had departed almost to a man, and for all practical purposes the program had run its course in Turkey.

Opium

In recent years a new divisive issue of major proportions has emerged to trouble Turkish-American relations: opium traffic. In 1932, after much interchange over this problem between Washington and Ankara at the end of the 1920s, Turkey finally adhered to the League of Nations convention to control the production and sale of narcotics. Accordingly, Ankara passed legislation on June 24, 1933, making the production and marketing of opium gum a state monopoly. Thereafter, the question largely fell into abeyance until the end of the Second World War. At that time, the United States solicited information on Turkey's attitude toward the handling of narcotics in the postwar world. On May 14, 1945, the İnönü government reiterated its position that opium production should be restricted to a handful of countries including Turkey. Within this context, the Ankara regime declared it would "consent to every limitation of production which may be contemplated under equal conditions for all producers," and requested that the manufacture of synthetic narcotic drugs be prohibited by international agreement.[45] This stand, designed to protect Turkey's profit from the

---

[44] *Cumhuriyet,* December 11, 1969.

[45] *Bulletin,* July 8, 1945, pp. 63–69. On the opium problem during the first two decades of the Turkish Republic, see John A. De Novo, *American Interests and Policies,* pp. 245–46.

legal opium trade, seemed generally satisfactory in the more or less relaxed atmosphere in regard to narcotics during this period.

It was only when drug abuse began to emerge as a matter of intense concern in American domestic politics that opium production again became an important bone of contention in U.S. relations with Turkey. The Bureau of Narcotics and Dangerous Drugs gradually reached the conclusion that about 80 percent of the heroin illicitly introduced into the United States was derived from opium diverted from Turkish production.[46] As a result, by the mid-1960s the Johnson administration had come to focus its diplomatic efforts on Turkey to shut off the illicit supply.

Drug addiction loomed as a far less important concern to the Ankara authorities.[47] There was no appreciable drug abuse among the sons and daughters of the elite in Turkey; nor was opium use obviously rampant among the poppy farmers or indeed on any level of Turkish society. The Ankara government, therefore, was not subject to compelling internal pressures to end poppy raising. Quite the reverse. Poppy planters earned far more from this crop—even selling it legally to the state—than they could expect from other produce grown on their land; hence to restrict or abolish the crop would be an economic blow to the traditional producers. Only a strong government with resolute leadership could disregard the popular discontent that would rise from a radical change in the pattern of poppy growing.

When the United States approached Turkey to discuss the issue of the opium traffic in the mid-1960s, it found Ankara none too enthusiastic. Prime Minister Suat Hayrı Ürgüplü, as nonpartisan head of a transition government, was reluctant to initiate any far-reaching moves.[48] After Demirel came to office at the end of 1965, conversations on this matter were renewed and the new prime minister showed greater willingness to assist in stamping out the illegal opium trade. Under his administration, the parliament ratified the 1961 Single Convention on Narcotics in December 1966, formally acceding to this instrument

---

[46] U.S., Department of State, Press Release no. 108, April 2, 1970, p. 13: "Address by the Honorable Elliot L. Richardson, Under Secretary of State...." For an early Turkish view which gave Turkish production scarcely more emphasis than that elsewhere in the world, see İsmail Baltacıoğlu, "Türkiye'de ve Dünyada Uyuşturucu Madde Kaçakçılığı," Ulus, June 17–21, 1967.

[47] Vedat Uras, "Opium Poisons Friendly Relations," Outlook, July 29, 1970, p. 4; "Opium Report," ibid., p. 5; M. A. Kışlalı, "Military Aid Against Opium Poppy," ibid., September 30, 1970, p. 4.

[48] "Opium," Outlook, September 16, 1970, pp. 6–7.

on June 22 the following year. There were press reports that at one point Demirel had even committed Turkey to eradicate all opium production by 1971.[49] In the end, however, the JP government undertook to reduce the number of provinces where poppy cultivation was legal, from twenty-one in 1967 to four in 1971; this timetable was actually followed. Turkish authorities also intensified cooperation with U.S. narcotics agents in tracking down opium diverted into illicit channels. For its part, the United States in 1968 extended a $3 million loan to the Turkish government to defray the foreign exchange costs for research into substitute crops and for vehicles and other equipment needed to police restrictions on the opium trade.[50] Already in the fall of 1966, American narcotics enforcement officers had joined Turkish police in action against smugglers (their efforts had resulted in one case in a well-publicized gun battle with Turkish traffickers in Istanbul).[51] Yet for some time the cooperation of the two governments aroused neither great comment nor criticism within Turkey. Rather, it would be the outrageous conduct of American addicts and opium traffickers that would be singled out from time to time for derision in the Turkish press.

By 1970 forces were converging that would turn the opium issue into an acute threat to the Turkish-American relationship. War on drugs had become an even higher priority matter under the Nixon administration than it had been for its predecessor. In this context Washington "now decided to try to pressure Turkey publicly to close down all of its opium fields." [52] Already the reduction in the number of provinces where poppy cultivation was permitted had reached a point where it was evoking domestic reaction. Given the disenchantment that had crept into U.S.-Turkish relations by this time, it was clear that opium had become an explosive issue.

---

[49] Felix Belair, Jr., "U.S. Loan to Turkey Dismays Narcotics Officials," *New York Times,* June 14, 1970.

[50] "Richardson-Çağlayangil ve Haşhaş Ekiminin Kısılması," *Devrim,* April 28, 1970, p. 3, was very critical of the use of any part of this loan for police controls. For an American commentary on this loan, see Barbara Ellis, "Talking Turkey on Opium," *Mid East,* December 1970, p. 30.

[51] *New York Times,* October 13, 1966.

[52] George Lardner, Jr., "Moynihan Recalls Prohibition Experiment: Drug Fight Seen as Another Crisis," *Washington Post,* March 9, 1970. See also his "U.S. Narcotics Unit to Press Turkey to End Opium Trade," ibid., March 6, 1970, which reported that the Bureau of Narcotics planned to "press Turkey . . . to close down all of its opium fields."

Turkish public attention became engaged in this problem in earnest at the time of U.S. Under Secretary of State Elliot Richardson's visit to Ankara in April 1970.. The Turkish press alleged that Richardson's talks were concerned in important measure with attempting to force Turkey to eliminate—not merely to restrict and control—opium production, both legal as well as illegal. These reports stirred up a storm in journals of both the left and the right.[53] Passions were further aroused when a story in the *New York Times* [54] triggered the rumor that U.S. narcotics officials advocated withholding future economic aid to Turkey in order to force a ban on opium production. Even former Prime Minister Ürgüplü felt impelled to attack any such tactics as inadmissible interference in Turkey's domestic affairs.[55] But the crowning blow, the news that finally provoked an explosion of exasperation in Turkey against the United States, was the report of Attorney General John Mitchell's testimony before the House Ways and Means Committee on July 20, 1970. In replying to a question by Representative Charles Vanik, Mitchell had given qualified approval to the concept of economic sanctions in order to shut off opium traffic from countries including Turkey. Immediately the Ankara government denounced the idea of imposing sanctions on Turkey; such measures, it declared, would harm "Turkish-American friendship and cast suspicion on the American attitude." [56]

[53] See *Devrim,* April 28, 1970, p. 3; *Ulus,* May 5, 1970. On April 2, 1970, in Philadelphia, Richardson had publicly mentioned "the elimination of opium production" in Turkey. U.S. Department of State, Press Release no. 108, p. 13.

[54] Belair, "U.S. Loan to Turkey," *New York Times,* June 14, 1970.

[55] *Cumhuriyet,* July 10, 1970. Noting this sentiment, the American press quoted a Turkish official as saying in exasperation, "the hell with" America! "U.S. Pressure to Ban Opium Annoys Turks," *Baltimore Sun,* July 6, 1970.

[56] Alfred Friendly, "U.S. May Finance Turk Opium Cutback," *Washington Post,* July 24, 1970. In hearings before the House Committee on Ways and Means, the director of the Bureau of Narcotics and Dangerous Drugs, John Ingersoll, assured Congressman Vanik that Turkey was the source of about 80 percent of the opium illegally introduced into the United States. Thereupon Vanik stated that "economic sanction" might be the best tool to combat the situation. He suggested to Attorney General Mitchell that "we ought to set up a system that would provide for an embargo, or suspension of trade, or even suspension of relationships" until Turkey should "control the problems" of drug traffic. Mitchell replied that he quite agreed with the concept: "We are all for cutting off the source in any way that is in the best interest of this country." He added that "any legislation or administrative action that can cut down the production and . . . the illicit traffic of opium . . . be the country Turkey or another, we, at the Justice Department, would be in favor of it. . . ." U.S., House, Committee on Ways and Means, *Controlled Dangerous Substances, Narcotics and Drug Control Laws,* 91st Cong., 2nd sess., July 20, 1970, pp. 247–48.

Public reaction took still stronger form. The Mitchell testimony led to a rare unanimity of feeling: even the more moderate Turkish commentators were aghast. Not a few likened the Mitchell statement to the famous Johnson letter of 1964.

Despite the comparisons with the Johnson letter, the Mitchell statement did not mark a comparably sharp dividing line in Turkish-American relations. The Department of State promptly denied any intention of applying economic sanctions against Turkey. The foreign trade bill which had contained provisions for such action expired in committee when the U.S. Congress adjourned at the end of 1970. But it was not primarily the mitigation of American remedial measures that limited the damage to the alliance. Rather it was the fact that the opium issue had risen too suddenly to seriously affect Turkish public opinion and was not in any case the basic national issue that Cyprus had been. After the momentary outburst of feeling against American interference in mid-1970, even some frequent critics of the United States were repelled on sober second thought by the undeniable immorality of the illegal opium traffic.[57] They accepted Turkey's obligation to curb this trade as a humanitarian gesture, regardless of American action. Finally, Turkish opinion was no longer shocked at the realization that even allies could have differences—as it had been during the Cyprus difficulties. In short, while the opium crisis unquestionably burdened the alliance with additional strain it brought no shattering disillusionment.

The emotional release over the Mitchell testimony did not clear the air. Even after recriminations had died down in Turkey, the positions of the two states on the opium issue remained far apart. Washington, for its part, took the view that under the Single Convention on Narcotics a country was obliged to abandon legal poppy cultivation if it could not successfully prevent the diversion of opium into illegal channels. On the other hand, at the U.N. Narcotics Committee meeting convened at U.S. initiative in September 1970, the Turkish delegate explained that regulation, not eradication, was his government's aim.[58] Accordingly, it was incumbent on the Ankara government to show itself moving effectively to curtail the illegal traffic. But Demirel had enjoyed such a thin margin of support in parliament since the defection

---

[57] See Ecvet Güresin, "Günün Yazısı: İğne ve Çuvaldız," *Yeni Gazete,* July 30, 1970.

[58] *Yeni Gazete,* October 1, 1970.

of the JP's conservative wing early in 1970 that he was reluctant to push ahead on the opium front, particularly as the votes of the opium-producing provinces were essential to the survival of his party's parliamentary majority. Thus although the Turkish representative at the U.N. narcotics meeting promised that a licensing bill would pass parliament without delay, no such regulatory bill was brought before the assembly for debate during the winter of 1970. On the basis of existing legislation, however, the Demirel government prepared a licensing decree which was issued on March 19, 1971, a week after the resignation of the JP administration.[59]

Meanwhile, urgency was mounting on the American side. Wide-circulation magazines, from *Saturday Review* to *Newsweek* and *Parade,* featured articles on the theme, "Let's Halt Heroin at the Source." [60] Members of the U.S. Congress as well propounded the view that the Turkish government had failed to take effective action to prevent opium trafficking. Pointing to the trifling revenue earned from legal opium commerce in Turkey—"less than one-third of one percent of Turkey's [total] foreign trade"—they argued that Ankara, which had received over $5 billion in aid from the United States since the Second World War, should be willing to forego the mere $5 million a year it earned from legal opium production.[61]

Faced with the rapidly rising emotion in the United States, Prime Minister Erim in his program statement before parliament declared that Turkey recognized its "humanitarian obligation" to prevent the illegal opium traffic.[62] Yet it was obvious, in view of the urgent domestic requirements of restoring effective government and reimposing law and order, that the new administration too would find it difficult to focus on poppy cultivation as speedily as Washington would have wished. Nonetheless, a month after Secretary of State William P. Rogers visited Ankara where, *inter alia,* he discussed the drug problem, the Erim regime

---

[59] *Resmî Gazete,* March 19, 1971, pp. 12–15. This act was issued the very day Nihat Erim was named to form the new government.

[60] Horace Sutton, "Drugs: Ten Years to Doomsday?" *Saturday Review,* November 14, 1970, pp. 18–21, 59–61; "America's Battle Against the 'White Death,'" *Newsweek,* March 29, 1971, pp. 41–43; Walter Mondale, "Some of Our Friends Are Killing Us with Drugs," *Parade,* May 23, 1971, p. 13. See also U.S. House of Representatives, *Heroin and Heroin Paraphernalia: Second Report by the Select Committee on Crime* (Washington, 1971), passim.

[61] William Schulz, "Let's Halt Heroin at the Source," *Reader's Digest,* May 1971, p. 99. See also U.S. Department of State, Press Release no. 108, p. 14.

[62] *Milliyet,* April 3, 1971.

did raise the government's purchasing price of opium by two-thirds in an effort to induce more producers to sell to the authorities.[63] And on August 18, 1971, the parliament finally passed the long-awaited bill providing strict licensing procedures with severe penalties for those who violated the terms of the act.[64]

From Washington's point of view, however, these moves came too late. Already in June 1971 Ambassador William Handley had been summoned to Washington to consult on opium matters. And following brief but intensive discussions with American officials during the weeks preceding the issuance of the annual decree regulating poppy cultivation for the ensuing year, Erim had agreed to use this authority to announce the prohibition of poppy planting in Turkey after the 1972 crop year.[65]

The bargain struck between the two sides was of advantage to both. Washington, of course, got the complete ban on opium production—and at a price which, though higher than it obviously had hoped to pay at the start, was nevertheless reasonable. The United States undertook to provide $35 million over a three-year period: $15 million to compensate the poppy growers in the provinces affected by the opium ban and $20 million for investments to orient poppy farmers to other crops.[66] For their part, the Ankara leaders apparently saw the poppy agreement as part of a larger revitalization design. Erim and his associates evidently hoped for sufficient aid to develop commercial agricultural projects and related industry as a pilot venture in a broad-scale effort to raise Turkey's low agricultural productivity.[67] However it was viewed, the agreement to end poppy cultivation seemed destined to slow the process of economic disengagement that had been under way over the past few years, for it created a new sphere of involvement in which the United States was committed to remain engaged for at least three years to come.

Salutary as the arrangement to ban poppy growing was in these ways, it did not, however, remove all problems. Public opinion in Turkey was by no means unanimous in praising Erim's action. Some

---

[63] *Milliyet,* May 17, 1971.

[64] The senate voted this bill August 18, 1971; the lower house had acted on June 21. See *Resmî Gazete,* August 25, 1971, pp. 1–2.

[65] *Bulletin,* July 19, 1971, pp. 74-77; *Resmî Gazete,* June 30, 1971, p. 5.

[66] Dana Adams Schmidt, "Poppy-Ban Cost to U.S. Disclosed," *New York Times,* November 21, 1971. For earlier Turkish estimates, see *Milliyet,* July 5, August 12, November 7, 1971.

[67] *Milliyet,* June 26, 30, 1971; *Cumhuriyet,* June 28, 1971.

Turks apparently were dissatisfied with the amount of financial assistance America was to extend. Their unhappiness on this score deepened when the foreign aid bill was rejected in the U.S. Senate in October 1971 and reports reached Turkey that foreign aid cuts might endanger financial asistance to poppy growers.[68] Moreover when U.S. Secretary of Agriculture Clifford Hardin paid a brief visit to Ankara in early November to explore agricultural plans and provide technical advice on the difficult transition from poppy cultivation, his mission was widely misinterpreted. A number of Turkish journalists had expected him to bring offers of substantial additional aid. During his visit the press carried estimates evaluating Turkey's direct losses from abandoning poppy cultivation at $100 million; the investment necessary for the transition to other crops, it was estimated, would amount to an additional $300 million. Turkish Minister of Agriculture Orhan Dikmen even found it necessary to issue a formal denial of a widely circulated report that the Turkish government had decided to permit a resumption of poppy growing if the United States failed to provide sufficient compensation.[69] And in this atmosphere of doubt concerning Washington's willingness to extend adequate assistance, a group of 21 deputies introduced a bill in parliament toward the end of December 1971 to authorize renewed opium production forthwith, though on a strictly controlled basis. [70] In these circumstances, it was clear that the issue of poppy cultivation had not been entirely laid to rest.

[68] *Cumhuriyet,* November 5, 1971.

[69] *Pulse,* November 29, 1971; *Milliyet,* November 19, 1971; "Turkey May Go Back on Opium Deal After Aid Cut, AID Warns," *Daily News,* November 5, 1971. The Hardin mission issued a joint report with its Turkish counterparts, *Improving Farm Income in the Poppy Region: Recommendations of the Joint Turkish/American Agricultural Mission,* Ankara, November 1971. Hardin's resignation immediately upon his return to Washington was interpreted by some Turkish journalists as an indication that the U.S. was "playing for time" to gain additional concessions from Ankara. See *Pulse,* November 15, 1971.

[70] *Milliyet,* December 23, 1971. Of the 21 signatories of the bill, 20 were from the RPP and one from the National Reliance Party.

Part Four:
SUMMING UP

9

Reflections on the Alliance

The foregoing chapters have described the problems which have troubled the Turkish-American alliance. Much of the difficulty arises from the fact that the relationship is in transition.[1] It is a defensive arrangement against what appears to be a waning threat. The view shared by both parties when Turkey joined NATO was that for all practical purposes they enjoyed a complete congruity of interests. This outlook has not stood the test of time. With the improved climate of Turkish-Soviet relations, both Washington and Ankara have come to feel more free to accord their own individual concerns priority over those of the other party. Today, as for some years past, there is no shared vision of what the alliance should be. Turkey's connection with the United States continues, carried along by a core of common concern fortified by momentum from the past. Yet the lack of explicitly affirmed ultimate purpose breeds uncertainty.

The need for some sort of continuing association between the United States and Turkey is still widely perceived and accepted by both states, but the value and nature of the collaboration have become matters of dispute. With advances in military technology, Turkey's strategic position has shifted. In an age of Soviet-American nuclear parity, Turkish forces, with their primarily defensive role, do not add dramatically to the deterrent; nor does it seem inevitable that Turkey would be an immediate target in a general war. As a result, the idea of

---

[1] See the prepared statement of Assistant Secretary of State Joseph J. Sisco, placed in the record of the hearings of the Senate Appropriations Committee, December 2, 1969. U.S. Senate, Committee on Appropriations, *Hearings . . . on H.R. 15149 . . .* (Washington, 1969), pp. 395–99.

reevaluating the alliance has gained ground in Turkey. Responsible opposition leaders, from İnönü on down, wonder aloud how they can be sure that Washington will put itself on the line to defend Turkey in the event—however unlikely they may view it—of conflict arising, for example, out of a border dispute with the U.S.S.R. Some thus advocate narrowing the scope of collaboration by removing weapons systems, i.e., nuclear weapons, that they believe might embroil Turkey in unwanted conflict or attract a Soviet first strike in the event of hostilities. Under these circumstances, pressures continue for even more rigorous limits on American freedom of action in Turkey.

Yet amid this uncertainty and narrowing cooperation, both partners have added new burdens to the relationship, and both have sought to turn the alliance to their own purposes. The Turks perennially attempt to use their intimacy with the United States as a means of solving the Cyprus dispute in their favor; the Americans have injected new concerns, such as opium traffic, into the framework of the alliance, and seem to the Turks to be willing to risk the whole U.S.-Turkish association for the sake of such issues. Where experience has led both sides to harbor reservations about the value of their cooperation, the endeavor of each to manipulate the other by appeals to the sanctity of the collaboration is thus risky and on occasion counterproductive.

These problems have been compounded by the tendency of the mechanism of cooperation to take on a life of its own. Once set in train, cooperative arrangements have not easily or quickly responded to change. As a result, the alliance partners have gradually fallen out of phase with each other. For example, while the United States was itself cautiously increasing contacts with the Soviet Union in the 1950s with the start of summit diplomacy, Ankara was not encouraged to move in a similar direction. Eventually, therefore, it was with a sense of grievance at having been left behind in normalizing relations with their northern neighbor that the Turks in the 1960s began to be more receptive to the Kremlin's overtures. Inevitably in this situation the association with the United States was blamed for having constricted Turkish freedom of action.

The history of Turkish-American cooperation clearly shows that peripheral accouterments of the relationship, such as arrangements for privileges and immunities of U.S. personnel, are not easily adapted to shifting popular attitudes in Turkey. U.S. Sixth Fleet visits also have been scheduled in places and at times which made them a liability to the alliance. While it is obvious that government-to-government relationships cannot shift with every breeze, no effective way has yet been devised to deal with such subsidiary matters before they become acute.

In addition to these bureaucratic problems there has been a tendency on both sides to give immediate goals priority over longer-range interests. There has always been the presumption that the strengths of the alliance would permit repair of any damage caused by attention to short-run problems. Hence President Johnson, in sending his strong letter to İnönü in 1964, focused his attention on the immediate question of forestalling a Turkish landing on Cyprus without giving great consideration to the ultimate implications of his message. The use of İncirlik air base in connection with crises in the Middle East, also apparently motivated primarily by the demands of the moment, has fostered suspicion and doubt which have undercut the larger relationship. Even the shift from grant aid to loans is a case in point. For however much this change may have seemed to alleviate the immediate U.S. balance-of-payments problem, the strains of repayment may engender serious difficulties for the Turks in the longer term. As for the Turks, their desire to get certain kinds of American equipment—for instance, naval vessels—which have large upkeep costs has already caused differences with the United States, and may again lead to controversy.

Underlying all these difficulties is the fact that the United States and Turkey are states of vastly disparate size and power. For its part, Turkey is a developing country, with all the shortcomings and needs of a nation caught up in that complex process. At the same time, however, it claims equal status with the developed states in NATO. In many respects, this ambivalent role has been impossible of fulfillment. It has often led Turks to judge the success of their Western ties by the degree to which Turkey has been accepted as an equal by its partners. Yet the continuing need for aid clearly undermines Turkey's pretensions to equality. On the other hand, Turkey's allies have shared this "double vision": when it suited their purposes they have required Turkey to behave as the most developed European state; at other times they have treated the Turks with the condescension of donor toward recipient.[2]

---

[2] John White, *Pledged to Development,* p. 94, makes this point with great elegance and cogency.

In fact, Turkey has been one of the world's principal beneficiaries of American foreign aid. Vietnam excepted, of all the less developed countries, Turkey ranks second in the amount of U.S. military aid received, and third in economic aid. While the pace of assistance is now slackening, overall the Turks have received nearly $6 billion from the United States since the Second World War. Grants of military equipment represent somewhat more than half of this amount. The remainder is divided about equally between grants of economic aid and loans ($1.5 billion) for which there is an obligation for repayment.

In a situation in which a flow of material aid plays a central part in the relationship between two states, it is always hard to escape entirely the suspicion that the smaller state has become the "client" or "satellite" of the larger. Indeed, where Americans have judged Turkey to be successfully developing its economic base, hence becoming less dependent on or influenced by U.S. aid, some vocal Turks have affected to discern the growth of subtle entanglements to increase Turkey's dependence. Thus most Americans find it highly ironic, if not incomprehensible, that Turkish leftists should trumpet the accusation that their land has become a colony just when the United States is retrenching in its activities and encountering greater difficulty in its efforts to continue what it could freely do in the past. The by now apparently widespread, though ill-founded, suspicion that the country has somehow lost a measure of its independence arouses deep resentment in Turkey. This at best complicates the forms of cooperation and at worst prevents what otherwise would be mutually profitable endeavors.

To keep nationalist sensitivity within bounds, successive Ankara regimes have found it essential to cultivate at least the appearance of independent action. In order to avoid attack by politicians seeking to gain advantage in the confused political scene, Turkish administrations have felt it necessary to appear not to be toadying to the United States on any matter. All international policies—from the most immediate concerns of Cyprus to less urgent matters of, say, routine votes in the United Nations—are thus calculated first on the basis of narrow national interest. While Erim's regime is undoubtedly less responsive to normal political pressures and vote-getting considerations than were those of his predecessors, there are nonetheless strict limits on the extent to which it can accommodate the interests of the alliance.

The virtually complete independence in terms of military and economic self-sufficiency that is often urged by Turkish critics of the

United States is clearly impossible. Nor has any government in Ankara set any such ideal condition as its goal. Even the major expansion of existing defense industry called for by a number of articulate Turks is increasingly viewed as out of the question. Many in the Turkish armed forces understand the practical limitations on what Turkey can achieve in this realm; hence the military establishment is the element of society which resists most stubbornly the suggestion of diluting or dismantling the alliance. According to one astute Turkish observer who has investigated the subject in some depth, the younger officers may at times chafe under continual dependence on U.S. support but their seniors are united in appreciating the lack of a desirable alternative.[3] In other sectors of Turkish society, where the American role is less obtrusive, there is more temptation to believe that Turkey could "go it alone" if need be. Few, however, yet subscribe to the prescription advocated by the TLP for their country to cut its bonds with Western Europe and the United States—and to increase them with the Soviet bloc.

It must not be supposed that in an association of a superpower with a smaller state the advantages all lie with the larger. As we have seen, starting with the original consummation of the alliance, Ankara has been able to maneuver the United States into carrying out its desires, on occasion even when Washington was not particularly eager to do so. Especially in recent years Turkey has been able to block or divert the United States from courses that Ankara believed served American interest at some risk to the smaller ally. Naturally, neither party has universally prevailed on disputed points. But in the calculus of national self-interest the score has not been heavily one-sided.

Among the important reasons for this is the fact that the relationship with the United States has been the central facet of foreign policy for the Turks. Thus the alliance has received urgent attention from Ankara's top leadership on a sustained basis. This has meant that in disputes with America the Turkish government has usually been able to mobilize impressive domestic support. In addition, the Turks have been at times quite uninhibited in their efforts to apply political pressure. The attempt to exploit Thomas Dewey's political influence to secure a $300 million loan in the mid-1950s was a particularly striking case in point. That incident triggered almost no reaction in

---

[3] Abdi İpekçi, "23 Yıldır Yardım Alma Ahlakı İçindeyiz," *Milliyet,* May 26, 1970.

America; the hue and cry in Turkey if an analogous maneuver had been attempted by the United States is not hard to imagine. In fact, Ankara has perhaps generally been more willing than Washington to see differences in the relationship escalate. Up to now these tactics have given the Turks a certain advantage in the bargaining process. At the same time, however, this approach has insured that the course of cooperation would be punctuated by troublesome disputes.

Washington, on the other hand, has frequently been obliged to let Turkey and the American association with it share attention with a host of other problems, many indeed far more demanding of high-level talent and energy. Often, though not invariably, Turkish problems have thus tended to become acute—such as the troubles surrounding the Sixth Fleet visits or the distribution and size of the American personnel assigned to Turkey—before the various elements of the U.S. government concerned could be brought together to take appropriate remedial action. In other words, in dealing with the Turks America has often seemed to be caught short by pressures or developments in Turkey rather than to take the lead in heading off difficulties before they can affect the collaboration.

The United States has also been hampered by the image of its personnel in Turkey. Particularly, memories of the U.S. intimacy with Menderes in the 1950s continue to dog the American diplomatic establishment to some extent, inclining a number of influential leaders in other parties to fear that Washington will take sides in Turkey's internal political affairs. This suspicion has firmly crystallized in the minds of many Turkish opinion makers, embarrassing those Turks labeled America's chosen friends and alienating those who are not. Feeding as it does on Turkish domestic political considerations, this legacy has proved difficult to escape.

In addition, the impression has gained currency among elements of the elite that American personnel are often disdainful of and uninterested in Turkey. This belief has been fostered by such factors as the separateness of many Americans in Turkey—persons whose lives revolve around facilities transplanted from the United States which make extensive contact with Turks unnecessary—and the failure of most Americans to acquire any substantial command of Turkish.[4]

---

[4] For a well documented study indicating the parameters of this isolation, see Charlotte Wolff, *Garrison Community: A Study of an Overseas American Military Colony,* passim.

Similarly, the U.S. failure to develop interchange with the Turkish press during the early years of the alliance, when Turkey's anti-Communist fervor and warmth of attachment to America made building such bridges seem not at all urgent, contributed to the alienation of a large part of the newspaper world. Turkish journalists were then eager to know more about their ally; they were baffled and not a little resentful at their rejection, as they saw it, by American officialdom. Surely it was no coincidence that in the end the press, like the universities which also had a legacy of bad experience, would become one of the segments of Turkish society most hostile to the United States.

Ongoing issues: aid programs

As we have seen, the U.S. economic assistance program for Turkey is likely to end during the 1970s. Termination of this activity, however well the ground may have been prepared for its eventuality, will have inevitable impact on the collaboration as a whole. For many years economic aid has been considered an integral part of the Turkish-American cooperation and the yardstick, along with military aid, by which the value of Turkey is measured. Its passing thus will leave a gap. Naturally, the severity of the "withdrawal symptoms" will be related to the general health of the Turkish economy at the time and to its ability to maintain a rather rapid pace of advance without large amounts of concessionary aid. In turn, such factors as the demand for Turkish labor in Europe and the success of Turkey's efforts at economic integration into the Common Market will play a major role in determining the success of Turkey's development plans. While the auguries may be cautiously seen as favorable in this regard, the Turks will in the next few years run into problems of debt repayment as past obligations come due in greater amounts. Already European aid has often included debt rollovers as an integral part of the assistance offered. As the American program winds down in the 1970s, this matter will command more urgent attention. While those who are now and are likely to be at the reins of the Turkish government may accept in principle the fact that U.S. economic aid will be terminated a few years hence, it is not clear what their attitudes would be toward the net outflow of resources to the United States that is implied by an end to the economic assistance program. Thus friction over the fate of the aid program is likely as America phases out its economic assistance to Turkey.

Military assistance also poses problems for the Allies. The McNaughton plan's five-year span is over. And although Turkey has now received materiel in amounts almost equivalent to what this program implied, and indeed more in the case of the navy, the matter of what broad military equipment strategy the Turkish military establishment will follow remains undecided. If the unbalanced force concept behind the McNaughton plan no longer obtains, it has not been replaced with any agreed alternative. Pressures within Turkey to cut the size of the armed forces appear to be growing; already the regime has responded by reducing the length of military service. But with an increasingly large contingent of draft-age men in prospect every year, the Turkish military establishment is up against some basic decisions that cannot indefinitely be postponed. Nor is it clear whether Turkey can afford to reequip all three services with the most modern weapons unless such items should be forthcoming from the United States in considerably greater quantities than in the past. But rather than even holding the line, Washington seems intent on cutting military aid to Turkey. Inevitably, then, the matter of the duration and aims of the military assistance program will be one of the more urgent questions to face the Turkish-American alliance.

The İncirlik air base

Amid all the uncertainties over just where the alliance is heading, the status of facilities used by Americans stands out as a particular point at issue. To be sure, some of the immediate questions concerning these installations in Turkey have been resolved by conclusion of the Defense Cooperation Agreement of 1969. But demands for further alterations are still being voiced by some parties. Moreover, certain kinds of accidents may give additional impetus to these pressures for change. For example, when the small plane carrying the chief of the military aid mission strayed into Soviet territory at the end of October 1970, this incident was widely portrayed by the Turkish press as involving Turkey unnecessarily in a dispute of real concern only to the superpowers. In this climate, it seems likely that continuing American access to Turkish facilities will be linked more or less directly to decisions on the term and level of military assistance.

Of all the remaining American activities in Turkey, the operation of İncirlik air base as a home for U.S. strike aircraft and training squadrons looms as the most controversial and the chief source of difficulty for the future.[5] Three different concerns converge to highlight the problem of the İncirlik facility: control of nuclear weapons, the presence of American strike aircraft, and the question of using the base for what could be construed as non-NATO purposes. All these matters relate integrally to the argument over whether or not the NATO alliance, as presently constituted, could drag Turkey into a war in which she did not wish to participate, and whether or not Washington would use nuclear weapons to defend Turkey. Moreover, despite the provisions of the Defense Cooperation Agreement and assertions by Ankara officials that the Turks have full control of the base at all times, fears that American activity at İncirlik would embarrass Turkey have not been completely stilled.[6] Given memories dating from the Lebanese operation in 1958, reinforced by subsequent incidents, public concern over this facility seems destined to remain, particularly as long as the Middle East is tottering on the brink of crisis.

Opium

Among the most divisive questions that have faced the alliance in recent years has been the opium problem. While much that is salutary has flowed from Erim's agreement to end poppy cultivation, some potential problems remain. Turkish public opinion has already staked out the claim that the justification for eradication of the poppy in Turkey rests on a rapid drying up of the illegal heroin trade in the United States. If opium producers elsewhere in the world should expand their exports to take up the slack caused by Turkey's move, and if the availability of heroin in the United States were to appear to be unaffected by the decision to end planting in Turkey, pressures on the Ankara government to resume legal production are certain to grow. In any event, enforcement of provisions directed against the diversion of opium into illicit channels is bound to be an abrasive process: the participation of U.S. narcotics agents can hardly fail to arouse resentment in time.

---

[5] This was also the finding of Abdi İpekçi in his series of articles analyzing the state of Turkish-American relations in *Milliyet,* May 18-27, 1970. See especially May 21, 22, 1970.

[6] Even relatively reassuring reports, such as Metin Toker, "Batı İttifakı İçinde Türkiye'nin Savunması," *Hürriyet,* December 12-17, 1971, testify to the continuing concern in influential Turkish circles over potential embarrassment from American use of İncirlik air base.

This activity is thus likely to offer a target for those political groups most hostile to the United States. And the issue of narcotics with its deep emotional overtones on both sides, may still prove disruptive of Turkish-American collaboration.

Outlook for the alliance

The outlook for the Turkish-American alliance indicates pressures for further disengagement. In view of the problems outstanding, it would be unrealistic to conclude that the process of loosening ties between Turkey and the United States has reached bottom.[7] Once martial law is lifted, domestic forces favoring a more distant relationship with America are likely to make their voices heard again. Time and repetition have spread the message of suspicion and doubt about American motives far beyond the limited leftist circles in which it originated. Reduction in U.S. personnel will doubtless help somewhat to reassure many Turks that Washington does not nurture evil designs on their country. Decrease in numbers will also cut the odds on accidents and other abrasive incidents. But this alone does not seem sufficient to wipe away the perceived threat of the American factor, resting as it does on the notion that a superpower can and will find the means to accomplish its desires. It is as much the myth as the reality that frays the bonds between the United States and Turkey. Current U.S. moves toward a foreign policy of limited overseas involvement help to restore confidence that America has no ulterior motives. Yet at the same time they instill doubts that Washington can be relied on; and retention of any special relationship by America in Turkey inevitably provides ammunition to those who want to attack the United States.

Nor can one be sanguine about solving the structural problems relating to the disparity in size of Turkey and the United States. Some inequality is inherent in the association of any two states at such different stages of development. The most that one can hope for is that both sides will avoid adopting emotional positions that will exacerbate the inevitable strains of alliance. With notable exceptions, this has been the pattern of the past; there seems a good chance that it will prove to be the pattern of the future as well.

---

[7] See the Sisco statement before the Committee on Appropriations, December 2, 1969, op. cit., p. 397.

Developments outside Turkey may also do much to determine the course of the alliance in coming years. Among these the Cyprus dispute obviously holds a leading position. No settlement agreeable to the parties to that controversy has yet been devised, nor does one seem likely to be hammered out in the near future. Fortunately the leaders involved appear to recognize the hazards of renewed fighting; there is no indication that any of them would deliberately risk triggering military action. Nonetheless, if by accident or miscalculation widespread violence were to recur, in the heat of the moment it would be hard to reconcile Ankara's determination to protect the Turkish Cypriot community with Washington's long-standing desire to see a solution reached by peaceful means. Under these circumstances, the prospects for serious damage to Turkish-American relations would be great.

Soviet expansion in the Middle East and the buildup of Soviet units in the Mediterranean are likely to speed the process of change in Turkey's Western alliance. Paradoxically, moves by Moscow which a decade ago would almost certainly have propelled Turkey into closer ties with the United States now exacerbate strains within Turkish society and between Turkey and America. On the one hand, the Kremlin's actions are stimulating Turkish military leaders to seek major improvements in their armed forces, improvements involving new demands on the United States and a continuing high level of maintenance and operating costs. Other elements of Turkish society, however, apparently do not see the Soviet expansion as requiring such a military response; these are the Turks who are concerned at the prospect of increasing friction in relations with the U.S.S.R. As a result, they oppose participation in the "on-call" force and favor avoiding confrontation with the Kremlin in the Mediterranean. They also do not want to be identified with the United States in the Middle East, not only for fear of provoking the Soviet Union but even more to avoid alienating the Arab states by the presumption of association with Israel that might ensue.

Finally, Turkey itself is being increasingly drawn into relations with Europe, a process that in time may dilute the American connection. Through the consortium the Turks have become directly involved with their NATO partners far more than in the past. With Washington's encouragement, West Germany in particular is emerging as an important source of aid to Turkey, and the presence of the several hundred thousand Turkish workers in Germany adds to the closeness developing in this relationship. These are healthy developments for Turkey's future, but inevitably they will distract the Turks from their heretofore single-minded concentration on cooperation with the United States and cut into the sum and substance of the special relationship with America.

There is, of course, a limit to how far disengagement between Turkey and the United States is likely to go. The forces at work do not seem to imply any breaking of the alliance. Rather they suggest that a gradual erosion of Turkey's special ties with America during the 1970s will turn the focus of Turkey's Western orientation more toward Europe. By the end of the decade, therefore, the United States may come to play a role roughly on a par with that of West Germany in relation to Turkey. In essence, this shift of emphasis can be accomplished without fanfare within NATO. And in this way the chances seem promising for a close, if not quite so intimate, association between Turkey and America to continue for many years to come.

Appendix 1

AID TO TURKEY AGREEMENT

Agreement between the United States of America and Turkey *(signed at Ankara July 12, 1947; entered into force July 12, 1947)**

The Government of Turkey having requested the Government of the United States for assistance which will enable Turkey to strengthen the security forces which Turkey requires for the protection of her freedom and independence and at the same time to continue to maintain the stability of her economy; and

The Congress of the United States, in the Act approved May 22, 1947,[1] having authorized the President of the United States to furnish such assistance to Turkey, on terms consonant with the sovereign independence and security of the two countries; and

The Government of the United States and the Government of Turkey believing that the furnishing of such assistance will help to achieve the basic objectives of the Charter of the United Nations [2] and by inaugurating an auspicious chapter in their relations will further strengthen the ties of friendship between the American and Turkish peoples;

The undersigned, being duly authorized by their respective governments for that purpose, have agreed as follows:

Article I

The Government of the United States will furnish the Government of Turkey such assistance as the President of the United States may authorize to be provided in accordance with the Act of Congress approved May 22, 1947, and any acts amendatory or supplementary thereto. The Government of Turkey will make effective use of any such assistance in accordance with the provisions of this agreement.

---

* Source: TIAS 1629.

[1] Public Law 75, 80th Congress.

[2] Treaty Series 993; 59 Stat. 1031.

Article II

The Chief of Mission to Turkey designated by the President of the United States for the purpose will represent the Government of the United States on matters relating to the assistance furnished under this agreement. The Chief of Mission will determine, in consultation with representatives of the Government of Turkey, the terms and conditions upon which specified assistance shall from time to time be furnished under this agreement, except that the financial terms upon which specified assistance shall be furnished shall be determined from time to time in advance by agreement of the two governments. The Chief of Mission will furnish the Government of Turkey such information and technical assistance as may be appropriate to help in achieving the objectives of the assistance furnished under this agreement.

The Government of Turkey will make use of the assistance furnished for the purposes for which it has been accorded. In order to permit the Chief of Mission to fulfill freely his functions in the exercise of his responsibilities, it will furnish him as well as his representatives every facility and every assistance which he may request in the way of reports, information and observation concerning the utilization and progress of assistance furnished.

Article III

The Government of Turkey and the Government of the United States will cooperate in assuring the peoples of the United States and Turkey full information concerning the assistance furnished pursuant to this agreement. To this end, in so far as may be consistent with the security of the two countries:

1. Representatives of the Press and Radio of the United States will be permitted to observe freely and to report fully regarding the utilization of such assistance; and

2. The Government of Turkey will give full and continuous publicity within Turkey as to the purpose, source, character, scope, amounts, and progress of such assistance.

Article IV

Determined and equally interested to assure the security of any article, service, or information received by the Government of Turkey pursuant to this agreement, the Governments of the United States and Turkey will respectively take after consultation, such measures as the other government may judge necessary for this purpose. The Government of Turkey will not transfer, without the consent of the Government of the United States, title to or possession of any such article or information nor permit, without such consent, the use of any such article or the use or disclosure of any such information by or to anyone not an officer, employee, or agent of the Government of Turkey or for any purpose other than that for which the article or information is furnished.

Article V

The Government of Turkey will not use any part of the proceeds of any loan, credit, grant, or other form of aid rendered pursuant to this agreement for the making of any payment on account of the principal or interest on any loan made to it by any other foreign government.

Article VI

Any or all assistance authorized to be provided pursuant to this agreement will be withdrawn:

1. If requested by the Government of Turkey;
2. If the Security Council of the United Nations finds (with respect to which finding the United States waives the exercise of any veto) or the General Assembly of the United Nations finds that action taken or assistance furnished by the United Nations makes the continuance of assistance by the Government of the United States pursuant to this agreement unnecessary or undesirable; and
3. Under any of the other circumstances specified in section 5 of the aforesaid Act of Congress or if the President of the United States determines that such withdrawal is in the interest of the United States.

Article VII

This agreement shall take effect as from this day's date. It shall continue in force until a date to be agreed upon by the two governments.

Article VIII

This agreement shall be registered with the United Nations.

Done in duplicate, in the English and Turkish languages, at Ankara, this 12th day of July, 1947.

Edwin C. Wilson
For the Government of the United States

Hasan Saka
For the Government of the Republic of Turkey

215

Appendix 2

AGREEMENT IMPLEMENTING NATO STATUS OF FORCES AGREEMENT, JUNE 23, 1954

Agreement, with Minutes of Understanding, between the United States of America and Turkey Implementing Status of Forces Agreement of June 19, 1951, between the Parties to the North Atlantic Treaty *(signed at Ankara June 23, 1954; entered into force June 23, 1954)**

For the implementation of the "Agreement Between the Parties to the North Atlantic Treaty, Regarding the Status of their Forces," dated June 19, 1951,[1] the two Governments have agreed as follows:

1. All persons who are relatives of, and in accordance with United States laws or regulations, depending for support upon and actually residing with any member of a United States force or the civilian component, except those who are not United States citizens, shall also be considered dependents and will be treated in all respects as those persons defined in Article I, paragraph 1, sub-paragraph c, of the aforesaid NATO Agreement.

2. For the purpose of the application of the aforesaid NATO Agreement and of the provisions of this Agreement, persons "who are in the employ of" the United States armed services, within the meaning of Article I-1 (b) of the aforesaid NATO Agreement, and without prejudice to the other requirements of that Article, shall include employees of United States military organizations, employees of United States Government departments, Post Exchanges, and recreational organizations for military personnel, Red Cross and United Services Organization personnel, and technical representatives of contractors with the United States forces who are assigned to United States military organizations in Turkey. All of these persons are subject to United States military law. Should any other specific categories become involved, the United States Government would wish to discuss their

---

* Source: TIAS 3020; 5 UST 1468, 1474-75.
[1] TIAS 2846; 4 UST, pt. 2, p. 1792.

inclusion in this paragraph with the authorities of the Turkish Government.

3. Residence documents to the members of the civilian component and the dependents described in paragraph 1 of this Agreement, as well as the dependents described in Article I, paragraph 1, sub-paragraph c, of the Agreement regarding the Status of NATO Forces, will be issued without fees, except for administrative expenses incurred in issuing the documents.

4. It is the agreed understanding of the Parties that reasonable quantities of provisions, supplies and other goods imported for the exclusive use of United States personnel, directly by special military agencies of the United States, such as post exchanges, commissaries, and officers' clubs, shall be accorded duty-free entry under the terms of Article XI, paragraph 4, of the aforesaid NATO Agreement in accordance with arrangements to be agreed with the appropriate Turkish authorities. It is understood that such provisions, supplies and other goods will be subject to agreed certification by an authorized United States official, and to inspection by Turkish customs for conformance with the certificates which shall be drawn up in accordance with the agreed arrangements mentioned above. It is further agreed that such special military agencies as post exchanges, commissaries, and officers' clubs will be permitted to operate at agreed locations without licenses, inspections or taxes and other charges. Categories of articles to be agreed between appropriate United States and Turkish authorities may be sold by these official United States military agencies only to authorized United States personnel. Administrative measures shall be taken by United States military authorities, in cooperation with the appropriate Turkish authorities, to prevent the resale or transfer in any way of merchandise sold under the provisions of this paragraph to persons not entitled to purchase items from such agencies, and generally to prevent the abuse of the facilities provided for in this paragraph.

5. In the implementation of Article XI of the aforesaid NATO Agreement, with respect to the duty-free entry of personal and household effects, it is understood that the free importation of such effects will be permitted from two months prior to six months after the arrival of the individual concerned or of any of his dependencies.

6. It is understood that sales of personal and household effects and automobiles, taking place between individuals entitled to customs-free entry, are not subject to Turkish taxes.

7. It is understood that in the case of any damages in Turkey, caused by persons referred to in paragraph 2 above who are not paid from appropriations made to the United States Department of Defense, which require, under the provisions of Article VIII of the aforesaid NATO Agreement, the payment of an amount in order to satisfy the claimant with respect to such damages, the Turkish Government shall pay such amount. Procedures with respect to the reimbursement to the Turkish Government of such amounts shall be the subject of special arrangements agreed between the two Governments.

In witness whereof the respective representatives, duly authorized for the purpose, have signed the present Agreement.

Done at Ankara, Turkey, in duplicate, in the English and Turkish languages, each of which shall be of equal authenticity, this twenty-third day of June, 1954.

For the Government of the
United States of America
Avra M. Warren

For the Government of the
Republic of Turkey
F. Köprülü

Minute of Understanding with Respect to Paragraph Four of the "Agreement between the United States of America and the Republic of Turkey Relative to the Implementation of the 'Agreement between the Parties to the North Atlantic Treaty, Regarding the Status of Their Forces' "

It is not the intention of the Turkish Government to prohibit the sale of articles normally sold through United States special military agencies.

A. M. W.   K.

Minute of Understanding Regarding Paragraph Seven of the Agreement between the Republic of Turkey and the United States of America Relative to the Implementation of the "Agreement between the Parties to the North Atlantic Treaty Regarding the Status of Their Forces"

It is understood that the United States Government is able to accept responsibility for repayment only with respect to claims arising from the acts of employees paid from appropriated funds of the Department of Defense. With respect to claims arising from the acts of all other members of the civilian component it is understood that the United States will exercise its good offices to make satisfactory arrangements with the responsible entities for reimbursing the Turkish Government. However, the United States Government under existing laws can accept no financial liability with respect to the latter category of claims.

A. M. W.   K.

Appendix 3

COOPERATION, MARCH 5, 1959

Agreement of Cooperation between the Government of the United States of America and the Government of the Republic of Turkey *(signed at Ankara March 5, 1959; entered into force March 5, 1959)**

The Government of the United States of America and the Government of Turkey,

Desiring to implement the Declaration in which they associated themselves at London on July 28, 1958; [1]

Considering that under Article I of the Pact of Mutual Cooperation signed at Baghdad on February 24, 1955,[2] the parties signatory thereto agreed to cooperate for their security and defense, and that, similarly, as stated in the above-mentioned Declaration, the Government of the United States of America, in the interest of world peace, agreed to cooperate with the Governments making that Declaration for their security and defense;

Recalling that, in the above-mentioned Declaration, the members of the Pact of Mutual Cooperation making that Declaration affirmed their determination to maintain their collective security and to resist aggression, direct or indirect;

Considering further that the Government of the United States of America is associated with the work of the major committees of the Pact of Mutual Cooperation signed at Baghdad on February 24, 1955;

Desiring to strengthen peace in accordance with the principles of the Charter of the United Nations; [3]

Affirming their right to cooperate for their security and defense in accordance with Article 51 of the Charter of the United Nations;

---

* Source: TIAS 4191; 10 UST 320.

[1] TIAS 4084; 9 UST 1077.

[2] British Command 9429, Miscellaneous No. 5 (1955).

[3] TS 993; 59 Stat. 1031.

Considering that the Government of the United States of America regards as vital to its national interest and to world peace the preservation of the independence and integrity of Turkey;

Recognizing the authorization to furnish appropriate assistance granted to the President of the United States of America by the Congress of the United States of America in the Mutual Security Act of 1954,[4] as amended, and in the Joint Resolution to Promote Peace and Stability in the Middle East;[5] and

Considering that similar agreements are being entered into by the Government of the United States of America and the Governments of Iran and Pakistan, respectively,

Have agreed as follows:

Article I

The Government of Turkey is determined to resist aggression. In case of aggression against Turkey, the Government of the United States of America, in accordance with the Constitution of the United States of America, will take such appropriate action, including the use of armed forces, as may be mutually agreed upon and as is envisaged in the Joint Resolution to Promote Peace and Stability in the Middle East, in order to assist the Government of Turkey at its request.

Article II

The Government of the United States of America, in accordance with the Mutual Security Act of 1954, as amended, and related laws of the United States of America, and with applicable agreements heretofore or hereafter entered into between the Government of the United States of America and the Government of Turkey, reaffirms that it will continue to furnish the Government of Turkey such military and economic assistance as may be mutually agreed upon between the Government of the United States of America and the Government of Turkey, in order to assist the Government of Turkey in the preservation of its national independence and integrity and in the effective promotion of its economic development.

---

[4] 68 Stat. 832; 22 U.S.C. § 1751 note.

[5] 71 Stat. 5; 22 U.S.C. §§ 1961–1965.

Article III

The Government of Turkey undertakes to utilize such military and economic assistance as may be provided by the Government of the United States of America in a manner consonant with the aims and purposes set forth by the Governments associated in the Declaration signed at London on July 28, 1958, and for the purpose of effectively promoting the economic development of Turkey and of preserving its national independence and integrity.

Article IV

The Government of the United States of America and the Government of Turkey will cooperate with the other Governments associated in the Declaration signed at London on July 28, 1958, in order to prepare and participate in such defensive arrangements as may be mutually agreed to be desirable, subject to the other applicable provisions of this agreement.

Article V

The provisions of the present agreement do not affect the cooperation between the two Governments as envisaged in other international agreements or arrangements.

Article VI

This agreement shall enter into force upon the date of its signature and shall continue in force until one year after the receipt by either Government of written notice of the intention of the other Government to terminate the agreement.

Done in duplicate at Ankara, this fifth day of March, 1959.

For the Government of the
United States of America
Fletcher Warren

For the Government of the
Republic of Turkey
Fatin Rüştü Zorlu

Appendix 4

DUTY STATUS AGREEMENT

Duty Status Agreement *(entered into force September 24, 1968)**

Republic of Turkey
Ministry of Foreign Affairs
Note No: 6302/5399   *Ankara, September 24, 1968*

Excellency:

I have the honor to acknowledge the receipt of Your Note of September 24, 1968 which reads as follows:

"Excellency:

I have the honour to refer to discussions between representatives of our two Governments concerning duty certificates in implementation of Article VII, paragraph 3 (a) (ii) of the Agreement between the Parties to the North Atlantic Treaty regarding the Status of Their Forces and have the honour to propose the following:

Article I

In case of offenses arising out of any act or omission done in the performance of official duty, the duty certificates will, in conformity with the spirit and the letter of the Agreement between the Parties of the North Atlantic Treaty regarding the Status of Their Forces and according to the practices in the other NATO countries, be issued by the authorities of the Sending State and will be put into effect by the authorities of the Government of Turkey in conformity with the spirit and the letter of the Agreement between the Parties of the North Atlantic Treaty regarding the Status of Their Forces, and according to the practices in the other NATO countries.

---

*Source: *Resmî Gazete,* July 24, 1969, pp. 2-6.

Article II

In implementation of Article I, the following procedures shall apply:

A. Upon being informed that the accused is entitled to benefit from the provisions of the aforesaid Agreement, the Public Prosecutor of the locality where the offense has been committed shall inquire of the Turkish General Staff, through the Ministry of Justice, whether the offense arose out of any act or omission done in the performance of official duty. The Turkish General Staff shall then inquire of the concerned authorities of the Sending State about this matter. (If the Sending State is the United States, the concerned authority will be the highest ranking commanding officer of the United States Forces in Turkey.)

B. If after investigation, the concerned authorities of the Sending State deem that a certificate, attesting that the alleged offense arose out of any act or omission done in the performance of official duty, should be issued in conformity with the provisions of Article I above, one copy of that certificate shall be forwarded immediately to the Turkish General Staff and another to the commander of the unit to which the accused is assigned or attached.

C. If accepted by the TGS the duty certificate will be sent through the Ministry of Justice, to the Public Prosecutor of the locality where the offense has been committed. Upon receipt of the duty certificate from the Ministry of Justice, the action against the accused shall be suspended by the competent judicial authorities, and the file of the accused shall be sent to the TGS. The TGS will then, except in cases covered by paragraphs (D) and (E) below, forward the file to the concerned authorities of the Sending State. The case against the accused will then be dismissed. The concerned authorities of the Sending State will officially inform the TGS of the outcome of the case.

D. If not found acceptable by the TGS and withdrawn by the concerned authorities of the Sending State, the TGS will, through [the] Ministry of Justice, so notify the Public Prosecutor of the locality where the offense has been committed. The Public Prosecutor of the said locality will, through the Ministry of Justice, inform the Turkish General Staff of the outcome of the case. The latter will in turn transmit this information to the concerned authorities of the Sending State.

E. If the duty certificate is not found acceptable by the TGS and not withdrawn by the concerned authorities of the Sending State, the

226

Ministry of Foreign Affairs will be informed with a view to reaching an agreement through negotiations with the diplomatic representative of the Sending State with the participation of TGS and a military representative of the Sending State and in consultation with other concerned Turkish authorities. In the meantime the duty certificate, as well as the legal action against the accused, will be suspended without affecting the availability of the accused for trial by Turkish courts if the duty certificate is not found acceptable. The outcome of these negotiations such as the acceptance of the duty certificate or its withdrawal by the concerned military authorities of the Sending State will be communicated to the Public Prosecutor of the locality where the offense has been committed, in the same manner as foreseen in paragraphs (C) and (D) above, for appropriate action."

I have the honor to propose that, if the foregoing is acceptable to the Government of Turkey, this note and Your Excellency's reply concurring therein shall constitute an agreement between our two Governments which shall enter into force on the date of Your Excellency's reply. It is the understanding of my Government that the agreement concerning duty certificates contained in the aides-memoire which were exchanged on July 28, 1956, will be considered terminated on that same date.

Accept, Excellency, the renewed assurances of my highest consideration.

His Excellency	His Excellency
İhsan Sabri Çağlayangil,	Parker Thompson Hart
Minister of Foreign Affairs	*Ambassador of the*
of the Republic of Turkey, Ankara	*United States of America*

Minute of Understanding

Republic of Turkey
Ministry of Foreign Affairs
Note No: 6302/5400   *Ankara, September 24, 1968*

Excellency:

I have the honor to acknowledge the receipt of Your Note of September 24, 1968, which reads as follows:

"Excellency:

I have the honour to refer to my note to you of this date, referring to discussion between representatives of our two Governments, concerning duty certificates in implementation of Article VII, paragraph 3 (a) (ii) of the Agreement between the Parties to the North Atlantic Treaty regarding the Status of Their Forces and wish to propose the following agreed minute:

The United States negotiators have indicated that the practices in other NATO countries are to accept the U.S.-issued duty certificate with provision for discussion of exceptional cases.

The Turkish negotiators have indicated that the phrase 'put into effect' corresponds to 'işlem görecektir' in Turkish.

In the interest of fulfilling the provisions of the NATO SOFA, which require than an accused person of the Sending State shall receive prompt and speedy trial, and in the interest of the proper and effective administration of justice, the Government of Turkey will permit the Sending State to take appropriate action under its own laws in the case at hand when negotiations have not resulted in an agreement within two months. The TGS will forward the duty certificate through the Ministry of Justice to the Public Prosecutor concerned. The case against the accused will then be dismissed. The file of the accused will be forwarded to the concerned authorities of this Sending State. The Government of Turkey will take the necessary steps with the appropriate authorities to give effect to this provision. The issues upon which agreement had not been reached shall continue to be the subject of discussion with a view to achieving a resolution to be applied in future cases involving similar issues.

I would appreciate being informed of the concurrence of Your Excellency's Government in the foregoing agreed minute.

Accept, Excellency, the renewed assurances of my highest consideration."

In reply, I have the honor to inform You that my Government is in concurrence with the foregoing agreed minute.

Accept, Excellency, the assurances of my highest consideration.

His Excellency
Parker Thompson Hart
Ambassador of the
United States of America
Ankara

His Excellency
İhsan Sabri Çağlayangil
Minister of Foreign Affairs

Appendix 5

REPORT OF TURKISH PRIME MINISTER SÜLEYMAN DEMIREL'S PRESS CONFERENCE, FEBRUARY 7, 1970*

Prime Minister Explains Bilateral Treaties and NATO

ANKARA—On Saturday at his 17th press conference the Prime Minister explained the bilateral agreements signed between Turkey and the U.S.A. under article 3 of the NATO Pact and the new NATO strategy. He said that over the 25 years of the alliance, 91 bilateral agreements had been signed and 54 of them had been in force when the JP had come to power in October 1965. Of these agreements 13 had been signed under the 1954 Military Facilities Agreement and were the most important.

"Above all I should like to point out that no bilateral agreement against the national interests has been signed in the JP period. On the contrary, intelligence flights, which were conducted on the basis of an agreement signed previously, were stopped on 28 December 1965, shortly after the JP came to office when an American intelligence aircraft was lost in the Black Sea. This incident was made the excuse to revise the agreements concerning bilateral defence setups.

"It is observed that while criticisms are made about bilateral agreements, points concerning multilateral setups are confused with bilateral agreements.

"At the talks we conducted with the U.S.A. we did not discuss the subjects concerning multilateral cooperation. As is known, multilateral defence setups in NATO are infrastructural, atomic support and communication arrangements. Under the infrastructural arrangements installations totalling TL4,000 m., such as airfields, communication installations, war headquarters, fuel pipelines, early detection radar systems, have all been turned over to the Turkish Armed Forces.

---

* Source: *Pulse* (Ankara), no. 1661, February 9, 1970.

"The subject to which our Government has given priority has been the Military Facilities Agreement signed on 23 June 1954 and the agreements concluded in connection with it."

Explaining the nature of the 13 agreements signed under the 1954 Military Facilities Agreement, Demirel said, "Some of these agreements concern the radar installations needed both for the defence of our country and that of our NATO allies. Because some of these have been taken over by the Turkish Armed Forces, at present only the Karamürsel, Sinop and Diyarbakır bases have a joint defence installation nature. Other of the agreements concern the cooperation between the Turkish and American Ground, Naval and Air Forces. The rest concern airfields. Of these only the İncirlik airfield in Adana is now in existence as a joint defence force.

"The aircraft in İncirlik which are located there in accordance with the NATO joint defence plans constitute part of NATO's general deterrent force. They come under the Supreme Allied Command for Europe (SACEUR) and this Command is attached to the NATO Council. As is known, Turkey is represented in the NATO Council. The NATO Council cannot take a decision without the participation of Turkey. And without the decision of the Council SACEUR cannot order the NATO-assigned aircraft in İncirlik to take action. It is out of the question for these aircraft to be used for any purpose other than NATO defence. For these reasons, it is impossible for these aircraft to drag Turkey into a war against her will, without any reason.

"The radar stations are passive defence installations. They are needed for both Turkey's and other NATO members' defence. They help to detect dangers against Turkey and NATO members. It is the most natural sovereignty right for every country to take measures concerning its defence. As is seen, there is nothing against sovereignty or provocative in these agreements.

"The NATO Armies, the Turkish Armed Forces among them, are equipped with nuclear arms in accordance with NATO resolutions. These arms menace no one. They are entirely defensive and short-range. They make deterrence more effective. They can be used in no way without Turkey's consent. They constitute no added menace or threat for Turkey. On the contrary, they gain for her an additional defence power."

Passing on to a comparison of what the situation was when the Justice Party came to power and what it was when it signed the Joint

Defence Cooperation Agreement on 3 July 1969, Demirel said, "I have explained above the nature and content of the 13 agreements. What did we do with the Joint Defence Cooperation Agreement of 3 July 1969?

"First we abrogated the Military Facilities Agreement of 23 June 1954. Secondly under the light of the past practice we introduced a discipline with a series of principles. We made a model covering all the agreements. This model will be applied to all 13 agreements and the adjustments that will be needed will be made. . . .

"At the end of 1965 there were airfields and installations, electronic intelligence centres, communications posts and support installations active in Turkey under the 1954 Military Facilities Agreement and other bilateral agreements signed within it. In these installations they used to run flight, periodic training, electronic intelligence, communications and scientific activities. In an area of 35,000 'donums (one 'donum' = 1,000 sq. meters) in more than ten places in our country, there were about 23,000 military and civilian Americans with their relatives.

"This was the actual situation when we took up office at the end of 1965. As for the legal situation: In the over ten years preceding 1965 there were scattered agreements concluded by several authorities not based on any principles. Besides, we were up against a practice whose legal grounds and content was not known and which led to great difficulty and complaints.

"What have we done in the question of the bilateral agreements? We stopped such flights: as from 28 December 1965 after an American reconnaissance aircraft was lost in the Black Sea. We have not allowed these flights since.

"After long and meticulous preparations and two years, four months of negotiations we signed the 3 July 1969 agreement and abrogated the 1954 Military Facilities Agreement.

"The agreements based on the Military Facilities Agreement will also be reviewed quickly and those which do not conform to the principles of the 3 July 1969 agreement will also be abrogated. The talks on this topic are continuing between the military authorities of the two countries."

Demirel then said that the JP Government had signed 15 bilateral agreements with the U.S.A. since it had taken over on 27 October 1965. All these agreements concerned military aid to Turkey under which

Turkey received over $600 m. aid in five years. None of the agreements concerned the foundation of a new installation or the expansion of the activities in any existing one. And none contained any provision that would drag Turkey into a war against her will.

"Since 1965, among the installations set up under the Military Facilities Agreement, the joint defence installations in Anadolukavağı and in Gölbası near Ankara have been completely turned over to our Armed Forces. Agreement has been reached for the total delivery to the Turkish Armed Forces of the Izmir (Çiğli) airfield and the Trabzon and Samsun radar installations. The actual units have now left Çiğli and only maintenance personnel and the persons in charge of delivery remain. By 30 June 1970 the base will be totally taken over by the Turkish Armed Forces and their resources and ability will thus be increased by approximately $40-45 m.

"At present there are joint defence installations run under the 3 July 1969 agreement in five places in our country. These are the radar installations in Kocaeli (Karamürsel), Diyarbakır (Pirincilik) and Sinop, the airfield in Adana (İncirlik) and the headquarters and logistics installations in Ankara (Balgat). The total area they cover is 19,500 'donum's. On 1 January 1970 the American military and civilian personnel, including the platoon-company size units in the transport terminals in Istanbul, Izmir and Iskenderun, totalled about 7,000. When the Samsun, Trabzon and Çiğli installations are completely taken over by our Armed Forces by 1 July 1970 the number will be reduced to about 6,000."

The Prime Minister also explained the principles which the Ministry of Foreign Affairs and the General Staff had established for the 3 July 1969 agreement. They had been approved by the National Security Council. The following were the highlights of the agreement which had been read in Parliament:

"1. All activities run in Turkey under joint defence cooperation will be based on the mutual cooperation foreseen in article 3 of the NATO Pact and will never exceed the limits of NATO commitments.

"2. The commitments in question will conform to the scope and principles of the U.N. Charter.

"3. The agreements and application of them will be run under the principles of mutual sovereignty and equality.

"4. No action can be taken for the foundation of a joint defence installation or its activities without Turkey's consent.

"5. The property rights of the areas where joint defence installations are set up belong to the Turkish Republic. The installations to be set up on them will also be the Turkish Republic's property. They are not even leased.

"6. The control of the Turkish Government over the joint defence installations and the activities from them will be full and absolute. Turkey will inspect all these installations as she finds it necessary to ensure that they are used in accordance with the agreements.

"7. Turkey will locate as many military and civilian personnel in these installations as she wishes.

"8. The foreign personnel in these installations will be subject to the NATO Forces' Status Convention signed on 19 June 1951 and the agreement signed on 23 June 1954.

"9. The Turkish Government will allow the U.S. Government to engage in any of the joint defence activities in Turkey only after it has full and detailed knowledge of them.

"10. The nature, scope and period of each of the joint defence installations have to be approved by the Turkish Government.

"11. The amount, arms and equipment and supply provisions of the American personnel to take up duty in the installations under the NATO Forces' Status Convention will be subject to the provisions which will enable the control of the Turkish Government.

"12. The Turkish Government will be able to take every restrictive measure for the maintenance of the national interests, throughout national emergency cases.

"13. The provisions of the Montreux Convention have been reserved.

"14. Joint defence installations are based on the principle of joint utilization.

"15. The principle in the construction, operation and maintenance of joint defence installations is to use a Turkish labour force.

"16. The material, equipment and supply goods to be required by the U.S. for the purposes of the agreement will be procured from Turkey, as much as possible.

"17. Foreign employees and their relatives to be employed by American personnel assigned to the joint defence installations will have to observe the legislation of the Turkish Republic.

"18. A special regulation conforming to the Turkish legislation will be in force in joint defence installations in connection with the hoisting of national flags.

"19. Disagreements concerning the application of the agreement will be solved through mutual negotiation and the Council of Ministers will be able to stop the practice pending the solution of the disagreement.

"20. Even though the agreement will be in force as long as the parties concerned are attached to the NATO Pact, each one of the parties will be able to ask for negotiations for the amendment or denunciation of the agreement.

"The U.S.A. has also pledged with the agreement to extend aid for Turkey's defence efforts, in accordance with her constitution."

Demirel also explained that the rules since 1956 about the trial of Americans committing crimes in Turkey had been changed and they now conformed to the rules of other NATO countries and further than this, still it was agreed through exchange of Notes on 24 September 1968 that the Turkish General Staff would have the last word on deciding whether or not the American concerned was on duty when the crime was committed.

"There is no provocative installation in Turkey that would attract lightning to Turkey. All joint defence installations are legitimate defence arrangements. They have no provocative or aggressive characteristic. To oppose such arrangements is tantamount to wanting Turkey to be blind and deaf. For the maintenance of the deterrence power of the Alliance certain intelligence information is needed. There are no strategic missiles in Turkey. The installations in Turkey are passive installations. The squadron allotted to NATO in İncirlik cannot be used outside NATO plans which are totally defensive. Turkey has a say in the preparation of NATO plans. It is natural that the procedure foreseen in our Constitution will be observed in taking these decisions."

Answering criticisms about the period of the 3 July 1969 agreement and the procedure concerning its denunciation, the Prime Minister said that it was normal and logical for the agreement to remain in force as long as the NATO Pact was in force. Yet Turkey had the possibility of denouncing the agreement even if NATO membership continued. "Also it was foreseen in the agreement that joint defence activities and installations have certain periods. These periods will be established by the application agreements concerned. The Government has the right to put an end to them before the periods stipulated in the application agreements, when necessary.

"The claim that putting an end to the 3 July 1969 agreement and other application agreements dealing with joint defence will take four and a half years is not true. It is understood that this conclusion is derived from adding together the maximum periods for the procedure involved in denunciation. When denunciation is found necessary first a six-month consultation period is accepted. If the situation necessitating the denunciation is not eliminated in this period, with a notification the denunciation will be made and then the liquidation period will begin. The durations of these periods will change in every special situation and will not in any case exceed two years. Under this the agreement will disappear in two years at the most, following the six-month consultation period. This is the maximum period and the term 'within' enables its realization before. Even under the maximum periods the denunciation is materialized in two and a half years, after which period all activities foreseen in the agreement stop. The liquidation period involves only activities about the liquidation."

The Prime Minister then said that ratification of the 3 July 1969 agreement by the Government was in conformity with article 65 of the constitution and Law 244.

Answering criticisms about NATO and the flexible response strategy, Demirel said that when a nuclear balance was struck between East and West the massive nuclear retaliation policy had necessarily been changed by the flexible response. "An aggression against Turkey will be of a nature to change the strategic balance of Europe. The geo-strategic characteristics of Turkey does not allow an aggression against our country to remain in a narrow area. Because an aggression against Turkey would change the strategic balance of Europe, the potential aggressor cannot risk an operation against her unless it risks engaging in a very extensive operation. When this is the case, aggressions against Turkey necessarily involve the general nuclear guarantee secured for Europe. Consequently it is impossible to envisage a local conventional or nuclear war against Turkey by any rational aggressor. There is no sign in the NATO strategy to indicate that Turkey or any other European country is considered a dispensable area."

Demirel then said that there was only one strategy in NATO and that there was no centre/wing differentiation in the new NATO strategy. The only difference being the existence of allied forces in the centre, in Germany and not in the wings. NATO had offered Turkey the same thing, by placing an allied division on the Soviet frontier but it had been rejected by Turkey.

He noted that Turkish forces had fought in Austria, Bulgaria and Rumania in 1916 in Ottoman times. "Under the NATO defence arrangements the Turkish forces are responsible exclusively for their own territory. It is out of the question for any of our units to take up duty outside Anatolia or Thrace.

"For the fulfillment of mutual aid commitments in the NATO alliance and for the execution of joint defence plans, infrastructural installations such as airfields, submarine shelters, oil pipelines and depots, early detection and warning systems, a joint communications network have been built in our country with NATO aid. Also passive land intelligence systems and logistics organizations are met with bilateral arrangements with the U.S.A. within the NATO Pact. Without such arrangements joint defence plans cannot possibly be executed effectively. Therefore the claims that Turkey undertook unnecessary commitments which do not come under NATO are untrue."

Turkey had been equipped with tactical nuclear arms according to NATO resolutions—"At present there are in Turkey ground launching devices and nuclear arms with limited ranges directed at the target from air and also the NIKE system against an air raid. All are to be used for tactical defence purposes. . . .

"In accordance with the established rules of NATO, tactical nuclear arms in Turkey are subject to the double key system and it is impossible to use them without Turkey's consent. The launching devices of tactical nuclear arms in Turkey are in the hands of the personnel of the Turkish Armed Forces and no other personnel has the right or possibility to use these arms. After NATO's decision to use these tactical weapons, taking over the warheads; placing them in devices and aircraft; directing and firing them at the target or flying the aircraft are entirely in the authority of the Turkish personnel and pilots."

Demirel said that in emergencies, NATO countries could use nuclear arms against a nuclear aggression without a decision of the NATO Council. The NATO Nuclear Planning Council had discussed the matter at its November 1969 meeting in Washington and taken very delicate and secret resolutions. NATO established the necessary procedure and certain criteria for the timely utilization of tactical nuclear arms by the members. "NATO countries are determined to further develop these procedures and criteria. It is our conviction that this stage attained in the alliance in this field is truly satisfactory under international realities today and they reinforce NATO's deterrence."

Answering the criticism that the U.S. could bomb Soviet targets from İncirlik and thus expose Turkey to a nuclear counter-blow, the Prime Minister noted that both the Soviet Union and the U.S. knew that even a limited nuclear aggression would soon lead to total nuclear retaliation by the other party, considering the importance of even seconds in such an eventuality. "When this is the case, the American desire to put Turkey in trouble would be tantamount to putting herself in trouble and it is inconceivable."

About the criticisms that NATO commitments and aid were not automatic under article 5 of the Pact, Demirel said that it was indeed so under article 5 but a necessary shortcoming. "In a collective security system formed by independent and sovereign States the agreement could not have been expected to have been otherwise. Like Turkey, other NATO countries are also tied by the provisions of their constitutions and the will of their parliaments." If it had been otherwise it would have been against article 110 of the Turkish constitution. However, there were certain measures to counter this shortcoming in NATO. These joint measures were: the NATO early detection and warning system; the communications and intelligence network; the joint defence plans; the Mobile Force of the European Allied Command.

He explained that under the Mobile Force arrangement light infantry battalions composed of German, U.S., Benelux, British, Italian and Canadian forces and NATO air support forces would come to the political tension area in NATO even before the outbreak of war. Thus the aggressor would find itself facing the forces of eight NATO countries in addition to the national forces of that country. This force was not very big, but it was a "live guarantee and assurance" that the countries concerned and NATO as a whole would be beside the member subjected to aggression.

Demirel said that the same was the case with the NATO naval "on-call force" which would be composed of U.S., British and Italian warships and would also be participated in by Turkey and Greece. The criticism that this would enlarge Turkey's responsibility area was not valid because Turkey was totally free about complying with each "call." Also, the mission of the Turkish participant would be established by Turkey herself. Therefore, there was no reason for anxiety. The matter was still under study, he added.

In conclusion, Demirel said, "Had Turkey felt secure enough outside NATO she would not have undertaken any commitment. It is also obvious that remaining outside NATO makes Turkey a more comfortable target for those who cherish aggressive ambitions. These calculations have been made today, as was done before, the answers have been given and the decision taken accordingly. . . . The claims that Turkey will be subjected to an aggression if she remains neutral should be taken as considerations with ulterior motives rather than valid ones."

Answers to questions: Jupiter missiles had come to Turkey with the 30 June 1960 agreement and had been removed because they had become obsolete according to one rumour and because of the Soviet-American bargaining during the Cuban crisis, according to another. The news reports were wrong that the American aircraft in Libya had been brought to İncirlik. The number of aircraft in the İncirlik base depended on the table of organization established, he said.

The Prime Minister ruled out the possibility that tactical nuclear arms would mean the destruction of Turkey. "Even if this consideration had been the case, still we could not have given up tactical arms," he pointed out.

Turkey had taken no initiative about concluding a non-aggression pact with anyone.

On being told that a Mr. Max Stuart had said that Turkey would be exhausted within four or five days in the event of an aggression, Demirel said that Turkey was no easy mouthful to swallow, as everyone had admitted. "We cannot accept such a fate of four or five days. Turkey's defence strategy is based on the defence of Turkey house by house, tree by tree, hill by hill, town by town, village by village, inch by inch," he said.

Milliyet reported from Berlin on Saturday that the renowned Dr. Mansholt of the EEC had said that he saw in Turkey's entry into the Common Market a "black end and bankruptcy" for her. He had said that Turkey could sell the Community no agricultural goods, nor was it anything but a dream to imagine that Turkey could sell cars to the EEC. Asked to comment on these words, Demirel said, "It is not right to seek abroad the authorities who think of Turkey better than us. Let everyone deal with his own affairs. Why should Turkey enter into a setup which would make her go bankrupt? Have we lost all wisdom?"

He wound up by saying that Turkey could use NATO arms herself and had done so in Cyprus.

Chronology

U.S.-TURKISH RELATIONS 1945-1971

1945	President İsmet İnönü Prime Minister Şükrü Saracoğlu Foreign Minister Hasan Saka	U.S. Ambassador Edwin Wilson (June)*	Feb. Mar. July	Turks declare war on Germany U.S.S.R. denounces 1925 Treaty with Turkey Potsdam Conference
1946	President İsmet İnönü Prime Minister Recep Peker Foreign Minister Hasan Saka	U.S. Ambassador Edwin Wilson	Jan. Apr. June Aug.– Sept.	DP founded USS *Missouri* visits Istanbul RPP wins elections Soviet notes on the Straits
1947	President İsmet İnönü Prime Minister Hasan Saka Foreign Minister Necmeddin Sadak	U.S. Ambassador Edwin Wilson	Mar. July Sept.	Truman Doctrine Treaty on U.S. aid to Turkey Devaluation of Turkish lira
1948	President İsmet İnönü Prime Minister Hasan Saka Foreign Minister Necmeddin Sadak	U.S. Ambassador George Wadsworth (Oct.)	July	U.S.-Turkish Treaty on Economic Cooper- ation (Marshall Plan)
1949	President İsmet İnönü Prime Minister Şemsettin Günaltay Foreign Minister Necmeddin Sadak	U.S. Ambassador George Wadsworth	Apr.	Formation of NATO (Turkey not a member)
1950	President Celâl Bayar Prime Minister Adnan Menderes Foreign Minister Fuat Köprülü	U.S. Ambassador George Wadsworth	May July Sept.	DP election victory Turkish brigade to Korea announced Turkey invited to join NATO Mediterranean military planning
1951	President Celâl Bayar Prime Minister Adnan Menderes Foreign Minister Fuat Köprülü	U.S. Ambassador George Wadsworth	Aug. Sept. Oct.	Law on Foreign Capital amended NATO agrees to Turkish membership Turkey joins Middle East Command

* Month named indicates date of presentation of credentials.

1952	President Celâl Bayar Prime Minister Adnan Menderes Foreign Minister Fuat Köprülü	U.S. Ambassador George McGhee (Jan.)	Feb. Turkey joins NATO
1953	President Celâl Bayar Prime Minister Adnan Menderes Foreign Minister Fuat Köprülü	U.S. Ambassador Avra Warren (Sept.)	May U.S.S.R. withdraws territorial demands on Turkey
1954	President Celâl Bayar Prime Minister Adnan Menderes Foreign Minister Fuat Köprülü	U.S. Ambassador Avra Warren	Jan. Bayar visits U.S. Mar. Petroleum law changed May DP wins elections June Menderes visits U.S. June Agreements on Status of U.S. Forces in Turkey and Military Facilities
1955	President Celâl Bayar Prime Minister Adnan Menderes Foreign Minister Fuat Köprülü	U.S. Ambassador Avra Warren	Feb. Turkey ratifies Baghdad Pact Sept. Riots over Cyprus in Istanbul and Izmir
1956	President Celâl Bayar Prime Minister Adnan Menderes Foreign Minister Ethem Menderes (acting)	U.S. Ambassador Fletcher Warren (June)	July Vice President Nixon visits Turkey July Status of Forces Agreement amended Oct.– Arab-Israeli war over Nov. Suez
1957	President Celâl Bayar Prime Minister Adnan Menderes Foreign Minister Fatin Rüştü Zorlu	U.S. Ambassador Fletcher Warren	Jan. Eisenhower Doctrine Oct. Narrow DP election victory Dec. NATO agreement to deploy MRBMs
1958	President Celâl Bayar Prime Minister Adnan Menderes Foreign Minister Fatin Rüştü Zorlu	U.S. Ambassador Fletcher Warren	July Iraqi revolution July Lebanese insurrection Aug. Devaluation of Turkish lira
1959	President Celâl Bayar Prime Minister Adnan Menderes Foreign Minister Fatin Rüştü Zorlu	U.S. Ambassador Fletcher Warren	Mar. Cooperation agreement Aug. Izmir blackmarketing scandal Nov. Lt. Col. Morrison auto accident Dec. President Eisenhower visits Ankara

1960	President, Prime Minister Cemal Gürsel Foreign Minister Selim Sarper	U.S. Ambassador Fletcher Warren	May May Nov.	U-2 shot down in U.S.S.R. Officers overthrow Menderes regime Junta purges 14 of its members
1961	President Cemal Gürsel Prime Minister İsmet İnönü Foreign Minister Selim Sarper	U.S. Ambassador Raymond Hare (April)	July Sept. Oct. Nov.	Constitution ratified Menderes, Zorlu, Polatkan hanged General elections: no party gains majority RPP-JP coalition government formed
1962	President Cemal Gürsel Prime Minister İsmet İnönü Foreign Minister Feridun Cemal Erkin	U.S. Ambassador Raymond Hare	Feb. June Aug. July Oct.	Abortive coup by Col. Aydemir RPP-NTP-RPNP coalition government formed Peace Corps agreement OECD consortium for aid to Turkey announced Cuban missile crisis
1963	President Cemal Gürsel Prime Minister İsmet İnönü Foreign Minister Feridun Cemal Erkin	U.S. Ambassador Raymond Hare	May Dec. Dec.	Second abortive coup by Col. Aydemir Intercommunal conflict on Cyprus begins RPP-independents coalition government
1964	President Cemal Gürsel Prime Minister İsmet İnönü Foreign Minister Feridun Cemal Erkin	U.S. Ambassador Raymond Hare	June June Aug.	"Johnson letter" warning Turks not to invade Cyprus İnönü visits Washington Acheson effort to mediate Cyprus dispute
1965	President Cemal Gürsel Prime Minister Suat Hayrı Ürgüplü (Feb.–Oct.) Prime Minister Süleyman Demirel (Oct.–) Foreign Minister Hasan Işık (Feb.–Oct.) Foreign Minister İhsan Sabri Çağlayangil (Oct.–)	U.S. Ambassador Parker T. Hart (Oct.)	Feb. Oct. Oct. Dec.	JP-NTP-RPNP coalition government formed JP election victory JP government formed RB-52 crash in Black Sea

1966	President Cevdet Sunay Prime Minister Süleyman Demirel Foreign Minister İhsan Sabri Çağlayangil	U.S. Ambassador Parker Hart	Feb. July	Assistant Secretary of Defense McNaughton visits Ankara Natural Senator Tunçkanat publicizes alleged U.S. intelligence documents
1967	President Cevdet Sunay Prime Minister Süleyman Demirel Foreign Minister İhsan Sabri Çağlayangil	U.S. Ambassador Parker Hart	June Nov. Nov.	Turkey adheres to the Single Convention on Narcotics Renewed Cyprus crisis Vance mission to mediate Cyprus dispute
1968	President Cevdet Sunay Prime Minister Süleyman Demirel Foreign Minister İhsan Sabri Çağlayangil	U.S. Ambassador Robert W. Komer (Nov.)	June Sept.	Turnover of "site 23" to Turks Amendment of Status of Forces Agreement
1969	President Cevdet Sunay Prime Minister Süleyman Demirel Foreign Minister İhsan Sabri Çağlayangil	U.S. Ambassador William Handley (July)	Jan. Feb. July Oct.	Komer's car burned "Bloody Sunday" riots in Istanbul during Sixth Fleet visit Defense Cooperation Agreement signed JP election victory
1970	President Cevdet Sunay Prime Minister Süleyman Demirel Foreign Minister İhsan Sabri Çağlayangil	U.S. Ambassador William Handley	Feb. Feb. Aug.	Demirel press conference on defense cooperation Demirel government budget rejected by parliament Turkish lira devalued
1971	President Cevdet Sunay Prime Minister Nihat Erim Foreign Minister Osman Olcay (Mar.–Dec.) Foreign Minister Ü. Halûk Bayülken (Dec.–)	U.S. Ambassador William Handley	Mar. Mar. Mar. June Oct. Dec.	4 U.S. airmen abducted Ultimatum by generals brings down Demirel government Nihat Erim forms government Ban on opium production announced Vice President Spiro T. Agnew in Ankara Second Erim cabinet formed

Selected Bibliography

I. PUBLIC DOCUMENTS

Central Treaty Organization (CENTO)

The Story of the Central Treaty Organization: CENTO. Ankara, September 1959.

Great Britain

Secretary of State for the Colonies. *Cyprus.* Cmnd. 1093. London, 1960.

North Atlantic Treaty Organization (NATO)

NATO Handbook. Brussels, 1971.

NATO Facts and Figures. Brussels, [1969].

Turkey

Başbakanlık. *Hükûmet Programı.* Ankara, 1961.

Dışişleri Bakanlığı. *Belleteni.* 1969–1970.

————. Organization for International Economic Cooperation. *Marshall Plan in Turkey.* Nos. 30–33. Ankara, 1958.

————. Organization for International Economic Cooperation. *Quarterly Report on the Marshall Plan in Turkey.* Ankara, 1951.

Joint Turkish/American Agricultural Mission. *Improving Farm Income in the Poppy Region: Recommendations of the Joint Turkish/American Agricultural Mission.* Ankara, November 1971.

Maliye Bakanlığı. Board of Financial Research. *Budget Speech Delivered by Mr. Hasan Polatkan, Minister of Finance.* Ankara, 1953.

Office of the Press Counselor. *Turkish Digest.* Turkish Embassy, Washington, D. C., 1967–1971.

Resmî Gazete. 1945–1971.

Turkish Information Office. *News from Turkey.* New York, 1948–1952.

————. *Turkey's Foreign Policy.* New York, 1951.

————. *Turkey's Foreign Relations in 1952.* New York, 1952.

————. *Turkey's Foreign Policy: 1958.* New York, 1958.

Türkiye Büyük Millet Meclisi. *Tutanak Dergisi.* 1945–1954. (*Zabıt Ceridesi,* 1954–1960; Temsilciler Meclisi, *Tutanak Dergisi,* 1961; Millet Meclisi, *Tutanak Dergisi,* 1961–1971; Türkiye Senatosu, *Tutanak Dergisi,* 1961–1971.)

Türkiye Cumhuriyeti Anayasası (promulgated July 20, 1961). English translation by Sadik Balkan, Ahmet E. Uysal, and Kemal H. Karpat, *Middle East Journal,* Spring 1962, pp. 215–35.

United Nations

General Assembly. First Committee. *Summary Records of Meetings.* 1947.

————. *Plenary Meetings: Verbatim Records of Meetings.* 1959–1967.

Security Council. *Official Records.* 1957–1968.

United States

AID. Office of Statistics and Reports. Bureau for Program and Policy Coordination. *U.S. Overseas Loans and Grants and Assistance from International Organizations.* Special Report Prepared for the House Foreign Affairs Committee, May 14, 1971, and earlier editions. Washington, 1971.

————. *Report to Congress on the Foreign Assistance Program for Fiscal Year 1962.* Washington, 1963.

————. *Turkey: Ereğli Iron and Steel Works Incorporated.* (Capital Assistance Paper, AID-DLC/P-567), June 6, 1967.

————. *U.S. Economic Assistance Programs Administered by the Agency for International Development and Predecessor Agencies: April 3, 1948–June 30, 1968.* Washington, 1969.

Department of the Army. *Nuclear Weapons and NATO: Analytical Survey of Literature.* DA Pamphlet 50-1. Washington, 1970.

Department of Defense. *Military Assistance and Foreign Military Sales Facts.* Washington, 1971 and earlier editions.

Department of Labor. *Labor Law and Practice in Turkey.* Washington, BLS Report no. 239, 1963.

Department of State. "Address by the Honorable Elliot L. Richardson, Under Secretary of State, to the Philadelphia Bar Association." Press Release no. 108. Washington, April 2, 1970.

————. *American Foreign Policy, 1950–1955: Basic Documents.* General Foreign Policy Series 117, Publication 6446, vols. 1 and 2. Washington, July 1957.

————. *American Foreign Policy: Current Documents, 1956–1967.* Washington, 1957–1969.

————. *Bulletin.* 1945–1971.

————. *Foreign Relations of the United States, 1945,* vol. 8: *The Near East and Africa.* Publication 8427. Washington, 1969.

————. *Foreign Relations of the United States, 1946,* vol. 7: *The Near East and Africa.* Publication 8490. Washington, 1969.

————. *Foreign Relations of the United States: The Conference of Berlin (The Potsdam Conference), 1945.* Publication 7015, vols. 1 & 2. Washington, 1960.

————. *Foreign Relations of the United States: The Conference at Malta and Yalta, 1945.* Publication 6199. Washington, 1955.

————. *Nazi-Soviet Relations, 1939–1941: Documents from the Archives of the German Foreign Office.* Publication 3023. Washington, 1948.

————. *The Problem of the Turkish Straits.* Near Eastern series 5. Publication 2752. Washington, 1947.

————. *Treaties and Other International Acts Series* (TIAS). 1946–1971.

————. *United States Foreign Policy, 1969–1970: A Report of the Secretary of State.* Publication 8575. Washington, 1971.

Economic Cooperation Administration. *Turkey Country Study.* Washington, 1949.

House of Representatives. Committee on Appropriations. *Hearings on ... Foreign Assistance and Related Agencies Appropriations for 1969.* 91st Cong., 1st session. Washington, 1969.

————. Committee on Armed Services. *Hearings on Military Posture ... 88th Cong., 1st session. Washington, 1963.

————. Committee on Foreign Affairs. *Hearings ... on H.R. 11792: Foreign Assistance Act of 1969.* 91st Cong., 1st session. Washington, 1969.

―――. Committee on Ways and Means. *Hearings . . . on Legislation to Regulate Controlled Dangerous Substances and Amend Narcotics and Drug Laws.* 91st Cong., 2nd session. Washington, 1970.

―――. Select Committee on Crime. *Heroin and Heroin Paraphernalia: Second Report.* House Report no. 91-1808. 91st Cong., 2nd session. Washington, 1971.

―――. Subcommittee of the House Committee on Armed Services. *Report . . . on the Military and Political Problems in Spain, Italy, Libya, Turkey, and Iran.* H.A.S.C. no. 91-42. 91st Cong., 2nd session. Washington, 1970.

Senate. *A Report on United States Foreign Operations by Honorable Allen J. Ellender.* 87th Cong., 1st session, Document no. 20. Washington, 1961.

―――. Committee on Appropriations. *Hearings on H.R. 15149: . . . Foreign Assistance and Related Programs. . . .* 91st Cong., 1st session. Washington, 1969.

―――. Committee on Foreign Relations. *Hearings . . . on S. 1656 . . . and S. 1657 to Consolidate and Revise the Foreign Assistance Act. . . .* 92nd Cong., 1st session. Washington, 1971.

―――. Special Committee to Study the Foreign Aid Program. *Foreign Aid Program; Compilation of Studies and Surveys.* 85th Cong., 1st session. Document no. 52. Washington, 1957.

―――. Special Committee to Study the Foreign Aid Program. *Greece, Turkey, and Iran: Report on United States Foreign Assistance Programs by Former Ambassador Norman Armour.* 85th Cong., 1st session. Washington, 1957.

―――. Subcommittee on Reorganization and International Organizations of the Committee on Government Operations. *Report of a Study of United States Foreign Aid in Ten Middle Eastern and African Countries Submitted by Senator Ernest Gruening.* 88th Cong., 1st session. Washington, 1963.

―――. Subcommittee on United States Security Agreements and Commitments Abroad of the Committee on Foreign Relations. *United States Security Agreements and Commitments Abroad: Part 7: Greece and Turkey.* 91st Cong., 2nd session. Washington, 1970.

II. BOOKS AND PAMPHLETS

Adalet Partisi. *Hükûmet Buhranı—Hükûmet Teşkili—Hükûmet Proğramı—Kıbrıs Olayları Karşısında Adalet Partisi.* Ankara, 1964.

Adams, Walter, and Garraty, John. *Is the World Our Campus?* East Lansing, Mich., 1960.

Aker, Ahmet. *Türkiye Endüstrisi ve Ortak Pazar.* Istanbul, 1970.

Akşin, Aptülahat. *Türkiyenin 1945'den Sonraki Dış Politika Gelişmeleri: Orta Doğu Meseleleri.* Istanbul, 1959.

Aktan, Reşat. *Analysis and Assessment of the Economic Effects of Public Law 480 Title I Program, Turkey.* Ankara, 1965.

Allen, Henry E. *The Turkish Transformation.* Chicago, 1935.

Altan, Çetin. *Onlar Uyanırken: Türk Sosyalistlerinin El Kitabı.* Istanbul, 1967.

―――. *Sömürcülere Savaş.* Istanbul, n.d.

Altıncı Filo Beklediğin Ekonomik Düzen. Istanbul, 1969.

Anadol, M. *Türkiyede Antiemperyalist Savaş Stratejisi.* Istanbul, 1968.

Ankara University. *Turkey and the United Nations.* New York, 1961.

―――. *The Turkish Yearbook of International Relations.* vols. 1–7. Ankara, 1961–1969.

Ansay, Tuğrul, and Wallace, Don, Jr. *Introduction to Turkish Law.* Ankara, 1966.

Arar, İsmail. *Hükümet Programları, 1920–1965.* Istanbul, 1968.

Ataöv, Türkkaya. *Amerika NATO ve Türkiye.* Ankara, 1969.

———. *Turkish Foreign Policy, 1939–1945.* Ankara, 1965.

Atatürk. See under Kemal, Mustapha.

Avcıoğlu, Doğan. *Türkiye'nin Düzeni (Dün—Bugün—Yarın).* Ankara, 1969.

Aybar, Mehmet Ali. *Bağımsızlık Demokrasi Sosyalizm.* Istanbul, 1968.

———. *Türkiyeyi Adalet Partisi Kalkındıramaz.* Istanbul, 1966.

Aydemir, Şevket Süreyya. *İkinci Adam,* vol. 3. Istanbul, 1968.

Başgil, Ali Fuad. *Le Révolution militaire de 1960 en Turquie (ses origines).* Geneva, 1963.

Baykurt, Fakir. *Amerikan Sargısı.* 2nd ed. Ankara, 1969.

Beer, Francis A. *Integration and Disintegration in NATO.* Columbus, Ohio, 1969.

Bekata, Hıfzı Oğuz. *Türkiye'nin Bugünkü Görünüşü.* Ankara, 1969.

Beşikçi, İsmail. *Doğuda Değişim ve Yapısal Sorunlar.* Ankara, 1969.

Bilge, A. Suat et al. *Olaylarla Türk Dış Politikası (1919–1965).* Ankara, 1969.

Boran, Behice. *Türkiye ve Sosyalizm Sorunları.* Istanbul, 1968.

Burk, Monroe. "Turkish Development and the Erim Government." Paper submitted to the Economic Planning Division, U.S. AID to Turkey, May 1971.

Byrnes, James F. *Speaking Frankly.* New York, 1947.

Campbell, John C. *Defense of the Middle East: Problems of American Policy.* New York, 1958.

Çaybaşı, Remzi. *Sosyalist Akım, Atatürk ve Anayasa.* Istanbul, 1967.

Çelik, Edip. *Türkiye'nin Dış Politika Tarihi.* Istanbul, 1969.

Cem, İsmail. *Türkiyede Geri Kalmışlığın Tarihi.* Istanbul, 1970.

Ceyhun, Demir-Taş. *Yağma Edilen Türkiye.* Istanbul, 1968.

Chenery, Hollis B.; Brandow, George E.; and Cohn, Edwin J. *Turkish Investment and Economic Development.* Ankara, 1953.

Cihan, Ali Faik. *Sosyalist Türkiye.* Istanbul, 1966(?). Translated as *Treatise on Socialist Turkey.* Joint Publications Research Service: 39,749. Washington, Feb. 2, 1967.

Cohn, Edwin J. *Turkish Economic, Social, and Political Change: The Development of a More Prosperous and Open Society.* New York, 1970.

Cumhuriyet Halk Partisi. *1961 C.H.P. Seçim Beyannamesi.* Ankara, 1961.

———. *C.H.P.'nin Rejim Konusundaki, Sosyal Konulardaki, Dış Politika ve Savunma Konularındaki Görüşleri.* Ankara, 1966.

———. *C.H.P. XIX Kurultayı Parti Meclisi Raporu.* Ankara, 1968.

———. *C.H.P. Programı.* Ankara, 1953.

———. *İnsanca bir Düzen Kurmak için Halktan Yetki İstiyoruz: CHPnin Düzen Değişikliği Programı.* Ankara, 1969.

———. Araştırma ve Yayın Burosu. *Dış Politika.* Ankara, 1961.

Davison, Roderic H. *Turkey.* Englewood Cliffs, N. J., 1968.

Demirel, Süleyman. *Başbakan Süleyman Demirel'in On Basın Toplantısı.* Ankara, 1968.

Demirer, Mehmet Arif. *Emperyalizm ve Biz. Bir Sömürge Midir Türkiye?* Ankara, 1967.

Demokrat Parti. *Bayar'ın Amerika Seyahatı.* Ankara, 1954.

———. *C. H. Partisi Liderlerinin Zararlı Tenkidlerine Cevap.* Ankara, 1954.

———. *Düşmanı Kore'de Karşıladık.* Ankara, 1954.

———. *Kalkınan Türkiye.* Ankara, 1954.

———. *Türkiye ve Atlantik Paktı.* Ankara, 1954.

DeNovo, John A. *American Interests and Policies in the Middle East, 1900–1939.* Minneapolis, 1963.

Dikici, Kenan. *Milli Doktrin: Milliyetçi Demokratik Sosyalizm.* Istanbul, 1969.

Dodd, C. H. *Politics and Government in Turkey.* Berkeley, 1969.

Ecevit, Bülent. *Bu Düzen Değişmelidir.* Ankara, 1968.

———. *Ortanın Solu.* Istanbul, 1966.

Erdemir, Sabahat, ed. *Muhalefette İsmet İnönü: Konuşmaları, Demeçleri, Mesajları, Sohbetleri ve Yazılarıyla.* Istanbul, 1956.

Eren, Nuri. *Turkey Today—and Tomorrow: An Experiment in Westernization.* New York, 1963.

Erişen, Necmeddin. *Türkiyede Altıncı Filo Hadiseleri ve Gerçek Emperyalizm.* Istanbul, 1969.

Erkin, Feridun Cemal. *Les relations Turco-Soviètiques et la question des détroits.* Ankara, 1968.

Eroğlu, Hamza. *Türk Devrimi Tarihi.* Ankara, 1967.

Evans, Laurence. *United States Policy and the Partition of Turkey, 1914–1924.* Baltimore, 1965.

Fahri, M. *Amerikan Harp Doktrinleri.* Istanbul, 1966.

Ford Foundation. *The Ford Foundation in Turkey, 1952–1967.* Ankara, 1968.

Frey, Frederick W. *The Turkish Political Elite.* Cambridge, Mass., 1965.

Giritli, İsmet. *Fifty Years of Turkish Political Development, 1919–1969.* Istanbul, 1969.

———. *Neden "NATO'ya Evet"?* Istanbul, 1968.

Gönlübol, Mehmet. *Dış Politika: İç Etkenler Açısından bir Dış Politika İncelemesi.* Ankara, 1969.

———. *Turkish Participation in the United Nations, 1945–1954.* Ankara, 1963.

Grew, Joseph C. *Turbulent Era: A Diplomatic Record of Forty Years, 1904–1945.* vols. 1 and 2. Boston, 1952.

Halil, Ali. *Atatürkçü Dış Politika ve NATO ve Türkiye.* Istanbul, 1968.

Hanson, A. H. *Public Enterprise and Economic Development.* London, 1959.

Hanway, Wayne E. "An Evaluation of the University of Nebraska Turkish University Program." Paper written in the Department of Political Science, University of Nebraska, Sept. 1970.

Harris, George S. "A Political History of Turkey, 1945–1950." Unpublished Ph.D. thesis presented to Harvard University, 1956.

Hartmann, Robert T. *Uncle Sam in Turkey.* New York, 1952.

Helseth, William A. "The United States and Turkey: A Study of Their Relations from 1784 to 1962." Unpublished Ph.D. Thesis presented to Fletcher School of Law and Diplomacy, April, 1962.

Hurewitz, Jacob C. *Diplomacy in the Near and Middle East: A Documentary Record, 1914–1956.* Princeton, 1956.

Iatrides, John O. *Balkan Triangle: Birth and Decline of an Alliance Across Ideological Boundaries.* The Hague, 1968.

İlkin, S. and İnanç, E., eds. *Planning in Turkey.* Ankara, 1967.

[İnönü, İsmet]. *1958de İnönü.* Ankara, 1959.

Institute for Strategic Studies, The. *The Military Balance, 1970–1971.* London, 1971, and earlier editions.

İpekçi, Abdi. *Liderler Diyor ki.* Istanbul, 1969.

İpekçi, Abdi, and Coşar, Ömer Sami. *İhtilâlin İçyüzü.* Istanbul, 1965.

Jaschke, Gotthard. *Die Türkei in den Jahren 1942–1951.* Wiesbaden, 1955.

———. *Die Türkei in den Jahren 1952–1961.* Wiesbaden, 1965.

Jones, Joseph M. *The Fifteen Weeks.* New York, 1964.

Kansu, Ceyhun Atuf. *Atatürk Devriminin Temeli, ya Bağımsızlık ya Ölum; bir Deneme.* Istanbul, 1964.

Karpat, Kemal H. *Turkey's Politics: The Transition to a Multi-Party System.* Princeton, 1959.

Kelly, Sir David. *The Ruling Few or the Human Background to Diplomacy.* London, 1952.

Kemal, Mustapha [Atatürk]. *A Speech Delivered by Ghazi Mustapha Kemal, President of the Turkish Republic,* October 1927. Leipzig, 1929.

Kennan, George F. *Memoirs 1925–1950.* Boston, 1967.

Kennedy, Robert F. *Thirteen Days.* New York, 1969.

Kılıç, Altemur. *Turkey and the World.* Washington, 1959.

Kinross, Lord. *Ataturk: A Biography of Mustafa Kemal, Father of Modern Turkey.* New York, 1965.

Kıran, Muzaffer, and Güneri, Gültekin. *NATO, Kanun ve Andlaşmaların Türkiyedeki Mukayeseli Tatbikatı.* Ankara, 1962.

Kıratlı, Metin. *Parlamanter Muafiyetler; Bizde ve Yabancı Memleketlerde.* Ankara, 1961.

Kirk, George. *The Middle East, 1945–1950.* London, 1954.

Kışlalı, Ahmet Taner. *Forces Politiques dans la Turquie Moderne.* Ankara, 1968.

Kissinger, Henry A. *The Troubled Partnership: A Re-appraisal of the Atlantic Alliance.* New York, 1965.

Knorr, Klaus, ed. *NATO and American Security.* Princeton, 1959.

Koçtürk, Osman Nuri. *Barış ve Emperyalizm.* Istanbul, 1968.

———. *Sessiz Savaş.* Istanbul, 1969.

Küçükömer, İdris. *Düzenin Yabancılaşması.* Istanbul, 1969.

Lenonian, Lutfi. *The Turkish Press, 1925–1931.* Athens, 1932.

Lewis, Bernard. *The Emergence of Modern Turkey.* London, 1961.

Lewis, G. L. *Turkey.* New York, 1955.

Magnus, Ralph H., ed. *Documents on the Middle East.* Washington, 1969.

Mango, Andrew. *Turkey.* London, 1968.

Markmann, Charles Lam, and Sherwin, Mark. *John F. Kennedy: A Sense of Purpose.* New York, 1961.

Mears, Eliot G. *Modern Turkey.* New York, 1924.

Merriam, John E. "Turkey, 1950 to 1956, and the Lessons of Inflation." Paper submitted to the Foreign Service Institute, 1956.

Millis, Walter, ed. *The Forrestal Diaries.* New York, 1951.

Ökçün, A. Gündüz. *A Guide to Turkish Treaties, 1920–1964.* Ankara, 1966.

———. *Türkiyenin Taraf Olduğu Milletlerarası Andlaşmalar Rehberi (1920–1961).* Ankara, 1962.

Özbalkan, Müslim. *Gizli Belgelerle Barış Gönüllüleri.* Istanbul, 1970.

Özkol, Sedat. *Geri Bıraktırılmış Türkiye.* Istanbul, 1969.

Özturk, Kâzım. *Cumhurbaşkanlarının T. Büyük Millet Meclisini Açış Nutkuları.* Istanbul, 1969.

Pearson, Kenneth, and Connor, Patricia. *The Dorak Affair*. London, 1967.

Powers, Francis G., with Curt Genty. *Operation Overflight*. New York, 1970.

Roberts, Thomas D. et al. *Area Handbook for the Republic of Turkey*. Washington, 1970.

Robinson, Richard D. *Developments Respecting Turkey*, vols. 1–4. New York, 1954–1957.

————. *The First Turkish Republic*. Cambridge, Mass., 1963.

————. *High-level Manpower in Economic Development; the Turkish Case*. Cambridge, Mass., 1967.

Sander, Oral. *Balkan Gelişmeleri ve Türkiye, 1945–1965*. Ankara, 1969.

Sarıca, Murat, and Devrim, Nurkalp, eds. *Türkiye İşçi Partisini Tanıyalım*. Istanbul, 1965.

Sayılgan, Aclan. *Bizim Radyo ve Hoparlörleri*. Ankara, 1969.

Sertel, Yıldız. *Türkiye'de İlerici Akımlar*. Istanbul, 1969.

Soysal, Mümtaz. *Dış Politika ve Parlamento*. Ankara, 1964.

Tamkoç, Metin. *A Bibliography on the Foreign Relations of the Republic of Turkey, 1919–1967*. Ankara, 1968.

Tansky, Leo. *U.S. and U.S.S.R. Aid to Developing Countries: A Comparative Study of India, Turkey, and the U.A.R.* New York, 1967.

Tevetoğlu, Fethi. *Dış Politika Görüşümüz*. Ankara, 1963.

————. *Türkiye'de Sosyalist ve Komünist Faâliyetler (1910–1960)*. Ankara, 1967.

Thomas, Lewis V., and Frye, Richard N. *The United States and Turkey and Iran*. Cambridge, Mass., 1951.

Thornburg, Max Weston; Spry, Graham; and Soule, George. *Turkey: An Economic Appraisal*. New York, 1949.

Trask, Roger R. *The United States Response to Turkish Nationalism and Reform, 1914–1939*. Minneapolis, 1971.

Truman, Harry S. *Memoirs:* vol. 1: *Years of Decisions*, vol. 2: *Years of Trial and Hope*. Garden City, N. Y., 1955–1956.

Tully, Andrew. *CIA: The Inside Story*. Greenwich, Conn., 1963.

Tunçkanat, Haydar. *İkili Anlaşmaların İçyüzü*. Ankara, 1970.

————. *Türk-Amerikan İlişkileri Üzerine Cumhuriyet Senatosunda Tabiî Senatör Haydar Tunçkanat tarafından Açıklanan Çok Gizli Rapor!* N.p., n.d.

Türkiye İşçi Partisi. *Programı*. Istanbul, 1964.

————. *Ankara İl Heyeti. NATO'ya Hayır*. Pamphlet, distributed 1968.

Ülman, A. Halûk. *İkinci Cihan Savaşının Başından Truman Doktrinine Kadar. Türk-Amerikan Diplomatik Münasebetleri, 1939–1947*. Ankara, 1961.

Umay, Tunç. *Düzenimizin Bir Mudafaası*. Istanbul, 1969.

Üstün, Nevzat. *Türkiyedeki Amerika*. 2nd ed., Istanbul, 1969.

Váli, Ferenc. *Bridge Across the Bosporus: The Foreign Policy of Turkey*. Baltimore, 1971.

Ward, Robert E., and Rustow, Dankwart A., eds. *Political Modernization in Japan and Turkey*. Princeton, 1964.

White, John. *Pledged to Development*. London, 1967.

Wolf, Charlotte. *Garrison Community: A Study of an Overseas American Military Colony*. Westport, Conn., 1969.

Xydis, Stephen G. *Greece and the Great Powers, 1944–1947: Prelude to the "Truman Doctrine."* Thessaloniki, 1963.

Yılmaz, A. Kemal. *Savulun Amerikalı Geliyor*. N.p., 1960.

III. ARTICLES IN MAGAZINES AND BOOKS

Açıkalın, Cevat. "Turkey's International Relations." *International Affairs* (London), Oct. 1947, pp. 477–91.

Aksoy, Muamer, "Atatürk'ün Işığında 'Tam Bağımsızlık İlkesi,' " in Ankara University, Siyasal Bilgiler Fakültesi, *Abadan'a Armağan.* 1969, pp. 689–799.

Alexander, Alec P. "Turkey," in Adamantios Pepelasis, Leon Mears, and Irma Adelman, eds., *Economic Development: Analysis and Case Studies.* New York, 1961, pp. 469–99.

Armaoğlu, Fahir H. "Recent Developments in Turkish Foreign Policy." *Dış Politika—Foreign Policy,* March 1971, pp. 85–94.

———. "Turkey and the United States: A New Alliance," in Ankara University, *The Turkish Yearbook of International Relations.* 1968, 6:1–15.

Armstrong, Hamilton Fish. "Eisenhower's Right Flank." *Foreign Affairs,* July 1951, pp. 651–63.

Ashworth, Selma. "Biz de mi Amerikan Elçisini Dağa Kaçıralım?" *Ant,* Sept. 30, 1969, p. 11.

Ataöv, Türkkaya, "Amerika Nereye Gidiyor." *Sosyal Adalet,* July 15, 1964, pp. 36–37.

———. "Doğu Avrupa'nın Sosyalistleşmesinden Truman Doktrinine kadar 'Soğuk Harb.' " *Siyasal Bilgiler Fakültesi Dergisi,* June 1968, pp. 189–222.

———. "Marshall Planından NATO'nun Kuruluşuna kadar 'Soğuk Harb.' " *Siyasal Bilgiler Fakültesi Dergisi.* Sept. 1968, pp. 275–310.

———. "The Origins of the Cold War: 1945–1949," in Ankara University, *The Turkish Yearbook of International Relations,* 1969, 7: 28–103.

———. " 'Soğuk Harb'ın Doğuşu: San Francisco'dan Mihver Barış Toplantılarına." *Siyasal Bilgiler Fakültesi Dergisi,* Mar. 1968, pp. 309–56.

———. "Turkish Foreign Policy," in Ankara University, *The Turkish Yearbook of International Relations.* 1963, 2: 103–42.

Avcıoğlu, Doğan. "Amerika ve Arab Sosyalizmi." *Yön,* Feb. 13, 1963, p. 3.

———. "Demagojiye Paydos!" *Yön,* Aug. 13, 1965, p. 3.

———. "Ereğli-Çelik Dosyası Açılmalıdır." *Yön,* Jan. 1, 1965, p. 3.

———. "Füze Üsleri." *Yön,* Oct. 31, 1962, p. 3.

———. "Milliyetçilere Sesleniş." *Yön,* Sept. 25, 1964, p. 3.

———. "Ortanın Solu ve Amerika." *Yön,* Apr. 14, 1967, pp. 8–11.

———. "Pusulası Gemi." *Akis,* Aug. 9, 1958, pp. 18–19.

———. "The Question of Bilateral Treaties and NATO." *Outlook,* Feb. 25, 1970, pp. 7–8.

———. "Sam Amca'nın Türkiyedeki Hazinesi." *Yön,* Apr. 25, 1965, p. 3.

———. "Tarafsız Dış Politika ve Türkiye." *Sosyal Adalet,* July 15, 1964, pp. 7–10.

———. "The Turkish Army and the United States." *Outlook,* Nov. 5, 1969, pp. 5–6.

———. "Türkiye'deki Amerikan Üsleri." *Yön,* Nov. 26, 1965, pp. 8–9.

———. "Türk Ordusu ve Amerika, 1947–1969." *Devrim,* Oct. 21, 1969—Feb. 24, 1970.

Aybar, Mehmet Ali. "Bugünkü Dış Politikamız Savunulamaz." *Sosyal Adalet,* July 15, 1964, p. 4.

Aydınlık. "TİP Nereye Geldi." *Aydınlık Sosyalist Dergi,* Nov. 1970, pp. 1–8.

B.C.Ü. "Kıbrıs Çıkmazı Dış Politikamızın Çıkmazıdır." *Sosyal Adalet,* Aug. 1964, pp. 4–5.

Birgi, Nuri. "The Atlantic Alliance: Its Present Problems and Its Aims." *NATO's Fifteen Nations,* Dec. 1970–Jan. 1971, pp. 31–38.

Borton, Nan, and James W. "Turkey," in Sargent Shriver et al., "Ambassadors of Good Will, the Peace Corps." *National Geographic,* Sept. 1964, pp. 330–33.

Bowen, Harold G. "Naval Aspects of the Mission to Turkey." *U.S. Naval Institute Proceedings,* Oct. 1951, pp. 1041–49.

Bradley, General Omar. "U.S. Military Policy: 1950." *Reader's Digest,* Oct. 1950, pp. 143–54.

Burnouf, Denis, "La Situation en Turquie." *Politique Etrangère,* 1971, no. 1, pp. 53–67.

Çelik, Edip. "Les Effets sociaux et économiques du stationnement des forces armées de pays membres de l'O.T.A.N. sur leur territoire respectif." *Annales de la Faculté de Droit d'Istanbul,* no. 19 (1963), 13:195–237.

Çetiner, Yılmaz. "Turkey Turns Anti-American." *Atlas,* Aug. 1965, pp. 107–108.

Cohn, Edwin J. "Middle East Studies Review: The Climate for Research in the Social Sciences in Turkey." *Middle East Journal,* Spring 1968, pp. 203–12.

Daniel, Robert L. "The Armenian Question and American-Turkish Relations, 1924–1927." *Mississippi Valley Historical Review,* Sept. 1959, pp. 252–75.

————. "The United States and the Turkish Republic before World War II: The Cultural Dimension." *Middle East Journal,* Winter 1967, pp. 52–63.

Davison, Roderic H. "Middle East Nationalism: Lausanne Thirty Years After." *Middle East Journal,* Summer 1953, pp. 324–48.

"Dış Politikanın Alfabesi." *Akis,* July 26, 1958, p. 11.

Ecevit, Bülent. "Dış Siyasetteki Ayrılığın Kaynakları." *Kim,* Aug. 8, 1958, pp. 12–13.

————. "Mektuplar." *Akis,* Jan. 22, 1966, pp. 8–9.

Edwards, A. C. "Impact of the War on Turkey." *International Affairs* (London), July 1946, pp. 389–400.

Eldridge, Robert H. "Emigration and the Turkish Balance of Payments." *Middle East Journal,* Summer 1966, pp. 296–316.

Ellis, Barbara. "Talking Turkey on Opium." *Mid East,* Dec. 1970, pp. 18–20.

Eren, Nuri. "Financial Aspects of Turkish Planning." *Middle East Journal,* Spring 1966, pp. 187–95.

————. "The Foreign Policy of Turkey," in Joseph E. Black and Kenneth W. Thompson, eds., *Foreign Policies in a World of Change.* New York, 1963. pp. 285–315.

————. "The Middle East and Turkey in World Affairs." *The Annals of the American Academy of Political and Social Science,* July 1951, pp. 72–80.

————. "Turkey: Prospects for Democratic Development." *Journal of International Affairs,* no. 2 (1965), pp. 170–80.

Ergin, Feridun. "A Friendly Remonstration: Anti-American Demonstration." *Turkish Economic Review,* Sept.–Oct. 1964, pp. 21–22.

Erkin, Feridun Cemal. "Turkey's Foreign Policy." *Proceedings of the Academy of Political Science,* Jan. 1952, pp. 562–72.

Eroğlu, Hamza. "La Constitution Turque de 1961 et les relations internationales," in Ankara University, *The Turkish Yearbook of International Relations.* 1963, 2: 62–90.

————. "Türkiye-Amerika Birleşik Devletleri İkili İşbirliği Anlaşması," in Ankara University, *The Turkish Yearbook of International Relations.* 1962, 1: 23–64.

Fernau, F.-W. "La Turquie, l'Alliance atlantique et la détent." *Europe Sud-Est,* Oct. 1970, pp. 13–25.

Flinn, Peter. "Turning Point for Turkey." *New Middle East,* Oct. 1969, pp. 13–16.

Fox, Colonel Clifton C. "Turkish Army's Role in Nationbuilding." *Military Review,* Apr. 1967, pp. 68–74.

Frey, Frederick W. "Socialization to National Identification Among Turkish Peasants." *Journal of Politics,* Nov. 1968, pp. 934–65.

————. "Surveying Peasant Attitudes in Turkey." *Public Opinion Quarterly,* Fall 1963, pp. 335–55.

Giritli, İsmet. "Coup by Memorandum." *New Middle East,* May 1971, pp. 40–42.

————. "Turkey Since the 1965 Elections." *Middle East Journal,* Summer 1969, pp. 351–63.

Gönlübol, Mehmet, and Ülman, A. Halûk. "Türk Dış Politikasının Yirmi Yılı, 1945–1965." *Siyasal Bilgiler Fakültesi Dergisi,* Mar. 1966, pp. 143–82.

Goodman, Seymour S. "Turkey's Trade Prospects in the Common Market: An Exploratory Study." *Journal of Common Market Studies,* June 1969, pp. 305–26.

Hadsel, Winifred N. "U.S. Aid to Turkey." *Foreign Policy Reports,* Oct. 1, 1947, pp. 182–84.

Harris, George S. "The Causes of the 1960 Revolution in Turkey." *Middle East Journal,* Autumn 1970, pp. 438–54.

————. "The Role of the Military in Turkish Politics." *Middle East Journal,* Winter-Spring 1965, pp. 54–66, 169–76.

Howard, Harry N. "The Turkish Straits after World War II: Problems and Prospects." *Balkan Studies,* no. 1 (1970), 11: 35–60.

————. "The United States and Turkey: American Policy in the Straits Question." *Balkan Studies,* 1963, vol. 4, pp. 225–50.

"Incident at Murted." *Outlook,* Jan. 28, 1970, p. 9.

İnönü, İsmet. "Son Hadiselere Dair Görüşüm. *Akis,* Aug. 2, 1958, pp. 6–7.

Karpat, Kemal. "Socialism and the Labor Party of Turkey." *Middle East Journal,* Spring 1967, pp. 173–86.

————. "The Turkish Left." *Journal of Contemporary History,* no. 2 (1966), pp. 169–86.

Kemal, Mehmet. "Ne Amerikan Dolları, Ne Moskof Rublesi." *Sosyal Adalet,* Oct. 1964, pp. 16–17.

Kışlalı, M. A. "Americans Do Not Like . . ." *Outlook,* Nov. 5, 1969, pp. 3–4.

————. "Military Aid Against Opium Poppy." *Outlook,* Sept. 30, 1970, p. 4.

————. "Tactical Nuclear Weapons and Turkey." *Outlook,* Dec. 17, 1969. p. 6.

Krueger, Anne O. "Some Economic Costs of Exchange Control: The Turkish Case." *Journal of Political Economy,* Oct. 1966, pp. 466–80.

Kurdakul, Şükran. "Atatürk Sosyalist Değil midir?" *Ataç,* no. 2 (1964), 21–23.

Lehman, Robert S. "Building Roads and a Highway Administration in Turkey," in Howard M. Teaf, Jr., and Peter G. Franck, *Hands Across Frontiers.* Ithaca, 1955, pp. 363–409.

Lerner, Daniel, and Robinson, Richard D. "Swords and Ploughshares: The Turkish Army as a Modernizing Force." *World Politics,* Oct. 1960, pp. 19–44.

Mango, Andrew. "Turkey and the Middle East." *Political Quarterly,* Apr.–June 1957, pp. 149–57.

McGhee, George C. "Turkey Joins the West." *Foreign Affairs*, July 1954, pp. 617–30.

Millen, Bruce. "Factions of the Turkish Labor Movement." *Monthly Labor Review*, June 1969, pp. 31–35.

Murarka, Dev. "The Soviet-Turkish Rapprochement." *Contemporary Review*, Nov. 1965, pp. 235–38.

Nicholls, William. "Investment in Agriculture in Underdeveloped Countries." *American Economic Review: Proceedings and Papers*, May 1955, pp. 58–73.

Okyar, Osman. "The Turkish Stabilization Experiment—Before and After." *Middle Eastern Affairs*, Aug.–Sept. 1960, pp. 238–46.

————. "Universities in Turkey." *Minerva*, Winter 1968, pp. 213–43.

Pool, Jonathan. "Yabancı Dil Sömürücülüğü." *Yön*, Oct. 8, 1965, p. 2.

Randall, Clarence B. "Can We Invest in Turkey?" *The Atlantic*, Nov. 1953, pp. 48–50.

————. "The Case for a Friend in Need." *Life*, May 7, 1956, pp. 115–16, 119–20.

"Robert W. Komer Geldi." *Tüm*, Dec. 11, 1968, pp. 7, 16.

Robinson, Richard D. "Impact of American Military and Economic Assistance Programs in Turkey." Report to the American Universities Field Staff, 1956.

————. "Turkey's Agrarian Revolution and the Problem of Urbanization." *Public Opinion Quarterly*, Fall 1958, pp. 397–405.

Roos, Leslie L.; Roos, Noralou P.; and Field, Garry R. "Students and Politics in Turkey." *Daedalus*, Winter 1968, pp. 184–203.

Sander, Oral. "The Balkan Cooperation in Perspective," in Ankara University, *The Turkish Yearbook of International Relations*. 1969, 7: 104–20.

Sar, Cem. "L'Association entre la Communauté Economique Européenne et la Turquie," in Ankara University, *The Turkish Yearbook of International Relations*. 1964, 3: 89–114.

Schulz, William. "Let's Halt Heroin at the Source." *Reader's Digest*, May 1971, pp. 97–103.

"Sealing off the Black Sea," *East Europe*, Mar. 1971, p. 11.

Sevig, Vedat R. "Le droit international privé turc en face du marché commun," in Ankara University, *The Turkish Yearbook of International Relations*. 1964, 3: 115–49.

Simpson, Dwight J. "Development as a Process: The Menderes Phase in Turkey." *Middle East Journal*, Spring 1965, pp. 141–52.

Sondern, Fredric, Jr. "Istanbul's Night of Terror." *Reader's Digest*, May 1956, pp. 185–92.

Soysal, Mumtaz. "Birlikte Yaşama." *Yön*, Nov. 28, 1962, p. 3.

————. "Bu Petrol Bizim!" *Yön*, Dec. 25, 1964, pp. 8–9.

Stone, Frank A. "Unrest in Turkey." *The Christian Century*, Sept. 23, 1970, p. 1131.

Sutton, Horace. "Drugs: Ten Years to Doomsday?" *Saturday Review*, Nov. 14, 1970, pp. 18–21, 59–61.

Sykes, John. "Fallible Human Turkey—Guardian of the Near Eastern Heartland." *New Middle East*, April 1970, pp. 31–35.

Szyliowicz, Joseph S. "Students and Politics in Turkey." *Middle Eastern Studies*, May 1970, pp. 150–62.

Tachau, Frank. "The Face of Turkish Nationalism as Reflected in the Cyprus Dispute." *Middle East Journal*, Summer 1959, pp. 262–72.

Tamkoç, Metin. "Turkey's Quest for Security through Defensive Alliances," in Ankara University, *The Turkish Yearbook of International Relations.* 1963, 2: 1–39.

Toker, Metin. "Amerikalılar." *Akis,* July 16, 1966, p. 5.

———. "Amerikalının Yanıldığı Nokta." *Akis,* Feb. 1, 1958, p. 5.

Tuna, Orhan. "Trade Unions in Turkey." *International Labor Review,* Nov. 1964, pp. 413–31.

"Turkey: A Friend in Trouble." *Time,* Oct. 24, 1955, pp. 24–25.

Ülman, A. Halûk. "Türk Dış Politikasına Yön Veren Etkenler (1923–1968)." *Siyasal Bilgiler Fakültesi Dergisi,* Sept. 1968, pp. 241–73.

———. "Türk Ulusal Savunması Üzerine Düşünceler." *Siyasal Bilgiler Fakültesi Dergisi,* Dec. 1966, pp. 201–25.

Ülman, A. H., and Dekmejian, R. H. "Changing Patterns in Turkish Foreign Policy, 1959–1967." *Orbis,* Fall 1967, pp. 772–85.

Ülman, A. Halûk, and Tachau, Frank. "Turkish Politics: The Attempt to Reconcile Rapid Modernization with Democracy." *Middle East Journal,* Spring 1965, pp. 153–68.

Uras, Vedat. "Opium Poisons Friendly Relations." *Outlook,* July 29, 1970, p. 4.

Üstünel, Besim. "Turkey's Attitude towards Common Markets," in Ankara University, *The Turkish Yearbook of International Relations.* 1966, 5: 13–18.

Xydis, Stephen G. "New Light on the Big Three Crisis over Turkey in 1945." *Middle East Journal,* Autumn 1960, pp. 416–32.

Yazoğlu, Cengiz. "Türk-Amerikan İlişkileri Üstüne." *Eylem,* Mar. 1, 1965, pp. 39–45.

Zorlu, Fatin Rüştü. "A Turkish View of World Affairs: A Bridge between East and West." *Vital Speeches of the Day,* Sept. 1, 1959, pp. 684–87.

IV. NEWSPAPERS AND PERIODICALS

Adalet. 1966.

Akis. 1954–1967.

Akşam. 1947–1971.

Ant. 1968–1971.

Aydınlık Sosyalist Dergisi. 1968–1971.

Ayın Tarihi. 1944–1952.

Bayram Gazetesi. 1969.

Cumhuriyet. 1947–1971.

Daily News (Ankara). 1970–1971.

Devrim. 1969–1971.

Dönüşüm. 1966.

Dünya. 1955–1959.

Economist, The (London). 1945–1971.

Emek. 1969–1971.

Eylem. 1965.

Evening Star, The (Washington). 1970–1971.

Gerçekler Postası. 1967.

Geveze. 1948.

Haber. 1967.

Halkçı. 1955.
Hürriyet. 1955–1971.
Kim. 1958–1965.
Kudret. 1961.
Meydan. 1965.
Middle East Journal, The (Washington). 1947–1971.
Millet. 1954
Milliyet. 1955–1971.
Monde, Le (Paris). 1970–1971.
New Times (Moscow). 1964.
New York Times, The. 1945–1971.
Öncü. 1960–1961.
Outlook (Ankara). 1969–1971.
Proleter Devrimci Aydınlık. 1970.
Pulse, The (Ankara). 1963–1965, 1969–1971.
Sabah. 1967.
Son Baskı. 1964.
Son Havadis. 1965–1966.
Sosyal Adalet. 1963–1964.
Tanin. 1947.
Tercüman. 1959.
Time. 1959.
Tüm. 1968–1969.
Türk Solu. 1969.
Ulus. 1947–1970.
Vatan. 1945–1961.
Washington Post, The. 1966–1971.
Yeni Gazete. 1966–1970.
Yeni Gün. 1960.
Yeni İstanbul. 1970.
Yeni Sabah. 1948–1950, 1960, 1964.
Yön. 1961–1967.
Zafer. 1951–1960, 1967.
Zincirli Hürriyet. 1947.

Index

and Soviet policy in Near East, 63;
Turkish role in, 67, 94, 128, 154, 203,
212;
and Turkish domestic politics, 83;
and Turkish junta, 86, 89-90;
and Cuban missile crisis, 92-94;
economic aid to Turkey, 100, 160;
and Cyprus, 108-109, 111, 115, 120,
123, 126;
and Soviet aid to Turkey, 126;
détente with U.S.S.R., 126-27, 158;
Turkish opposition to, 129, 141-43,
147, 156, 209;
and nuclear weapons, 151-53;
fleet visits, 169;
maneuvers, 185.
See also Bilateral agreements, Military Facilities Agreement, Defense
Cooperation Agreement, Status of
Forces Agreement, "On-call" force.
North Vietnam. See Vietnam
Nuclear Planning Group, 152. See also
NATO, strategy
Nuclear weapons, 14, 141-42, 151-53,
158

Official Gazette, 168
Oliver, Gen. Lunsford, 31
"On-Call" force, 158-59, 211
Opium. See Narcotics
Organization for Economic Cooperation
and Development (OECD), 100
Ottawa, 43
Ottoman Empire, 10, 27, 45, 58, 144
Özdağ, Muzaffer, 87

Pakistan, 62, 68, 70
Palestinian fedayeen, 145
Pan-Turanists, 12
Papandreou, George, 117, 139
Parade, 196
Paris, 32, 57, 141
Patterson, Robert P., 13
Peace Corps, 137, 188-91
Peace partisans, 39-40
Pentagon, 158, 161
"People's Liberation Army," 145
Perez Jiménez, Marcos, 82
Petroleum, 73
Poland, 23
Polaris submarines, 94, 151
Porter, Lt. Gen. Robert W., 119
Portugal, 82
Potsdam Conference, 16-18
Powers, Gary, 57

Pratt, 172
"Prometheus Plan," 139

Qasim, Abd al-Karim, 66

Ramparts, 135
Randall, Clarence, 72
Reader's Digest, 41
Regional Cooperation for Development
(RCD), 70
Reliance Party, 183
Republican Peasants Nation Party
(RPNP), 91, 131-32. See also National Action Party
Republican People's Party (RPP): and
DP, 23, 38, 69, 84, 98;
and Truman Doctrine, 28;
and NATO, 36, 37, 67, 141-43, 156;
and Mediterranean pact, 37, 40;
fall of, 38;
and Korean War, 39;
and U.S., 44, 67, 69, 81-83, 131, 134;
and Near East, 63, 66;
and economic planning, 71, 98;
and foreign capital 72-73, 140, 187;
and military establishment, 84;
coalition governments, 91;
and Cyprus, 113, 131;
left-of-center stance, 131;
and CIA, 136;
and Komer, 140;
and Erim, 146;
and DCA, 163-64;
and European Communities, 183-84;
and narcotics, 198
Revolutionary Youth Organization (Dev
Genç), 145
Rhee, Syngman, 83
Richardson, Elliot, 194
Robert College, 10
Rogers, William, 196
Roosevelt, Franklin D., 15

Sadak, Necmeddin, 36, 37
Saigon, 133, 139. See also Vietnam
Salazar, Antonia de Oliveira, 82
San Francisco Conference, 16
Sarper, Selim, 29, 92
Saturday Review, 196
Scandinavians, 37, 94
Second World War, 10, 12, 13, 191
Single Convention on Narcotics, 192,
195
Sinop, 88, 167
"Site 23," 167

¹ 57349 M

Cover and book design: Pat Taylor